LABOR OF
LOVE

LABOR OF LOVE

MOIRA WEIGEL

FARRAR, STRAUS AND GIROUX   NEW YORK

Farrar, Straus and Giroux
18 West 18th Street, New York 10011

Printed in the United States of America
First edition, 2016

Library of Congress Cataloging-in-Publication Data
Names: Weigel, Moira, 1984– author.
Title: Labor of love : the invention of dating / Moira Weigel.
Description: New York, NY : Farrar, Straus and Giroux, 2016.
Identifiers: LCCN 2015041606 | ISBN 9780374182533 (hardback)
  | ISBN 9780374713133 (e-book)
Subjects: LCSH: Dating (Social customs) | Interpersonal relations.
  | BISAC: SOCIAL SCIENCE / Sociology / Marriage & Family.
Classification: LCC HQ801 .W6285 2016 | DDC 306.73—dc23
LC record available at http://lccn.loc.gov/2015041606

Designed by Abby Kagan

www.fsgbooks.com
www.twitter.com/fsgbooks • www.facebook.com/fsgbooks

1   3   5   7   9   10   8   6   4   2

For everyone who has taught me about love,
especially Mal and Ben

CONTENTS

LABOR OF LOVE

INTRODUCTION: **DATES**

The con was up. Or about to be. That was what it felt like in my midtwenties. I was not sure who I had been fooling, or why, or how exactly I was going to slip up and get caught. The self-help books and my Irish Catholic mother said it was the drumbeat of imminent spinsterhood I heard approaching. I did not want a lonesome, loveless future; who does? But the dread I felt was not about that.

I was starting to realize I did not know *how* to want.

The first sign came one swampy New York evening early in the summer I was twenty-six. I was walking around Chelsea with a man I had been seeing, and like actors in a romantic comedy we ended up on the High Line. Surrounded by tourists and millionaires, we watched the sun sink into Hoboken, New Jersey.

He was older, handsome, and (I thought) maybe a genius. Also selfish in a way that was that much more destructive for being unintentional. For weeks he had been trying to break off our thing in order to commit to another, longer-standing thing with an ex-ex he had started to call his girlfriend again, and then changing his mind. He wanted to keep us both apprised of his thought process.

He was saying something about the ideologically suspect qualities of long-term romantic love, when a question I had been avoiding caught up with me. Its footsteps quickened.

What should I want?

At the time, I felt miserably torn between my awareness of what a cliché the Maybe Genius and I were and my equally acute awareness that knowing clichés were clichés could not protect me. He was breaking my heart. But like many women, I had been well trained to focus on what other people might want—if not to make them happy, then at least to make myself desirable. So even my feelings came with *should*s in front of them. *Should* had become a reflex.

"What should I want?" I asked the Maybe Genius later, as he walked me back toward the subway. I was trying not to sound too anything, and it must have worked, because he laughed.

"Doesn't everyone just want to be happy?"

I winced. It was not just that he was brushing me off, probably so he could go spend the rest of the night with his ex-ex-girlfriend. It was that it was such a banal answer. Did he not have any better information than I did? He was so confident that he had a right to want, even when he wanted to be indecisive. I wanted to want, but what?

Why was I always asking some man?

I had learned to do it by dating. I say "I." I could mean any one of many women I know. I belong to a generation that grew up hearing that we girls could do anything. Yet in many ways we grew up dispossessed of our own desires. In school, our textbooks told us that feminism was something that had already happened: if we worked hard, we could now aspire to the same things that our male classmates did. Dating trained us in how to be if we wanted to be wanted.

Since we were children, we had heard that romantic love would be the most important thing that ever happened to us. Love was like a final grade: Whatever else we accomplished would be meaningless without it. We knew that we were supposed to find love by dating. But beyond that there were no clear rules. Nobody even seemed to know what dating was.

As grown-ups, most of my friends agreed that dating felt like experimental theater. You and a partner showed up every night with different, conflicting scripts. You did your best. Those of us who were women looking for men were flooded with information about how we should go about it. Books and movies, TV shows and magazines, blog posts and advertisements all told us how to act.

Pink covers and curly scripts, and the fact that these instructions came stuck between perfume samples, clearly announced that they were trivial. *Come on*, the pink and curlicues and perfume said. *Dating is not serious.* But what could be more serious than the activity you are told is your one way to fulfillment—and the main way your society will reproduce itself?

The more I thought about it, the more it felt like a conspiracy. *Here is how to be if you want to be loved*, the advice said, *which is to say, if you want to be worth anything.*

Now don't ask any questions.

Female desire is not a trivial subject. Neither is happiness. As I recognized how many of my assumptions about what I should want and how I should act had come from dating, I realized that I wanted to find out where dating itself came from. To do this, it would not be enough to survey the present. The welter of beliefs that friends and I held had accumulated over decades, if not centuries. So I set out to investigate the past.

My first Google search yielded some bad news.

Dating was dead.

On January 11, 2013, *The New York Times* confirmed it. "The End of Courtship?" a headline asked. Citing conversations with twenty- and thirty-something women from several East Coast cities, the paper of record announced that "hookups" and "hangouts" had replaced the ritual of the date.

"The word 'date' should almost be stricken from the dictionary!" one source exclaimed.

The author posed a series of questions that he seemed to imagine any single girl longed to hear. Then he shot them down.

"Dinner at a romantic new bistro? Forget it."

"A fancy dinner? You're lucky to get a drink."

"Nobody dates anymore!" parents who have children in high school or college often protest when I tell them that I am writing a book about dating. Meanwhile, countless singles across America sign up for online matchmaking services every day.

At restaurants across the country, pairs of strangers meet every night, each earnestly hoping that the other might be The One, or at least *someone* to make a life with. Brimming with information they have gleaned about each other, two people sit down. They start, a little stiffly, asking questions.

Are they doing it right?

One person laughs too loud.

"First online dates." My friend rolls her eyes. "You can always tell." She has been working as a waitress since losing a job in PR and says she sees dozens of such daters every week. She can tell an OkCupid from a Match.com meet-up. She says that subtle differences distinguish JDaters from those who met on Hinge.

If dating is dead, the owners of the apps and restaurants must say, *long live dating!*

Have reports of the death of dating been greatly exaggerated?

All human societies, and many animal ones, have always had courtship rituals. They have not all had dating. The male blue-footed booby does a mean mating dance, but he does not date. Neither did Americans until around 1900. Since then, experts have constantly declared that dating was dead or dying. The reason is simple. The ways people date change with the economy. You could even say dating is the form that courtship takes in a society where it takes place in a free market.

The story of dating began when women left their homes and the homes of others where they had toiled as slaves and maids and moved to cities where they took jobs that let them mix with men. Previously, there had been no way for young people to meet unsupervised, and anyone you did run into in your village was likely to be someone you already knew.

Think what a big deal it is when one new single shows up in a Jane Austen novel. Then think how many men a salesgirl who worked at Lord & Taylor in the 1910s would meet every day. You start to appreciate the sense of romantic possibility that going to work in big cities inspired.

The ways people work have always shaped the ways they date. *I'll pick you up at six* made sense at a time when most people had jobs with fixed hours. Today, a text asking *u up* may be asking basically the same thing. But dating is not only influenced by work. Dating *is* work. Some of that work is physical. Take all the things that glossy magazines suggest a straight woman must do to be baseline datable. Shop for attractive clothes, exercise to fit into them, eat well, and stay well groomed—nails polished, everywhere waxed, face made up, hair styled, etc. Work at a job to earn the money to pay for it. All daters are advised to make and monitor online dating profiles and maintain winning social media presences. Their efforts do not end there.

The work of dating is not only physical. It is emotional. My old roommate Travis used to refer to his first-date routine as "The Travis Show." He would punctuate this with an ironic flutter of jazz hands. But it does take work to perform the version of yourself who might charm a stranger. The hardest part can be making that work seem effortless.

The fact that dating is work is not necessarily a bad thing. Labor is how we shape the world around us. Desire is the chance each of us gets at birth to bind ourselves with others and make our shared world new. Most writing about dating only addresses certain people: straight white middle-class kids or college graduates who live in cities. Because I want to investigate dating culture, which is produced for and marketed to such people, I will talk a lot about them, too. But I will also try to show how their stories intersect with others.

Attraction and affection can leap across lines set by identity. Over the past century, dating has given people exhilarating new freedoms. Daters have gone out and fought for their rights to look for love that is interracial, straight, gay, both, neither, monogamous, or polyamorous, without risking criminal prosecution. It has become possible to imagine doing so without fear.

There is no better life than a life spent laboring at love—exerting effort not because we have to, but because we believe that what we are bringing into being is valuable and we want it to exist. Yet because our culture tends to misunderstand the nature of labor and of love, we undervalue both.

If marriage is the long-term contract that many daters still hope to land, dating itself often feels like the worst, most precarious form of contemporary labor: an unpaid internship. You cannot be sure where things are heading, but you try to gain experience. If you look sharp, you might get a free lunch.

CHAPTER 1. TRICKS

A free lunch is getting harder to come by in business or pleasure. When I ask people how they would define what "a date" is, they usually say that it involves a person inviting another person out to eat or drink something, or to consume some other kind of entertainment. Then they note wistfully how rare this has become. Articles that lament the death of dating frequently cite the absence of such excursions as evidence of the decline of romance. Yet at the dawn of dating, the idea of a man taking a woman somewhere and paying for something for her was shocking.

Previously, looking for love had not involved going out in public or spending money. So around 1900, when the police started to notice that young people were meeting up on city streets and going out together, they became concerned. Many early daters—the female ones, anyway—were arrested for it. In the eyes of the authorities, women who let men buy them food and drinks or gifts and entrance tickets looked like whores, and making a date seemed the same as turning a trick.

The word "date" first appeared in print in the sense that we now use it in 1896. A writer named George Ade dropped it in a weekly column that he wrote for *The Chicago Record*. The column was called "Stories of the Streets and Town." It promised to give his middle-class readers a glimpse into how the working classes lived.

The protagonist of the column is a young clerk named Artie. When Artie suspects that his girlfriend has been seeing other people, and is losing interest in him, he confronts her. "I s'pose the other boy's fillin' all my dates?"

In an installment published three years later, he gawks at another girl's popularity. "Her Date Book had to be kept on the Double Entry System."

The girls a boy like Artie would have dated were a brand-new type. In Chicago, people called them "women adrift."

Starting in the 1880s, more and more women who had grown up on farms or in small towns began leaving their homes to go look for work in cities. When they arrived, they crashed with distant relatives or found cheap rooms in boardinghouses. Changes in the economy were creating more and more opportunities for them. They could make garments and other light goods in factories. They could become salesgirls in department stores or day servants in the homes of rich families. They could learn shorthand and become office secretaries. Or they could work in the laundries, restaurants, and cabarets.

African American women were even more likely than white women to be looking for work outside their homes. After the Civil War, a huge population of former slaves tried to find jobs. Discrimination kept many black men from earning living wages, and black women in cities often ended up stuck in positions that nobody else wanted. In 1900, 44 percent of them worked in domestic service. Most were desperate to leave it. While in a white household, they remained vulnerable to physical, emotional, and sexual abuse. Many tried to transition to "day work." Others even opted for heavy labor.

In the 1890s, a stock market crash set off the worst economic crisis that the United States had ever experienced. This sped up the flood of single women into cities. At the same time, a huge wave of immigrants arriving from Italy and Eastern Europe crammed into tenements alongside the Irish who already lived there. The female members of these families joined the job hunt.

In the 1960s, the second-wave feminist movement canonized the appeal that Betty Friedan made in *The Feminine Mystique*. Friedan told housewives to flee the suburbs and take on paid work. So today it is easy to forget that by 1900, more than half of American women were already working outside their homes. Many of them were unmarried. At work, or on the way to and from work, they crossed paths with men. It is hardly surprising that some of these singles were interested in flirting and pursuing relationships with one another. And it made sense for them to do so in public places. Where else did they have?

The son of a rabbi, Samuel Chotzinoff came with his family from Vitebsk, Russia, to New York when he was seventeen years old. They lived in a housing project on the Lower East Side of Manhattan. Chotzinoff grew up to be a well-known music critic, and in his memoirs he described their home in the Stanton Street Settlement.

"The average apartment consisted of three rooms: a kitchen, a parlor, and a doorless and windowless bedroom between.

"The etiquette of courting was strict," he added.

If a young man came to call on his older sister, the two of them would have to crowd in the kitchen. If his parents were out, they made Samuel stay in to spy on his sister and any suitors who turned up.

"Privacy in the home was practically unknown," the grown-up Chotzinoff recalled. "Privacy could be had only in public."

Of course, traditional parents would have preferred to set up their children through family members or matchmakers. In the Old Country, your family and community had controlled courtship. Many ethnic and religious groups funded political and theatrical clubs in the hopes that their children would meet there. But even strict parents tended to trust their children not to do anything too untoward outside. Many courting couples were allowed to go walking and attend concerts, balls, and plays together. When young Samuel headed out to the park near his home, he saw young men and women everywhere. They strolled hand in hand and squeezed next to each other on benches. They tucked themselves between trees to steal kisses and caresses. English, Russian, and Yiddish drifted through the air.

The girls mostly worked in laundries and textile factories. The boys worked in industrial sweatshops. As soon as they punched out, they met up. As twilight wore on, the streets became like one large party, into the darkening corners of which couples slipped. Someone might see you, but nobody was likely to. The risk you took became part of your bond. It was a secret that you shared.

For people who could afford it, there were a growing number of other date spots. In cities across the country, saloons, restaurants, dance halls, and amusement parks were springing up to cater to new arrivals.

The more daters went out, the more destinations they had to choose from. There were penny arcades packed with games. As films grew in length and quality, the owners of such establishments added projectors and started charging five cents admission. By 1908, there were ten thousand "nickelodeons" across America.

———

Earning money gave young women a new degree of freedom to decide where they would go with whom. Still, their wages did not amount to much. Despite the record numbers of women entering the workforce, the belief remained widespread they were working not to support themselves but only to supplement the earnings of fathers or husbands. Employers used this misconception as an excuse to pay women far less than they paid men. In 1900, the average female worker earned less than half of what a man would earn in the same position. This meant that women adrift hardly made enough to eat, much less to spend on leisure.

"If I had to buy all my meals I'd *never* get along," a young woman living in a boardinghouse in Hell's Kitchen told a social worker in 1915. The social worker, Esther Packard, was preparing a series of reports on the lives of women and children in the neighborhood.

"If my boyfriend did not take me out," another woman asked, "how could I ever go out?"

Packard saw her point. In her case file she noted: "The acceptance on the part of the girl of almost any invitation needs little explanation, when one realizes that she often goes pleasureless unless she accepts 'free treats.' "

Most middle-class onlookers were less sympathetic. They had their own system of courtship. It was called "calling," and around 1900, it still followed an elaborate set of rules. When a girl reached a certain age, usually around sixteen, she became eligible to receive suitors. For the first year, her mother would invite men to call on her on one of several afternoons per week that they both spent at home. After that, if she met a man she liked at one of the social gatherings she attended, she could ask him over to the house herself.

A man might simply show up at the home of a young lady he

admired. In this case, however, decorum required him to present his card to the servant who opened the door. Until the beginning of the First World War, it was common for even households with average incomes to employ one servant. She would ask him to wait while she saw whether the young lady was "in."

If the girl did not want to see her visitor, she could tell her servant to say she was not there. If she did, he could come into her parlor. There, the pair could talk, or sing and play the pianoforte, chaperoned by her mother and other relatives and friends.

Today, calling sounds like holding an awkward kind of office hour. But to the people who did it, it offered the comforts of clear conventions and a community to watch over you while you performed them. It also reinforced a set of strong beliefs about the proper places of men and women. The ritual made men into agents in pursuit. It made women the objects of desire.

Some called it the "doctrine of separate spheres." It held that women should stay in their homes, tending lovingly to their families. Men, by contrast, should compete with one another to earn money in public. Political conservatives now call these gender roles "traditional" and claim that they have been hardwired into us by evolution. But there is nothing timeless about them. In fact, the idea that men and women were so fundamentally different would have made little sense to people who lived even a few hundred years ago.

Before the Industrial Revolution, most people in Europe and the United States subsisted by running small farms or businesses with members of their extended families. The men and women assumed different responsibilities. He plowed the fields; she killed the chickens. She churned the butter; he took it to town to sell. But both were clearly engaged in the same endeavor. So were their children. It's no accident that in English we call childbirth "labor." After the physical burden of pregnancy and giving birth, there is all the work that follows: feeding and caring for your offspring, teaching them enough to get by and get along with others. You had children because you expected them to help you at work and to care for you during your old age. In this way, the goals of labor and the goals of love dovetailed.

When masses of people began to leave farms for factories and family businesses for large corporations, the work that women did having and raising children and caring for their husbands continued to create economic value. Women sustained and replenished the workforce. And they drove consumption. As industrialization progressed, and lighter industries began mass-producing items like clothing and food, it became vitally important that there be households—meaning *housewives*—to buy them. But as working for a salary became standard practice, the reality that housewives contributed to the economy became harder to see. The idea arose that work was what someone else paid you money to do. Not-work was what you were not paid to do. Work was what men did out in public. Not-work was what women did at home.

According to this theory, women had no desire to be compensated. They did all they did out of instinct. We give our time and energy to others as automatically as a cow grazes or the grass grows. Our caring is a natural resource. It follows, from this worldview, that female labor did not count. Of course women should do their work for free. Many women even came to believe that it was simply in their natures to do anything for love.

The Calling Class had a lot at stake in the idea that women cherished being confined at home, providing attention and affection to the men around them. So they were both repulsed and fascinated by "public women." Whores went out and demanded to be paid for what wives had to give away for free. Their existence challenged everything that middle-class people believed about female nature.

Prostitution has been called "the world's oldest profession." But, like many professions, it was changing dramatically around the turn of the last century. In the late 1800s, more and more women, struggling to get by in the industrializing economy, took on sex work. Individual prostitutes had once operated like artisans, small-business owners, or housewives who dabbled in freelance consulting. But as cities grew, brothels began to be organized on a corporate basis. Men were the bosses. By the 1890s, several cities had large, well-organized, and officially tolerated red-light districts. In New Orleans, the city government printed brochures listing the names of establishments in its vice quarter, Storyville, the acts they offered, and the going rates for each. The San Francisco Tenderloin included multistory brothels that incorporated light shows.

Critics who were horrified by these places said there was no way women could be choosing to work in them. The belief became widespread that vulnerable girls were being abducted and sold into "white slavery." In the summer of 1910, the newly founded Bureau of Investigation (BOI), the precursor to the FBI, launched an investigation into brothels around America. Agents warned women that making dates with strangers could send them down a slippery slope toward disrepute, disease, and death.

It took a spitfire like the anarchist Emma Goldman to point out that the white slave hysteria seemed a little misplaced. In a scathing article criticizing the popular obsession with prostitution, Goldman quoted the famous British sexologist Havelock Ellis: "The wife who married for money, compared with the prostitute, is the true scab. She is paid less, gives much more in return in labor and care, and is absolutely bound to her master."

———

Our culture remains fascinated by the myth of the all-giving wife and mother and her twin, the prostitute. Trashy pleasures like *The Real Housewives* franchise appeal to viewers precisely because they play on cherished convictions saying that love and money should not mix, while also winking at the fact that they often, obviously, do.

On an episode of *The Real Housewives of Beverly Hills* that became notorious, one of the housewives, Yolanda, hosted a group of friends in her recently remodeled kitchen. Over white wine, she delivered some real talk on the importance of keeping sexual passion alive in marriage.

"Let's get it straight," Yolanda said. "Men love beautiful women and beautiful women love rich men. They will fuck your husband for a Chanel bag." This, she seemed to be saying, was why it is imperative to fuck your husband first.

"If you have found your true love, it should be easy."

According to Yolanda, "true love" is what you share with a man who finds you as sexy as you find him rich. It makes that exchange—of sex for financial security, consumer pleasure, and social status—easy. Not like work at all.

The irony of course is that all of the housewives who appear on *Real Housewives* thereby become *professional* housewives. Impersonating themselves, they gain credentials that let them leverage their stay-at-home identities into lucrative careers as consultants and businesswomen. In that capacity, they sell products to enrich the housewife experience, like Skinny Girl Margaritas.

No wonder the Real Housewives are so beloved. We live in an era that tells people to do what they love and let their passion take care of their profession. Yolanda is a heroine for an age that believes in getting rich by turning your feelings into assets.

———

The old-fashioned practices of chaperoned courtship and calling had drawn clear lines between the worlds of men and women. Dating undid them. It took courtship out of the private sphere and into public places. It transferred control over the process from the older generation to the younger generation, from the group to the individual, and from women to men.

It all seemed highly suspicious to the authorities. In the early 1900s, vice commissions across the country sent police and undercover investigators to check out spots where people went to make dates. As early as 1905, private investigators hired by a group of Progressive do-gooders in New York City were taking notes on what we can now recognize as the dating avant-garde.

At the Strand Hotel, in Midtown, an agent named Charlie Briggs saw many women who did not seem to be prostitutes, exactly, but who definitely seemed shady. The majority were "store employees, telephone girls, stenographers, etc."

"Their morals are loose," he wrote, "and there is no question that they are on terms of sexual intimacy with their male companions."

When a female investigator named Natalie Sonnichsen and her male colleague T. W. Veness went to an uptown dive called the Harlem River Casino several months later, they deemed the floor to be too small and "much too crowded for decent dancing." Sonnichsen was appalled by how the women were dressed.

"Two girls [wore] very tight knickers," she noted. Another had "a very décolleté costume with practically no sleeves, tights, with very short and skimpy knickers."

The idea that young women might want to go out and enjoy themselves—and, maybe, even enjoy sex—was a lot for the Calling Class to process.

In the 1910s, John D. Rockefeller Jr., the son of the Standard Oil founder, funded investigations into the commercialized vice industries of more than a dozen American cities. The reports that they produced are full of anecdotes about young people making dates.

The Chicago committee found that many young girls often used their charms as a ticket to a day's entertainment at boardwalks and amusement parks: "Some young girls go regularly to these parks. They come with the price of admission and carfare, and as they have no money for amusements, seek a good time at some one's expense."

The write-up on New York described a cruise that took place in August 1912, between New York and New Haven. Two girls, accompanied by a woman who seemed to be their mother, rented a stateroom on the boat, where they stayed all day and were visited by different men. At some point on the trip, "the girl became friendly and offered to make a 'date' with the investigator." The report does not mention whether he said yes.

Early dating slang stressed that what was taking place was some kind of transaction. "Picking up" made a date sound like a casual purchase. Other terms romanticized dating as an exchange of gifts. Take "treating," for instance. The word "treat" was commonly used as both noun and verb to describe a date or the action of taking someone on one. When a woman accepted "a man's treat," she could later brag to her girlfriends that "he treated."

Women who did this were called Charity Girls. A 1916 *Sexual Dictionary* included "*Charity cunt*, n. Woman who distributes her favors without a price." Meaning for only the price of a date. By the 1920s, the prostitutes at New York's Strand Hotel complained that Charity Girls were putting them out of business.

The key fact that distinguished a Charity Girl from a prostitute—and still legally distinguishes an escort from one— was that she did not take cash. Undercover investigators in bars and dance halls reported that many women refused to discuss money with them. Instead, they would bring up things they wanted.

When one investigator in New York started to negotiate the terms of leaving a bar with a woman late at night, she demanded that he buy her a pack of cigarettes and a bottle of whiskey. And while he was at it, could he come with her to the butcher to pay an outstanding bill? (It never seems to occur to the investigators that the women they write up might have recognized them for what they were, and decided to mess around.)

"I told her all butcher shops were closed now," he wrote, "and I didn't care to travel around from store to store, she got sore at me and called me a piker and told me to beat it."

To be treated to food or drinks or even articles of clothing was one thing. But when offered money for their services, many women balked. *Who did he think she was?*

In the 1910s, many women arrested for dating protested that they had been wrongly accused.

At Bedford Reformatory, an institution founded to rehabilitate female delinquents in upstate New York, an Irish woman told her jailers again and again that she had "never taken money from men." Instead men took her "to Coney Island to dances and Picture Shows."

An African American inmate admitted to having had "sexual intercourse with three different friends" but swore she had "never taken money from any of them." Instead, she said, they "sent her presents and have taken her out to dinner and the theater often."

As the years passed, the vice squad had to accept it. Daters did not see these exchanges as tawdry. They saw them as romantic.

Dating still suffers from a kind of prostitution complex. I have heard many debates about whether you "owe" someone

"something"—meaning some act of physical intimacy—in return for an evening out. The people who say these things do not
usually seem to think that they are negotiating a price for their
time or access to their bodies. But it would be difficult to pinpoint
what exactly makes sleeping with someone because he bought you
dinner different from sleeping with someone because he paid you
what that dinner cost. At the same time, the very ambiguity that
is supposed to make a date different from a sex-for-money transaction makes people nervous. Who has not wondered: *Does he like
me? Is she just using me? What is the other person* really *in this for?*

American English still has a huge store of slang that describes
dating as transactional. Expressions like "damaged goods" no
longer fly in polite company, and few people I know wonder why
a man would "buy the cow when he can get all the milk he wants
for free." But we do say that both men and women should shop
around. If you really like someone, you should play hard to get.
If you let a partner get some for nothing, you risk selling yourself
short. He or she may just want to seal the deal. Friends with benefits offer a sense of security. But they come with trade-offs. Wait
too long and you may have to settle. If you're on the market, it's
wiser to invest in a relationship.

This is before we even get into all the increasingly common
ways of talking about dating that self-consciously borrow concepts from economics. People conduct "cost-benefit analyses" of
their relationships, and cite the "low risk and low investment
costs" of casual sex. They try to "position themselves" to "opti-
mize" their romantic options.

A large sector of the advice industry encourages people to
approach their love lives equipped with a business strategy.
In 2003, a dating coach named Rachel Greenwald published a
"15-step action program": *Find a Husband After 35 (Using What
I Learned at Harvard Business School)*. Greenwald promises to
teach daters of a certain age "to see the problem of finding a

husband through the eyes of a marketer." Blogs about online dating obsess about ROI, short for "return on investment."

There is one other rich set of metaphors used to describe dating. These imply that dating is like playing a sport. It is not just the bases. We take long shots. Losers aim too high and strike out. *Don't hate the player, hate the game!* If you ask a friend to be your wingman, or to run interference, that friend must take one for the team. Friends do not let friends get cock blocked. They help them score.

People may use these expressions half-jokingly. But the fact that so many of them remain current shows that our culture still sees dating as a transaction that takes place on uncertain terrain between work and play. It also tells us something about the gender roles that many daters still feel pressured to perform.

Theoretically, these two sets of metaphors are equal opportunity. In many social circles, a young woman can now call herself a "baller" and assume she will be understood. A young man can joke about playing "hard to get" and expect the same. But the cows and milk and allusions to testes make clear that we still associate these opposing attitudes toward love and sex more "naturally" with one gender or the other. A female "player," like a "man slut," adopts a kind of drag by professing to be so.

In other words, our slang suggests that we still think dating is work for women and recreation for men.

Over the past few decades, it has become commonplace to observe how dramatically the Digital Revolution is disrupting dating. Yet many of the disruptions that new sites and apps have brought about recall the changes that brought dating into being in the first place. I have seen a sandwich board outside a bar joke that they had "3-D Tinder." It took me a minute to realize that by saying that they served the "3-D" version of a popular dating app, all the owners meant was that there were people inside.

Like Tinder, the first dive bars and dance halls that the working classes created when they flooded into cities were forms of social media. A bar is still a dating technology. It brings strangers together and enables them to connect. It also structures the possible ways that they can interact. The streets around the overcrowded tenements where the first daters lived were platforms, as the Internet is a platform.

In their unruliness, they resembled the early World Wide Web. In the 1990s, marketplaces like Craigslist's "adult services" and Backpage became notorious for making it easy for those looking to buy sex to find people selling it. Law enforcement eventually shut these pages down. But new digital technologies continue to create new kinds of erotic transactions. Many sex workers who engage in them still refer to meetings with clients, and clients themselves, as "dates."

The year I got my first job out of college, in the immediate aftermath of the 2008 financial crisis, the trend that I heard people giggling about the most was "findoms." Through webcams, men who called themselves "pay pigs" were hiring women to "financially dominate" them for a fee. Mostly they seemed to want to be verbally abused and told to offer gifts.

In the years since, the spread of smartphones and mobile dating apps has made it easier for sex workers to find clients directly and thus avoid the risks associated with streetwalking—including surveillance and harassment by police.

One man I talk to says that he finds the women he hires to come to his apartment the same way he finds the women he takes out to drinks or dinner: by using Tinder. The only things distinguishing the dates he pays from the ones he does not are the discreet links that appear on their profile photos. Click, he explains, and you find yourself at a website with a short bio and a local phone number. Text it and someone shows up within thirty minutes. When she finishes working for the night, she will deactivate the account.

"They don't even bother to use burners." He shrugs.

Recently, mobile phone apps that facilitate "sugar dating" have captured the popular prurient imagination. The most notorious is SeekingArrangement. The concept is simple. SeekingArrangement provides a platform for "Sugar Babies" and "Sugar Daddies" to find one another. According to the site, Sugar Daddies are "successful men and women who know what they want . . . and enjoy attractive company by their side." Sugar Babies are "attractive people looking for the finer things in life."

Mostly SeekingArrangement connects younger women who want money with older men who want sex. Opening an account and setting up a profile is free. Both Babies and Daddies post photos, stats like weight, height, and ethnicity, and charming self-descriptions. Then they indicate their "Expectations": how much a Daddy is willing to pay and how much a Baby asks. You select from a drop-down menu.

> *Select Assistance Level:*
> *Negotiable*
> *Minimal*
> *Practical*
> *Moderate*
> *Substantial*
> *High*

In addition, Daddies list their net worth and annual income.

If you are serious about sugar dating, you will want to upgrade to a Premium Membership. These currently run between $15.95 and $29.95 per month, depending how long you commit to. Once you upgrade, the site will prioritize your profile in the searches of others, bringing you more traffic. It will also perform background checks, allowing a Baby to verify that a Daddy is who he says he is and has roughly as much money as he claims.

In the past two years, SeekingArrangement has attracted more and more media attention, for the way it targets college students. One section of the site, "Sugar Baby University," explains the advantages of having a Daddy to support you, so that you can graduate without debt. It offers free Premium Memberships to anyone who signs up using a .edu address.

The CEO, Brandon Wade, says he is proud of the function his company serves. In early 2015, he announced that around 1.4 million college students had used SeekingArrangement to earn money during the previous year, and that that figure was up 42 percent since 2013. Every year he now releases a list of the top ten "Fastest Growing Sugar Baby Universities." They are all schools that you have heard of. There may be one in your city.

The Sugar Baby I meet in San Francisco graduated from Princeton. She says that her years sugar dating have taught her to recognize that almost all romantic relationships are transactional. "People are always getting something out of each other."

Her SeekingArrangement profile describes her as "a half-hispanic super sweet bisexual metal chick." I can see why she is good at hustling (her verb). Her presence is magnetic. Since she graduated five years ago, she has dipped into and out of different sites in different cities. She was on a lesbian Sugar Mommy site called Mutual Arrangements for a while but could not make it work. She was living with her parents in Florida at the time; there were not enough Mommies within driving distance.

She says that sugar dating is better in San Francisco than anywhere else she has tried it. Since moving here nine months ago, she has used an app called StrawClub to make paid dinner dates with a few businessmen from out of town. But most of her regulars are married Sugar Daddies she found on Seeking-Arrangement. She sees them for one to two months. She usually meets them in a hotel room they have rented, for a few hours between when they work and when they go home. She takes a flat fee of around two hundred dollars per meeting.

"These are men who just want to feel seen," she says. "They like me because I make them feel like they matter." She likes married men because they pay well. To do so reassures them that their "incentives are aligned." They want to know that she will not get angry and run to their wives.

The copy on SeekingArrangement admonishes Sugar Babies that they must not fall for their Daddies. But the women I speak to who have done this kind of work—where you see someone regularly, and get to know him, providing a "girlfriend experience" as well as sex—say that in practice it almost always goes the other way.

A professor, now in her forties, tells me about a client she met while working as a dominatrix in a private "dungeon" during grad school. He would come once a week, bringing her books and theater tickets. She made the mistake of telling him her real first name. Then one day he came in with an experimental play he had written. It ended with a scene of her whirling around an empty room in a tattered wedding dress. When she moved to another city soon after, he tracked her down. Packages started showing up at her apartment. He even called the university where she was working. He pleaded with her to come back.

I ask whether it surprised her.

She shakes her head. "For most of them, there was only one of me, and usually they were cheating. So I was this very big deal in their lives. I was seeing a dozen of them a week."

The Princeton Sugar Baby says that almost every one of her

long-term Daddies has ended things because he says he is developing feelings.

She laughs. "I guess I'm too good at my job."

Ever since the invention of dating, the line between sex work and "legitimate" dating has remained difficult to draw and impossible to police. Around the end of World War I, the reformers who had vowed to stop the tide were starting to accept that they could not. Dating had spread far beyond the recognized vice districts. A waitress who had been arrested for making dates explained to an Illinois court how easily you could fall into it while working.

"You wait on a man and he smiles at you. You see a chance to get a tip and you smile back. Next day he returns and you try harder than ever to please him. Then right away he wants to make a date, and offer you money and presents if you'll be a good fellow and go out with him." If this was how a woman fell into sex work—*smiling*, and trying harder than ever to please customers— then turning tricks was just part of her job.

When a Sugar Baby invites me to log on to her Seeking-Arrangement account to look at her messages, what strikes me are not the messages. Those actually seem like pretty standard online dating fare:

> *What do you do in your free time?*
> *Write. I hike on weekends.*
> *What do you write?*
> *Sci-fi and fantasy, mostly. How about you?*
> *I like to sail.*
> *I've always wanted to learn! Maybe you can give me lessons.* ☺

What shocks me is the vanilla corporate language the company uses to tout itself as a kind of job-training center.

All paid dating sites are laden with euphemisms. They have to be. This is how they stay on the right side of the line that divides (legal) escort services from (illegal) prostitution. But SeekingArrangement goes to extraordinary lengths to promote the idea that sugar dating prepares you for a career.

The ex-dominatrix tells me she bluffed her way through interviews at several dungeons she applied to by alluding to "rope and needle skills" she did not actually possess. It did not matter. All that the people hiring cared about was your physical type: white, Asian, black, or Hispanic; short or tall; curvy or thin. Once she got hired, coworkers taught her during downtime how to stimulate clients to orgasm without directly touching their genitals. The dungeon did not pay for the hours that employees spent receiving this kind of on-the-job training or waiting for clients to show up. Like Uber drivers, the "girls" bore the up-front expenses of costumes and makeup and regular waxes, manicures, and pedicures, and they paid a portion of their earnings for the opportunity to work.

SeekingArrangement encourages Babies to think of the site as a source of opportunity for personal development, describing the Daddy's role as "mentorship." Near major Sugar Baby universities it hosts meet-ups, where women are invited to talk about sugar dating as a route to financial empowerment over coffee and chocolate fondue. The last time I logged on to the site, the most recent post on its blog was called "Your Application Has Been Unsuccessful."

"Consider the position of an employer looking to hire new staff," the anonymous author begins. "This is basically what the process of meeting a potential Sugar Daddy is like." The 7 mistakes that make a profile a miss include "poor communication skills," "poor presentation skills," "asking the wrong questions," and "no wow factor." That is, the same things that would make you sink a job interview.

As the first decade of the twentieth century gave way to the second, the middle classes gradually accepted dating as a legitimate form of courtship. In 1914, *Ladies' Home Journal*—the largest-circulation magazine in the country, with more than one million readers—ran a short story about a sorority sister and her love life. The author put the word "date" in scare quotes but did not see a need to explain it further. By the early 1920s, stories about college students going out to dinners and dances and vaudeville shows and movies had become widespread.

Soon, nobody seemed to remember that these activities ever appeared dubious. Today, authorities like *The New York Times* refer to them offhand as "traditional." Americans seem to have gotten over the ambiguities that once made vice squads worry that dinner dates were just another form of sex work. Yet other ambiguities remain. If daters are often unsure about what it is they are trading "on the market," there is also a lot of uncertainty regarding the point of dating.

What is dating for?

The rituals of calling had served a clear purpose: marriage. The parents and relatives who oversaw the process had a clear incentive to make sure that courtship led to the formation of new couples, who would start new households and produce heirs. Not only would this make their children happy. It also would enlarge and extend their family property.

The first entrepreneurs to create dating platforms had different incentives. The success of restaurants, bars, and amusement parks did not depend on the quality of marriages that resulted from dates there. It depended on the volume of daters who came and went. Unlike your mother, a bartender did not care if you ended up making babies with the guy you came in with. In fact, the best thing would be if no one ever settled down.

By bringing courtship out of the home and into the market-place, dating became a lucrative business. The practice made it possible to take basic human needs for sex and attention and af-fection that can never be sated and turn them into engines of potentially endless demand.

For the first time in human history, dating made it necessary to buy things in order to get face time with a prospective partner. This remains true today. Even if we find dates on apps that cost nothing to download, we pay in the hours that we spend creating and updating our accounts. We pay in the attention that the owners of the apps sell to advertisers. It may be a symptom of the confusion about work and play that dating first created that it would be hard to say whether we are working or enjoying leisure. Updating your OkCupid profile seems like both and neither.

For OkCupid, getting us into a relationship that might take us off the app is, at best, a secondary goal. The first priority is to harness our desires in order to increase their profits. In this sense, every dater is still a Charity Girl even if you pay for it, and even if you think you are just having fun. These are the tricks dating now plays on everyone.

CHAPTER 2. **LIKES**

D ating moved courtship from the home onto the market. As it became possible to shop for your own mate, it also became necessary to sell yourself. Taste became a key way that a dater could create her brand.

"What really matters is what you like, not what you *are* like."

In the movie *High Fidelity*, John Cusack says these words directly to the camera. His character, a thirty-something record store clerk, wouldn't dream of sleeping with a woman who preferred recent Sting to a classic Police record. When the indie rom-com *Garden State* came out in 2004, the group the leading couple bonded over was the Shins. By the time *500 Days of Summer* followed, five years later, the 1980s were cool again, so it was the Smiths.

The editors of the "girl-on-girl" blog Autostraddle agree with Cusack.

"It's not what you're like, it's what you like," they wrote in a post on Valentine's Day 2012. "It might take you a while to be sure, but one day you'll just know that it's time to lend her your copy of *Birds of America* and hold your breath while you wait to see if she likes it." Either she will "get" it, or she won't. Either your girl-friend gets *you*, or she doesn't.

Celebrity couples like Kim Kardashian and Kanye West publicly declare that they get each other.

"Kanye has the most amazing taste in the world," Kardashian recently gushed to a reporter at *Extra*.

Her husband concurred, "It's really all about dopeness at the end of the day."

Ordinary daters dream of finding someone who shares their (amazing) taste, too. At least they yearn for someone who does not actively offend it. A sad smile of recognition crosses my face when I overhear a girl on the train complaining to her friend about her one-night stand with a man who started playing Limp Bizkit on his laptop in the morning. Though the sex had been good, there was no way she was giving him her number.

"I want the guy I like to like the things I like," she sighed.

"Oh, *that*," my friend groans when I quote the line from *High Fidelity* to her. "You wouldn't believe how many men put that on their OkCupid profiles."

Over the past ten years, the rise of online dating has given "likes" an increasingly central role to play in courtship. Different sites and apps take stock of what you like in different ways. But they all give information about your taste a prominent place in the profile that prospective partners see.

Match.com asks users to share their "Interests," "Favorite Hot Spots," and "Favorite things." Even celebrities answer dutifully. When Martha Stewart joined in 2013, under her Interests she listed "Cooking, dining out, fishing/hunting, gardening/landscaping, movies/videos, museums and art, shopping/antiques, travel/sightseeing." She said her Favorite Hot Spot was somewhere called "sushi yasuda." Her favorite things are "British *House of Cards*, American *House of Cards*, *Homeland*, all the food, the symphony, opera & rap."

Martha's profile skillfully deploys just the right mix of self-revelation and elusiveness. Anyone who happened upon her profile was likely to know that she enjoyed "all the food." But who knew she liked hip-hop? Likes may be especially important for famous people who want to use online dating services while preserving their anonymity.

An attractive, successful professional in her forties who uses several apps to date in New York City tells me about getting approached on OkCupid by someone who liked the same books she did. He did not have a profile picture; when she asked why, he entreated her to believe that he had "a very good reason." They traded messages about historical nonfiction for a few weeks before he asked to meet her. She showed up to the café prepared for the worst. It turned out she had been chatting with the comedian Rick Moranis!

Virtually all dating sites ask users to supply information about what they like. Dozens of specialized services take things further—promising to match you with someone who has similar files in his or her iTunes or laughs at similar jokes. If you are the type to develop a crush on an Instagram account, there's an app for that, too. It is called Glimpse. It asks users to enter only the most basic information: age, gender, and sexual orientation. Then it lets you select a set of photographs pulled from your Instagram profile and start browsing the photos of other users, without any other identifying information.

The idea that the way someone shoots brunch plates and bathroom selfies might tell you all you need to know takes the idea that *what you like* reveals *what you are like* to its logical conclusion. It suggests that aesthetic choices like selecting filters and writing captions might capture your personality more effectively than you could do in words. It also shows how the most apparently trivial aesthetic decisions can end up determining who likes you.

Favorite books and bands have not always guided courtship. A monkey does not marvel that his mate shares his taste for bananas. Adam did not sidle up to Eve, refill her Solo cup, and ask her if she, too, liked the punk band Hüsker Dü.

For most of human history, the idea that a preference for one consumer product over another could serve as a predictor of romantic compatibility between two people would not have made any sense. For one thing, there were not many nonessential goods to choose among. The criteria that guided courtship were far more limited: family, religious background, social class. *Likes* were freighted with little of the significance that they have now.

In the late eighteenth century, these facts began to change. Within two decades, the American and French Revolutions took place; the anticolonial revolutions in Latin America soon followed. Combined with the beginnings of industrialization, these upheavals helped create a new middle class. As they rose to power, they claimed the high culture that had once belonged to princes as their own. The revolutionaries who beheaded King Louis XVI in Paris made the emblematic gesture of seizing the royal art collection and turning his palace, the Louvre, into a public museum.

It was in this environment that philosophers and critics of art and literature began to talk a great deal about what they called *gusto*, *goût*, *Geschmack*, or "taste." Theorists like Immanuel Kant claimed that judgments of taste were objective and based on reason. Although the reaction that a given person experienced before an object depended upon the sensations of pleasure or displeasure that that object caused him or her personally,

Kant said this appraisal should have "universal validity." That is, it should hold true for anyone and everyone. In retrospect, the obsession with taste looks a lot like snobbery—a tool for distinguishing people by social class. Taste was a way for an aristocracy with waning political power to assert its superior cultural capital. As the nineteenth century went on, criticizing the bad taste of nouveau riche upstarts became one way for the first members of the middle class to hold their ground.

"Taste classifies, and it classifies the classifier," the French sociologist Pierre Bourdieu has observed. Information about class remains useful on the dating market.

In an age when most of us no longer rely on our families to select partners for us from our own social set, or crow openly about "how many pounds a year" a love interest expects to inherit from his bachelor uncle, inquiring after taste is a way to select someone from the "right" background. Someone who announces a love of opera says that she is wealthy enough to buy opera tickets, or at least sophisticated enough to know about standing room. Accurately pronounce the name of the Bordeaux you order, or linger on your description of its terroir, to show that you know about France or French or at least know enough to drop the final letters.

A lifetime of socialization causes many of us to send and receive these kinds of signals about class background without thinking about it. A savvy dater can use them to telegraph status. And if you understand these rules of taste well enough, you can manipulate them in order to date up. This is precisely what the first women who dated tried to do.

Women who went to work at department stores, restaurants, and other businesses in the early twentieth century often hoped to snag one of the men they served. Flirting at work was the best chance many of them had at a happy—or at least financially stable—future.

A gig as a salesgirl or a waitress put a young woman on public display and brought her into contact with countless eligible men every day. If she was lucky, some of them might be rich. Just a decade or so earlier, it would have been nearly impossible for a working-class girl to catch the eye of a millionaire, much less converse with him. Now she could get close enough for long enough to get asked out. Maybe she could even make him fall in love.

Shortly after moving to New York from Texas and beginning his prolific career writing short fiction, O. Henry published a portrait of "The Secret Life of Shop Girls." The story appeared in 1906, in a weekly column that he wrote for the *New York World Sunday Magazine*. It told of two "chums" who "came to the big city to find work because there was not enough to eat at their homes to go around."

A short preamble related that Nancy was nineteen; Lou was twenty. Both were "pretty, active, country girls who had ambition to go to the stage." But both got jobs in service. Instead of memorizing scripts, they spent most of their time studying the kinds of men they would like to date and the kinds of wives who had managed to win them.

Nancy works as a salesgirl behind the handkerchief counter at a luxurious department store. Her colleagues go on dates, drinking and dining on the dime of "swell gentleman friends," without compromising their virtue—or at least without revealing that they have. She makes only $8 per week, but she knows that the real value of her position is the visibility it gives her.

"Look what a chance I got!" she exclaims. "Why, one of our glove girls married a Pittsburg—steel-maker, or blacksmith or something—the other day worth a million dollars."

Lou works ironing clothes in a laundry. Although she makes

$18.50 her first week, she is less ambitious than Nancy when it comes to courtship. She pokes fun at her friend's plans to marry a millionaire. But she, too, tries to use her job to meet men. When Lou gets asked out at work, Nancy is skeptical.

"What show would a girl have in a laundry?" It turns out that there is a coveted position at the *front* of the laundry where you can get some exposure.

"He came in for his Sunday shirt and collars and saw me at the first board, ironing," Lou explains. "We all try to get work at the first board."

O. Henry was not making this up. Frances Donovan, a University of Chicago–trained sociologist who taught at Calumet High School on the city's South Side in the 1920s, interviewed senior girls about their plans after graduation.

"I would like to be a stenographer," one announced. "I'm going to be an executive secretary and marry the boss."

After spending two summers working behind the counter at a Chicago department store as research for her 1929 book *The Saleslady*, Donovan believed that one of her students could do just as well there.

"I knew of several marriages and heard of a great many more where the husband was far above the wife as measured by the economic scale," Donovan reported. About coworkers who managed to make a "fine marriage," Donovan's research subjects expressed frank envy. "He's a millionaire from Kansas City. She has a Packard car and did you notice that sparkler on her left hand? Isn't she the lucky kid! And you and I go right on workin'."

The legends of girls in their position who had married rich encouraged many service workers to daydream. The British annual magazine *Forget-Me-Not* promised to reveal to its readers "How Shop-girls Win Rich Husbands." Department store managers even got in on the game. *Sparks*, an in-house newsletter published for employees of Macy's in New York, regularly summarized selling-floor gossip.

"Have you noticed a gentleman wearing spats stopping at Miss Holahan's counter every day, leaving a spray of lily of the valley? Best of luck, Ide!"

Landing the job was a start. To make the most of her position, however, the Shopgirl had to become a highly informed consumer of the kinds of goods she sold. She learned to read the signals that men sent through the appearances they cultivated and the kinds of things they bought.

In the O. Henry story, Nancy learns to look for hints about whether her customers are in fact rich. She spies on them as they slip in and out of their automobiles. "A 12 H. P. machine and an Irish chauffeur!" she scoffs when she sees this dead giveaway. "Give me the real thing or nothing, if you please."

In addition to scrutinizing customers, women in service positions strove to send the right messages themselves. To do this they studied their female customers—the wealthy housewives they dreamed that they, too, might become if they played their likes right. By dressing tastefully, they aimed to attract the attention of desirable men and to demonstrate that they deserved something better than their current station.

Dress for the job you want, not the job you have, career advisers tell us today. Shopgirls were the first to realize that it was not where you came from but what you wear that determines how far you can go.

In an earlier era, a girl from humble origins could not hope to look like the wife or daughter of a millionaire. But a job in a department store or a laundry gave anyone opportunities to become well versed in the signs of wealth. After all, the salesladies and laundresses were the ones selling the handkerchiefs and ironing the cummerbunds that made the rich look rich. A growing number of inexpensive fashion labels offered to help them imitate their customers. So did beauty products.

The cosmetics industry exploded in the 1920s. Previously, only prostitutes and actresses "painted." Victorians had viewed "natural" outer beauty as a sign of clean living. But around 1900, more and more women were starting to apply cosmetics. By 1912, *The Baltimore Sun* reported that even respectable society women "are seen on our streets and fashionable promenade with painted faces."

The cosmetics industry invented a new term to free its products from all the negative associations they once had: "makeup." Not only was "making yourself up" permissible; advertisers were soon claiming it was positively virtuous. By making herself up, a woman showed that she valued her femininity and was willing to spend time and money on her appearance. The results not only made her look pretty. They also demonstrated that she had a good attitude—the kind that her employer, as well as her customers and romantic prospects, wanted.

Driven by anxiety, as well as romantic ambition, the Shopgirl drove a kind of arms race. The more effectively she sold fashion and beauty culture to her clients, the more mandatory participation in that culture became. It was just what the economy needed.

By the end of the nineteenth century, the United States had become a consumer society. New technologies and labor practices had made shoes and shirtwaists easier than ever to produce. All that was needed was a population who shopped for new shoes and shirtwaists as quickly as factories churned them out.

In 1925, for the first time, individual consumption of nonessential goods accounted for the majority of the GDP. Economists started to measure growth and health not in terms of manufacturing capacity but rather by the public's ability, and desire, to buy things. In a market that required consumers to constantly develop new likes for things they did not need, the Shopgirl's work was essential. While on the clock, she helped others consume. Off the clock, she kept her own consumption up to speed.

In "The Frog and the Puddle," a short story that she published in 1912, Edna Ferber described how exhausting it could get. Gertie, the heroine, works at the men's glove counter at a department store in Chicago. Her manager is particular about hair and fingernails. Gertie quickly learns that "you cannot leave your hair and finger nails to Providence. They demand coaxing with a bristle brush and an orangewood stick." When she returns home to her boardinghouse every night, she is exhausted, but she knows her work is far from over. She must manicure her nails, mend her undergarments, apply cold cream to her face, and brush her hair the regulation one hundred strokes with a bristle brush.

"The manager won't stand for any romping curls or hooks-and-eyes that don't connect," Gertie explains. "Sometimes I'm so beat that I fall asleep with my brush in the air."

The Shopgirl who worked tirelessly to maintain her professional appearance was also striving to achieve something that went beyond looks. In *The Saleslady*, Frances Donovan explained why dress was so important to the colleagues whom she studied: "Without pretty clothes, a girl cannot hope to realize her personality."

The idea that your personality might be part of what made you desirable was a new one. In the nineteenth century, Americans had used concepts like "character" and "virtue" to describe themselves. These terms had moral valences. A person revealed her character through kind acts, true friendships, and deeply held convictions. Nineteenth-century advice literature admonished women that when they received gentleman callers, in order to make their best impression, they should wear something dark, modest, and nondescript. They should not let anything superficial distract attention from the soul within.

"Personality" was different. Personality was something that manifested on your surface. The word comes from the Latin *persona*, meaning mask. Personality was like "painting"—a way a woman could make herself up in order to appeal to men. Turn-of-the-century psychologists had diagnosed patients with abnormal minds as having "personality disorders." Starting around 1920, however, experts began to grant that healthy individuals had personalities, too. Suddenly, the word was all over the popular press.

Authors who wrote about romance used it to refer to outward expressions and behaviors. In the context of dating, to have a "good personality" or to simply "have personality" meant to have charisma. This was an asset whether you were selling handkerchiefs or selling yourself. But what exactly it was, was difficult to capture.

The popular writer Elinor Glyn simply called it "it." In a two-part short story that appeared in *Cosmopolitan* magazine in 1926, Glyn defined "it" as a mysterious kind of animal magnetism. "With 'It,'" Glyn wrote, "you win all men if you are a woman—and all women if you are a man."

The story was adapted into a movie of the same title in the following year. Clara Bow plays a shopgirl who has "it"—and has her eye on her manager, Cyrus. Cyrus is the son of the owner of the department store where Clara works. He will inherit it someday, and Clara is determined to marry him. The "It Girl" uses "it" like a currency, to obtain the best man it can afford her. Yet Glyn insisted that an It Girl was above all effortless.

"Unselfconsciousness, and self-confidence, and indifference as to whether you're pleasing or not, and something in you which gives the impression that you're not at all cold," she wrote. "That makes 'it.'"

This suggested that It could not be learned. But the fact that personality was external meant that you could endeavor to improve it. Between 1910 and 1930, a growing number of books of dating advice promised to tell young women how.

In 1915, *The New York Times* reported on a lecture that Susanna Cocroft, the bestselling author of *Beauty a Duty*, gave at the Astor Theatre in New York. She was promoting her new book, *What to Eat and When*, but she ended up telling the packed house that "poise" could be more effective than a diet.

She encouraged her fans to develop poise by studying and mimicking the appearance of fashion models who possessed it.

"Place a beautiful figure on your wall, and compare that with the lines of your own body," she instructed. "Express your ideals with your body as in the pictures you express your ideals on your walls."

"Beauty is no longer vanity; it is use," Cocroft said. A waitress or a shopgirl could be fired at any time simply because someone her boss found prettier showed up and asked for her position.

Nineteenth-century writers on health, hygiene, and etiquette had offered women plenty of wisdom regarding courtship and marriage. But they did not teach *strategies* for winning and keeping a man by manipulating his emotions. Indeed, they denounced such calculated approaches to romance as coquetry. In the age of personality, however, the experts declared that it was perfectly acceptable—indeed, absolutely necessary—for a woman to *work* to win a lover. She just had to make it seem effortless. Otherwise she risked committing one of the cardinal sins of the era of taste: She would look like she was trying too hard.

The skills that helped a Shopgirl like Clara Bow in her romantic life also served her well at work. Personality was an asset on the sales floor as well as on the street. Bosses hoped that their employees would inspire desire for what they sold.

Samuel Reyburn, the president of Lord & Taylor, claimed the Shopgirl could improve her personality simply through her "daily observations of customers in the building." After spending enough time in the store, "she will lower the tone of her voice, grow quiet in manner, exhibit better taste in the selection of her clothes, become more considerate of others." Reyburn described this process as if it took place unconsciously, as a matter of course.

Shopgirls themselves knew better. A Shopgirl knew that the personality she expressed through her likes and her behavior was not something she was born with. Personality consisted of myriad effects that she had to work hard to produce. Anyone who ventures into online dating relearns this lesson. To construct a picture of yourself through photographs and likes and other gestures takes a lot of effort and requires constant tweaking to maintain.

"A friend, Derek, told me that if I listed *Sleeping Beauty* among my favorite movies on OkCupid, I would attract creeps and weirdos," a writer for *New York* magazine recounted of her own dating profile. "He went on. For instance, to list *Gilmore Girls* among my favorite TV shows was fine, but I should balance it with something more aggressive, like *The Sopranos*. My favorite foods should include something savory, not just 'pie' and 'jam.'"

In O. Henry's story, Nancy tailors her personality as craftily as she stitches up her knockoff clothes. She studies her customers' habits, adopting "the best from each." "From one she would copy and practice a gesture, from another an eloquent lifting of an eyebrow, from others, a manner of walking, of carrying a purse, of smiling, of greeting a friend, of addressing 'inferiors in station.'"

In Frances Donovan's *Saleslady* study, one fellow department store worker described the thrill of using her charisma to sell frocks. "My great joy was to be so nice to them it would put them to shame. Very soon I had them eating out of my hand."

The skills that you developed at work made you better at dating, and vice versa. It turned out that selling handkerchiefs and selling yourself required young women to do many of the same things. The most effective women could do both at once.

In the 1930s, the renowned sociologist C. Wright Mills interviewed dozens of shopgirls as part of the study that would eventually become his book *White Collar*. The typology he created included the kind of shopgirl he called the "Charmer," who perfected the art of flirting while selling and selling by flirting.

"It's really marvelous what you can do in this world with a streamlined torso and a brilliant smile," one Charmer told him. "People do things for me, especially men when I give them that slow smile and look up through my lashes. I found that out long ago."

It is difficult to tell whether she is talking about picking up a date or attracting a customer—what exactly the "things" she wants from men are. Her desire to be desirable creates a feedback loop. "I spend most of my salary on dresses which accentuate all my good points," she confesses. "After all, a girl should capitalize on what she has, shouldn't she? You'll find the answer in my commission every week."

Today it is a commonplace that "sex sells." The Shopgirl pioneered the practice of activating sexual desire in order to make consumers want to buy anything and everything—whether or not a given product has anything to do with sex. She was the predecessor to the models who posed in a bikini next to 1950s sports cars, and the women who winked *You've come a long way, baby* in the 1960s Virginia Slims ads while cheekily tonguing their cigarettes. Her sales floor flirtations paved the way for the Herbal Essences commercials, where women cry out in orgasm at the scent of their shampoo, and the Perrier spots in which the voluptuous burlesque star Dita Von Teese pours sparkling water over her breasts.

As women went to work as salesgirls, they mobilized the primal forces of attraction and the new rituals of courtship in order to drive shopping habits. Like latter-day, better-dressed Midases, they turned romantic longing into longing for consumer products. They performed this magic on customers, and they did it to themselves.

As economic activity—buying and selling things—became eroticized, so, too, did erotic and romantic life seem to require more work. Both their jobs and dating required the same kind of work.

Not only did they toil to earn the money to buy clothes and products and maintain stringent diets and elaborate beauty regimens. Women also had to work on their feelings. The most important part of a waitress or shopgirl's job was to *seem* a certain way. This meant expressing some emotions while repressing others. It meant being able to smile even when you felt low. It meant acting friendly toward all your customers without actually making friends with any of them. And it meant not getting angry when they behaved badly.

At work, as in dating, it was crucial not to be too spontaneous. "Many salesgirls are quite aware of the difference between what they really think of the customer and how they must act toward her," Mills wrote. "The smile behind the counter is a commercialized lure . . . 'Sincerity' is detrimental to one's job."

In the 1980s, the sociologist Arlie Hochschild coined a term for the kind of efforts that the salesgirls were expending when they cast slow smiles and batted their eyelashes across the selling floor: "emotional labor." Hochschild defined emotional labor as work that required workers to manage their feelings in order to display particular emotions. We speak of "service with a smile," but in many jobs, the smile *is* the service, or at least the most important part of it. Today, more and more of us sell these kinds of feelings—from the stockbrokers who hype a stock to clients, to the personal trainers who cajole them into working out, from call center receptionists who calm down customers to bill collectors who terrorize them, from baristas to brand managers. In an age where very few Americans make a living making anything, dating trains us for our careers, and vice versa.

In work and love, we sell ourselves in order to sell what we are selling. We strive to become the way we want to come across. We are all Shopgirls now. We enjoy the pleasures the first Shopgirls enjoyed and we run the risk they ran: that our efforts do more for consumption than for courtship. For all our *likes*, we get too little love.

CHAPTER 3. **OUTS**

Shopgirls knew that dressing and speaking the right ways would help them get a job, and that the right job could help them find a man. People who did not want what authorities said they should used many of the same tactics. They, too, chose clothing and gestures to express their desires.

Around 1900, the German Jewish physician Magnus Hirschfeld received a letter at his practice in Berlin. Hirschfeld was gaining an international reputation for defending the rights of men who had "female spirits" and women who had "male" ones. The letter came from a Jenny O. in San Francisco. The law said Jenny was a man. She said she was a woman and preferred to wear women's clothing. But she did so only at home. Jenny had been arrested once for the crime of "masquerading in feminine attire." She dreaded its happening again.

"Only because of the arbitrary actions of the police do I wear men's clothing outside the house," she wrote. "Skirts are sanctuary to me."

Hirschfeld was one of the first advocates of "coming out." He argued that if several thousand prominent homosexuals would only reveal themselves to the police, they would blaze the way to strike down laws that criminalized them. Public opinion was sure to follow.

Hirschfeld later traveled to the United States and photographed Jenny O. When his study *Transvestites: The Erotic Drive to Cross-Dress* came out in 1910, it included four images of her, both clothed and naked. These now look like proud declarations. But Jenny O. knew that she was lucky that the book was published only in German. A person who appeared in public in "a dress not belonging to his or her sex" could easily end up in jail—and all over the yellow press.

As dating ceased to be seen as a form of vice and became the main way that young people expected to find partners, cities filled with venues to go out to. But the mainstreaming of dating also drew lines between who was "out" and who was "in."

Some likes were more important than others. According to the magazines and books and movies that were canonizing the laws of dating, only some people could participate. This has remained true for a long time—even if the best dates seem to take place at the margins.

What is it about *out*?

Even now, in an age when a smartphone can pipe countless prospects into your pocket, "going out" still plays a key role in how we think of dating. After the end of a long relationship, friends soon urge you to "get back out" and "put yourself back out there." If you have no one to take you, some say, go alone. Who knows? You might meet someone. You can get "asked out" when you are already there.

Couples who go out for a long time and then move in together are told that they must continue to schedule nights out with their friend groups, and "date nights" with each other. Leaving behind the drudgery of the home where you wash dishes or fix radiators or raise kids lets you rediscover the spark that made you want to live together in the first place. In 2012, the National Marriage Project, a conservative think tank at the University of Virginia, released a study showing that scheduling at least one date night per week was one of the most statistically significant predictors of marital satisfaction. Going out lets longtime partners feel briefly mysterious to one another again.

Yet the reason to go out is not necessarily to seek or strengthen a cohabiting relationship. When you are out, you can seek anything. Samuel Chotzinoff said that growing up in the tenements of New York's Lower East Side around 1900, immigrants like him could find privacy only in public. Being out among strangers not only lets you feel anonymous. It also can create moments of serendipity.

After Prohibition passed in 1921, the speakeasies that sprang up around New York and other major cities became places where people from different backgrounds could mix beyond the reach of the law. The atmosphere was exciting—and a little dangerous. You were surrounded by strangers you could not necessarily trust. The thing was, you did not have to.

"What does it matter if an unsavory Irish politician is carrying on a dull and noisy flirtation with the little blond at the table behind us?" Ellin Mackay wrote in *The New Yorker* in 1925. "What does it matter if the flapper and her fattish boy friend are wriggling beside us as we dance?"

Mackay signed her essay "A Post-Debutante." She was the heiress to a mind-boggling mining fortune. Starting with the "coming out" ball that her parents threw for her when she was sixteen, she attended an endless string of engagements with her mother. The young men she met at these events were all highly eligible. They were all on the Social Register. But they were all boring. "Hundreds of pale-faced youths, exactly alike," Mackay called them. So after the balls finished, she would take her father's car and tell the driver to take her downtown.

One night early in the spring of 1925, she caught sight of a man sitting alone at a popular speakeasy called Jimmy Kelly's. Her friend whispered what the bartender had just told her: "That man sitting alone over there is Irving Berlin!"

Just a few years earlier, the idea of an heiress crossing paths with a popular songwriter would have been unthinkable. Like Chotzinoff, Berlin was a Russian Jewish immigrant who grew up in a tenement; he got his start singing in Chinese restaurants for tips.

That was exactly what attracted Ellin Mackay. She walked over and introduced herself. Irving bought her a drink. It was the beginning of a whirlwind romance. Within a year, the pair had eloped to the Municipal Building. The paparazzi had taken to following his car, so they took the subway downtown. Her family's disapproval made the front page of *The New York Times*. "Ellin Mackay Weds Irving Berlin; Surprises Father." But they stayed together for sixty-three years, until her death.

Singles have headed out hoping to find this kind of luck ever since.

Ralph Werther moved to New York to study medicine around 1900. In his autobiography, he described his amazement at discovering the city's open secret: It was full of men like him. "Adhesive" personalities, the great, adhesive poet Walt Whitman had called them. The medical literature of Werther's time called them "inverts." Both terms meant men who were sexually attracted to other men.

In a textbook he wrote in the 1890s, the famous sexologist Havelock Ellis claimed that there were large communities of inverts scattered across the United States. In the largest American cities, Ellis wrote, they had their own "'clubs,' really dance-halls, attached to *saloons*, and presided over by the proprietor of the saloon, himself almost invariably an invert, as are all the waiters and musicians." Ellis reported that the authorities tended to look the other way—or more. "It is not unusual," he wrote of the clubs, "for the inquiring stranger to be directed there by a policeman."

In New York, Werther met dozens of gay men in bars and cafés. Late at night, the most ordinary-looking cafeteria could turn into "a gathering spot for that nocturnal clan, the third sexers," as the tabloid *Broadway Brevities* called them. Crowds gathered every night at Childs, a large twenty-four-hour cafeteria near Columbus Circle. In establishments like Childs, Werther saw powdered and rouged men who called themselves "fairies," construction workers whose biceps bulged out of rolled-up shirtsleeves, and men in suits playfully debating the merits of new literary magazines. There was always at least one group of female prostitutes clustered around a table. The rest of the space teemed with boisterous cliques of Bohemians, male and female. Some were there with queer friends; others came simply to take in the scene. After the cafeteria, they could move on to one of the saloons called "black and tans," where interracial couples cavorted openly.

It was not always easy to tell who was who, or what they wanted. Was the man quietly sipping his coffee at the counter just passing time? Or was he looking to get picked up? The uncertainty was exciting, but it could be dangerous. Just weeks before the first time he went to Childs, Werther noted in his diary that the police had raided the Hotel Koenig, a bar in the East Village. They had found a room packed with men who danced together and kissed. Twenty-three were charged with "degenerate, disorderly conduct," and sentenced to ten days in the workhouse.

To stay safe, you had to learn to hide in plain sight. As

shopgirls did their hair and chose their clothes in order to broad-cast their personalities and attract the attentions of eligible customers or colleagues, men who wanted to attract other men developed a secret language. Like shopgirls, they often used their taste to speak it.

Werther recalled wearing white kid gloves and a red bow tie to identify himself as a "fairy" to the working-class youths on Fourteenth Street. Other "inverts" were known to favor green. These articles of clothing served as badges of identification. To don them was a way of announcing your sexuality to those in the know, without giving yourself away to straight colleagues or acquaintances. If a man like Werther wore his red tie to a lecture or a laboratory, the men he worked with might raise an eyebrow at his eccentric fashion sense, but they would not think to call the cops about it. And if Werther liked the look of a man in a red tie he saw sitting on a park bench smoking a cigarette, he could safely approach him, asking, *Do you have a match?*

The signals that men like Werther used to flirt turned ordinary streets and parks into a kind of secret theater. The subculture supplied the costumes and the scripts. This color. That hand gesture. In 1951, the psychologist Edward Sagarin described how it worked. Published under the pseudonym Donald Webster Cory, *The Homosexual in America: A Subjective Approach* became the most famous of a series of gay manifestos that appeared over the decade. It also served as a how-to manual for many nervous cruisers.

Cory explained that a "gay street" might look like any other street. If you were a man interested in men, when you struck up a conversation on such a street, you had to pay close attention. So would your interlocutor, if he was what you hoped. "In the exchange of words," Cory wrote, "each is seeking a clue. Neither desires effeminacy, yet each needs just a suggestion of it, in a softness of tone, an over enunciation of word sounds, an affectation in the movement of the hands or in the method of holding the cigarette."

To get what you wanted, you had to recognize, while being recognizable. And so you played it, slightly, up. Men learned to imitate the signals they saw other men send: the lift of a voice, the tilt of a head. But to out yourself in the 1940s or '50s was still dangerous. You had to walk a thin line.

The homosexual man, Cory said, looked for a "mere iota of the mannerisms of the opposite sex, or to be more exact the mannerisms of the outcast group, in order to reassure himself that this is no trap, no folly that will lead to frustration or even worse."

Slang, too, could do the trick. When Cory was writing—and, presumably, cruising—the word "gay" was just starting to be used as a synonym for "homosexual." To most people it still just meant "bright" or "fun." When a man worked up the courage to drop a hint like *You should come here more often; it's a gay place!* or *This bar looks gay!,* he subtly tipped his hand. If the man he said it to replied by saying something like *Yes it does look gay,* Cory explained, "the *word* has been uttered . . . From that moment on, there is no doubt as to the direction of the evening."

The hope was that if you learned these scripts, you became freer to choose your role. Not only could you meet anyone, you also could *be* anyone. Going out let you imagine it, anyway. Who, gay, straight, or otherwise was not wearing some kind of costume?

During the era of the speakeasy, "drag balls" became wildly popular among black gay men in New York City. The most famous one took place in Harlem, at a hall called Hamilton Lodge (full name: Hamilton Lodge No. 710 of the Grand United Order

of Odd Fellows). Starting in the early 1920s, Hamilton Lodge began throwing an annual party that quickly became a highlight of
the Harlem social calendar. Its official title was the "Masquerade
and Civic Ball." By the late 1920s, however, it was widely known as
the "Faggots Ball." Every year it drew hundreds of drag queens
and thousands of spectators.

Like the Village and the Bowery, Harlem was a haven for
homosexuals during Prohibition. Sure, African American leaders
who preached the importance of "respectability" condemned the
participants. But other authorities gave winking approval, and
even encouragement. At the Hamilton Lodge Ball, every year,
thousands of "queers" were openly applauded.

"It was fashionable," the great poet Langston Hughes later
wrote, "for the intelligentsia and the social leaders of both Harlem and the downtown area to occupy boxes at this ball and look
down from above at the queerly assorted throng on the dancing
floor." Hughes was known to be a little queer himself. But osten-
sibly straight socialites from the Astor and Vanderbilt families
attended, too. So did the actress Tallulah Bankhead.

Large black newspapers like the *Amsterdam News* covered
the Hamilton Ball. In 1931, the *Baltimore Afro-American* ran
"Debutantes Bow at Local 'Pansy' Ball." They described it as "coming out . . . into homosexual society." Other papers picked it up.
In 1932, the tabloid *Broadway Brevities* scandalized its readers
with the headline "Fag Balls Exposed: 6,000 Crowd Huge Hall as
Queer Men and Women Dance." By that point, "pansy parades"
were taking place at mainstream locations including Madison
Square Garden and the Astor Hotel downtown.

Adopting a drag persona was a good way for inverts to keep
the lives they led "out" a secret from their families. In the 1930s,
Mae West was the rage with queens. A man could introduce himself to people he met out at the Hamilton Lodge as Mae West or
the "sepia Mae West" (meaning the nonwhite one), and even get

quoted in the paper that way, and still return home unrecognized. He could go out and do what he wanted without endangering his "real" life.

The real Mae West was all for it. In 1926, she wrote a play called *The Drag*, which featured dozens of gay singers and dancers. In preparation, she asked them questions about the apartments they lived in in Greenwich Village and the constant police raids on their favorite bars. She used material and one-liners that she elicited from the cast to build her script. *The Drag* sensationalized gay life, but also sympathized with its challenges. The third act included a drag show. Rumor had it that a wealthy, well-connected high-society man offered West an enormous pile of money for the chance to play in it one night.

Can you imagine? the chorus boys gossiped. *Some Vanderbilt or some guy onstage!* The man had been willing to pay a high sum for a chance to step out in women's clothing. Because no one would recognize him, he could keep his desires secret, even as he boldly declared them to the world. After try-out performances in Connecticut and New Jersey, *The Drag* was deemed too salacious for Broadway; it soon closed. But the daydreams it inspired remained. Not only could you find privacy in public. Performing in public might also give you a chance to find new versions of yourself.

Going out to a speakeasy or a drag ball created opportunities to demand new kinds of recognition. But it had its disadvantages, too. Then, as now, you could get priced out of the very spots you had made cool.

By the middle of the 1920s, many Harlem residents could not afford to go out in their own neighborhood. The black journalist Wallace Thurman complained that by 1927, the legendary Harlem clubs were becoming "shrines to which white sophisticates, Greenwich Village artists, Broadway revellers, and provincial commuters make eager pilgrimage . . . In fact," he continued, "the white patronage is so profitable and so abundant that Negroes find themselves crowded out and even segregated in their own places of jazz."

In the famous cabarets, the daily wages of a day maid would hardly buy a soda. But most young black women in the 1920s and '30s were working as "domestics." Unlike (mostly white) shop-girls or waitresses, maids did not meet men they could date at work. If they hoped to find love, they had to go out and look for it.

Luckily, "rent parties" offered alternatives to the pricey clubs. These gatherings took place in private homes. White landlords had long charged Harlem residents above-market rates, confi-dent that segregation would keep black tenants from fleeing to cheaper neighborhoods. As prices rose, a new trend developed: If you were struggling to afford your rent, you might throw a party, charging a small admission fee at the door.

These parties usually had good cheap food and drink; some-times musicians from the expensive jazz clubs came by to play after hours. Some people even began making careers of hosting rent parties, turning their homes into permanent "buffet flats." They distributed invitations to friends, and friends of friends.

> We got yellow girls, we've got black and tan
> Will you have a good time?—YEAH MAN!

A Social Whist Party

—GIVEN BY—

MARY WINSTON

147 West 145th Street   Apt. 5

Saturday Eve., March 19th, 1932

GOOD MUSIC   REFRESHMENTS

Langston Hughes went to rent parties almost every Saturday that he spent in Harlem. "I met ladies' maids and truck drivers, laundry workers and shoe shine boys, seamstresses and porters," he wrote. Along with writers and intellectuals and some of the best musicians of their day, these workers met and flirted at rent parties, and they took their dates to them.

This Harlem, Hughes wrote, "didn't like to be stared at by white folks." These parties allowed members of the black working classes "to have a get-together of one's own, where you could do the black-bottom with no stranger behind you trying to do it, too."

The hosts and guests at rent parties had discovered an important law of going out: Not everyone can rely on getting the same kind of access to public space. The institutions of dating have often excluded many people. In the decades that followed, daters would use semiprivate places to create new social movements.

After World War II, gay daters began gathering in places that they slowly made their own. It started in just a few cities and a few neighborhoods. But the energies that it unleashed would eventually change laws across America.

During the war, the armed forces had been eager to enlist recruits, and many young gays and lesbians who felt isolated in their hometowns saw military service as a chance to escape. In the 1978 documentary *Word Is Out*, the lesbian actress Pat Bond recalled the determination she felt as a teen growing up in Davenport, Iowa, to join the Women's Army Corps. "I was in love with this woman who wasn't in love with me," Bond said. "So the thing to do was to go into the Women's Army Corps, and go to Paris, where Gertrude Stein had been."

Bond never made it to France. But in the WAC she did find an environment that welcomed lesbians. Everyone knew it. Girls showed up at recruitment centers wearing short haircuts and corduroy suits; they winked their way through interview questions.

"Have you ever been in love with a woman?"

Wide-eyed. "What's a woman?"

On paper, the WAC discouraged homosexuality. But in practice, it also discouraged persecution. A training manual assured officers that lesbians "are exactly as you and I, except that they participate in sexual gratification with members of their own sex." Many WAC officials had no need to be reminded. Pat Bond could tell at once that the officer who enlisted her was gay, even though she wore a skirt, stockings, and high heels.

"She looked like all my old gym teachers," Bond exclaimed, "but in drag!"

That was during the war, when the army needed people. As the war wrapped up, it started purging hundreds of gay men and women. Five hundred lesbians were expelled from the WAC in Tokyo. Most received a shameful "blue" discharge, which was given for "psychiatric problems," including "sexual deviance." Pat Bond returned to the port of San Francisco. Like many other gay men and women, she stayed. Soon others started showing up, drawn by rumors of new kinds of freedom.

Some came from Washington, D.C., where many gays and lesbians had worked in the State Department and developed a thriving nightlife scene. On April 27, 1953, President Eisenhower signed an executive order demanding that all homosexuals working for the government be purged. The justification was that the dark secret of their lifestyle made them susceptible to blackmail by Communist agents. Although it drew far less media attention than the witch hunt being led by Senator Joseph McCarthy, to the people it targeted, the "Lavender Scare" was just as devastating as the Red one. Finding their professional lives ruined, many men and women cast out of the government looked for oases in friendlier cities.

Pat Bond recalled that in the 1950s, on Broadway in San Francisco, there were at least five bars where women could flirt with one another without being expelled or harassed by management. Every night, she hopped among the five, gathering gossip from old friends and scanning the crowd for new faces. She never worked nights and she never stayed in. Otherwise, she said, she "might miss something."

These were not quite "lesbian bars." During this era, the police still mixed many different kinds of "vice" together; they treated homosexuality and drag like sex work or drug deals. Drunken GIs who had recently returned from overseas and sailors on shore leave crowded into them. These men stared at and pestered the regular patrons for dances. But the women had the power to say no. In the 1920s, Ellin Mackay had written that one of the joys of going out to a speakeasy was being able to ignore anyone who did not interest you. Being in public offered the same opportunity to women who had no interest in men.

"Go away, I'm a lesbian! Get out of my life!" Pat Bond would shout when one of these men approached her. She felt both gleeful and enraged. The protection that being in the bar offered was not foolproof. Sometimes the men got angry when they realized that she was not pretending. Sometimes they waited outside to beat up dykes. Sometimes the cops raided the place. When they did, the women they abused and insulted had little recourse.

Even in the best-case scenario, having to repeat *I'm a lesbian! Get out of my life!* again and again got tiring. But bit by bit, as women who wanted to date women continued to do so, and to tell off gawkers, they started to create something new: publicly recognized lesbian spaces.

The uncertainties involved in going out are a big part of its allure. The fun of flirting is that you are never sure what it means.

The people we meet out, we approach because something attracts us. It might be his hair, or her glasses, or simply a beautiful face, the gender of which we cannot pin down. Often it is something intangible that we glimpse in the moment of our encounter. A gesture. A laugh. A way of ordering a drink. Something gives us a sense that we want to know more.

In many ways, this wanting to know is the most exciting part of going out. It has an edge of risk. Not only do we not know whether the other person is interested in us. We cannot really know how interested *we* are until we have flirted. Our own level of interest is one of the things we are trying to gauge by flirting. Smiling back at a stranger across the room, you know little about her apart from the fact that you like her smile. This not knowing is an appealing change from the obligatory feel of many setups, Internet dates, or workplace intrigues, the rote feel of the questions you ask and the answers you get.

Some risks, however, are not exciting to run at all. Almost everyone who goes out who is not a straight, white, and gender conforming man will at some point fear that a flirtation has put him or her in danger. To worry all the time weighs on you, oppressing you even if you never actually meet with violence.

"Men do not text one another that they got home safe," one friend points out.

"If a guy wants to know what it feels like," another jokes, "he should try watching *Fatal Attraction*. For the rest of his life, he should watch it before every time he goes out."

This was why José Sarria wanted to make the Black Cat Café a gay bar. Owner Sol Stouman hired Sarria as a waiter in the early 1950s. By that time, the Black Cat was already famous as a destination for Beats and Bohemians. The Armed Forces Disciplinary Control Board had added it to a list of establishments that military personnel were forbidden to enter, and Allen Ginsberg declared it "the best gay bar in America."

But at that time it was not quite "gay" yet.

"It was very subtle," Sarria recalled. "Not like it was in later years."

In the 1950s, the Black Cat was a "wide-open" bar that allowed *any* kind of dress and behavior. Famous gay men like Truman Capote visited, but so did the Hollywood actors Bette Davis and Gene Kelly.

"Everybody" went there, Ginsberg wrote. There were "all sorts and kinds of people": "heterosexual and homosexual." There were "gay screaming queens," "longshoremen" and even "heterosexual gray flannel suit types." "All the poets went."

Jack Kerouac set part of his seminal Beat novel *On the Road* in the Black Cat. The scenes where it appears make clear that the mix Ginsberg loved could be a liability as well as a source of excitement. The protagonist, Sal Paradise, admits to getting his kicks by threatening men who flirt with him.

"Several times I went to San Fran with my gun and when a queer approached me in a bar john I took out the gun and said, 'Eh? Eh? What's that you say?' He bolted." The boast then turns into bewilderment: "I've never understood why I did that; I knew queers all over the country."

Sal apologizes for his bad behavior. Like many homophobes before and after, he insists, *I have gay friends!* Like many homophobes, and like Jack Kerouac, he is also clearly sexually interested in men. It would not take an especially skilled psychoanalyst to point out the symbolism. *I just had to show him my penis—I mean, gun!* He goes to the Black Cat hoping to get picked up and then snarls at the first person to approach him.

Sarria quickly worked his way up the Black Cat hierarchy. He started greeting guests, singing arias, and eventually performing as the club's general emcee. By 1960, he was doing four drag shows a night. In the spotlight, he improvised clever ways to disarm anyone who he feared might make queer patrons feel threatened. Around the turn of the millennium, Sarria boasted to historians of the Black Cat: "I *made* it gay. It didn't get gay until I got there." How do you make a bar gay? By creating an atmosphere where everyone who enters is assumed to be gay. During his show, Sarria addressed himself to a gay audience, regardless of exactly who was present.

Wearing a sign that said I'M A BOY, he poked fun at the legal pretext that was often used to arrest cross-dressers: "female impersonation with intent to deceive." (Having to wear such signs had also often been a form of punishment for people arrested for "masquerading in attire not proper to his or her sex.") Sarria told dirty jokes, spilled gossip about prominent members of the gay community, and sang snippets of opera, altering the lyrics to make them raunchy. Sometimes Sarria made his act overtly political. He would read aloud from the newspaper and interpret recent events. If he caught sight of someone he suspected was slumming, he would storm over to the table, high heels clicking, while everyone stared. Years later, he remembered taking one tourist and his cardigan-wearing wife by storm.

"Oh *you*!" he exclaimed. "So you're *bisexual*, are you? I didn't know I was merely another woman!"

The man bristled; the wife blushed. But after a moment, they had to acknowledge that Sarria was right. Everyone in the bar was gay, and gay was good. Straight people could come if they wanted, but they would have to accept that they were the outsiders. They could learn what that felt like.

At the Black Cat and countless other "homophile" bars, daters went out and claimed new kinds of public spaces. By going out, people who had long been made to feel like outcasts found or created new communities. And as they became confident that these places were *theirs*, and felt the strength of their numbers, they fought back against authorities who had long tried to control them. The new movement made "coming out" a powerful rallying cry.

Many of the most famous scenes of the gay liberation movement took place spontaneously, in the places where people went to socialize. Popular histories often date the beginning of the movement to the riots that erupted at the Stonewall Inn in New York's West Village during the early hours of June 28, 1969. When plainclothes police officers raided the bar, a group of trans women and butch lesbians refused to go to the bathroom to have their sex inspected. Other customers began to refuse to line up to have their IDs checked. Soon the crowds in the bar and the streets were in open revolt.

Other historians offer other starting points for the swell of LGBT activism in the 1970s. The clash between a group of queens and street hustlers and the Los Angeles Police Department at Cooper Do-nuts in May 1959. The riot that a group of trans women started at Compton's cafeteria in the Tenderloin district of San Francisco in August 1966. Small protests that erupted spontaneously could draw the attention of a broader public.

Going out gave energy and visibility to LGBT causes. But where some saw going out as the chance to start a revolution, others saw it in terms of commercial opportunity.

In the early 1960s, a young entrepreneur named Alan Stillman moved to New York. He was full of high hopes but found it was a struggle to meet single women. Yet he knew that the city was full of them. Secretaries and typists squeezed into shared apartments on the Upper East Side. Hundreds of flight attendants gravitated toward the "girl ghetto" just above the Fifty-ninth Street Bridge, because it was a quick trip to the airport. Yet the same women who flew all over the world could not go to many local bars without a man. The Oak Room at the Plaza did not admit women until 3:00 p.m. McSorley's Old Ale House banned them entirely until 1970. Signs posted around the bar read: GOOD ALE, RAW ONIONS, AND NO LADIES. Countless other places allowed women only if they were "escorted." Meaning, by a man. That meant, in effect, that single women could not go out to *meet* men. Being on a date with one already was the one way you could get in.

Stillman wanted to change that. Walking through the West Village one night, he had a eureka moment: He would make a gay bar, but for straight people. It was a brilliant idea. Soon after, he opened the first T.G.I. Friday's on the Upper East Side, First Avenue and Sixty-third Street. With it, the "singles bar" was born. Simply by providing a place for singles to mix, Stillman started a craze. He had to install velvet ropes outside the front door in order to wrangle the crowds of young men and women who showed up every night of the week. Across the street, another singles joint, called Maxwell's Plum, soon opened. Two more quickly followed. By the summer of 1965, the police had to come every Friday and close down the block from 8:00 p.m. until midnight, because there were so many patrons going back and forth between the bars that cars could not get through.

By 1967, *Life* magazine announced that the singles bar had become an "institution." "All over Manhattan and in a growing number of other cities there are swinging, noisy gin mills which cater exclusively to young single males and females and which function more or less as perpetual college proms." By the early 1970s, researchers at Stanford University found that between 20 and 25 percent of American couples had met at bars.

In 1971, Stillman sold the T.G.I. Friday's franchise, and it gradually became what it is now: a chain of family-friendly restaurants you might visit in a strip mall or storefront in any one of dozens of countries. If you woke up in a T.G.I. Friday's, you would have a hard time telling whether you were in Tokyo or

Tuscaloosa based on the decor. High-backed leather chairs separate diners. Gay bars may have become starting points for social revolutions, but when the counterculture they created was co-opted, it quickly became a chain of the least sexy restaurants on earth.

A similar fate befell disco music. The roots of disco were planted at a permanent rent party in the Bronx called "Love Saves the Day" that the DJ David Mancuso hosted at his apartment, the "Loft," from 1970 onward.

"I used to go to bars that were open to the public," Mancuso told the music historian Terry Williamson. "But I preferred rent parties because they were a little more intimate and you would be among your friends."

At the Loft, Mancuso charged $3 per entry and offered free snacks and dancing. "There was no one checking your sexuality or racial identity at the door. I just knew different people . . . It wasn't a black party or a gay party. There'd be a mixture of people. Divine used to go. Now how do you categorize her?"

The DJ Nathan Bush was one of Mancuso's guests. As a high schooler, he feared going to gay bars. *What if a friend or relative saw him entering or exiting?* He wanted a space to explore his sexuality and his artistic interests, away from the watchful eyes of his family and neighbors.

"The Loft was a completely different world," he said. "You met all types of people—artists, musicians, fashion designers, bankers, lawyers, doctors. Male, female, straight, gay, it didn't matter."

It was at the Loft that Nathan ran into Larry Levan again. Larry had been a friend in middle school. Bush had always suspected that he was gay. He guessed right; the two became romantically involved and went on to found Paradise Garage, a legendary club in the West Village.

As the disco craze seized New York, however, people went out less to mix with people they would not have met otherwise than to affirm their membership in a crowd that they belonged to already. You went out in order to be part of the scene that party photographers captured. Later you could smile and say, *I was there*.

As being seen became its own end, going out became the means to reach it. The most popular discotheques became media phenomena. At Studio 54, a bouncer would usher a group of celebrities and regulars inside, then select from the countless other hopefuls based on their clothing and appearance. All of the popular discos carefully curated their nightly guest lists in order to create the right environment—the kind that would attract more media attention.

The gay actor Richard Brenner recalled popular discos like Arthur and Cheetah. "They weren't gay clubs. They just let in a certain number, a kind of quota, to give the place more of a party atmosphere."

The entrepreneurs who lifted the disco sound and look from gay African American DJs often ended up excluding the very kinds of people who had pioneered it. Just as T.G.I. Friday's repackaged the gay bar as the singles bar, discos like Buster T. Brown's stole Paradise Garage's music and sold it to the Midwest.

Buster T. Brown's was the only singles bar in Cincinnati in the early 1970s. In 1974, it was sued for racial discrimination. Off the record, some waitresses and patrons admitted to the press that they thought the real issue was sexual insecurity among white men, who felt intimidated by black men who dressed and danced better than they did. On the record, however, they defended the management.

"Oh, we don't really discriminate against blacks," one waitress told the *Cincinnati* magazine reporter Dan Bischoff. "It's just that when too many start to pack the place in, we just start

playing Beach Boys music. That usually makes them move on."
In the absence of laws segregating daters, unofficial techniques
can still do it.

It has long since become a cliché to observe that the lines between
public and private are disappearing, or that, in an age of ubiquitous mobile digital technologies, privacy does not exist. We take
photographs of our food and share them with thousands of
people. We tweet a clever joke while our date is in the bathroom.
The smartphone has dramatically changed what it means to go
out. By making it possible to leave home with the entire Internet
in our pockets—with the profiles of everyone we love, or have
loved, or might ever love, on hand and able to be contacted in
an instant—the smartphone makes it possible never to be fully
out or in.

At the same time, many more people who were once "outsiders" to dating can now go out openly. Gay men, bisexuals, and
lesbians no longer need to hide from the police. In many parts of
many cities, couples who might previously have risked arrest as
"degenerate deviants" if they expressed their affection openly,
can now do so without fear.

These are triumphs. Yet the spaces we call "out" are still not
for everyone. Over the past few years, there have been many signs
that trans people are gaining greater acceptance from the general American public. Yet trans daters are constantly threatened
with hostility and violence. Trans women often become the targets
of the very men who feel attracted to them—scapegoats for the
confusion and self-loathing that such attraction can inspire. Many
states still have laws on the books that make "trans panic"—a
freak-out experienced upon realizing that someone is not the
gender you thought—a legitimate legal defense that can be in-
voked to downgrade a murder charge to manslaughter. The life

expectancy of a trans woman of color in the United States is around thirty-five.

Going out is always about being among others. In this way, it creates a relationship between more than two people. And it is always potentially political. What we hope for when we go out is to be surprised. The surprise may be as ordinary as the slight thrill of jealousy you feel when someone else looks at your longtime partner. Or it might be the delight you feel when you yourself draw such a look. At bottom, a dater goes out to be recognized, even if it is as someone she did not know she was yet.

When strangers catch each other's eyes across a room, however briefly, they become a *we*. Whatever form our relationships take, and for however long they last, it is with a desire for *we* that they begin. *We* is the beginning of every story. And so people who go out create new kinds of community. Going out to date is one way to demand that the world recognize the right of everyone to desire.

CHAPTER 4. **SCHOOL**

As gay bars inspired the first straight singles bar, the success of the first dating app for "gay, bi, and curious" men launched an arms race to develop an equivalent for straight people. Released in 2009, Grindr uses geolocation technology to show members other members in their vicinity; it indicates precisely how far away they are and lets them initiate multiple simultaneous chats. In 2012, Tinder launched and quickly became the most successful of the products promising straight daters a similar experience.

If every dating app re-creates some earlier, predigital dating experience, Grindr lets users relive the thrills of the speakeasy. Like an "invert" of yore, you scan a crowded bar for hints. Could *he* have the waxed and sculpted torso that appears headless on the profile you're eyeing? Or is *that* stuffed shirt hiding it? Even if your phone avers that he is only ten feet away, the idea of walking up to the wrong stranger and asking "Sw33tbun?" might make you nervous.

A night out on Tinder, however, feels less like cruising than like college. And Tinder facilitates a mode of interaction that has mostly replaced formal dating on college campuses: hooking up.

Those who say that romance is dead often point to college "hookup culture" as the culprit that killed it. Like the language of "treating" and "charity" that the first daters developed, the term blends an exchange of goods and services with an act of intimacy. Linguists have found that among African Americans, "hook up" still usually means something like "give" or "arrange." *Can you hook me up with a light? So and so got us the hookup on these backstage passes.* But in the 1990s, white suburban kids started using it to refer to sexual encounters.

As is the case with much slang, the power of the expression lies in its ambiguity. For a teen to say that she *hooked up* with a boy from her class might mean anything from that they had cuddled while watching a movie, to that they had had sex in the bathroom at a house party. I remember using "hook up" mostly as a term of discretion. *Yeah, we hooked up* was a gentle way to reproach the friend who kept fishing for details about your weekend.

To speak of hookups made us feel grown-up, like we had finally outgrown the Truth or Dare? years when we kissed and told everything. But this vagueness gave prying grown-ups the pretext they needed to imagine the worst.

In 2000, the celebrated chronicler of mores Tom Wolfe used *Hooking Up* as the title of a book of essays whose subtitle was *What Life Was Like at the Turn of the Second Millennium*. For Wolfe, hooking up was the perfect metaphor for an America that had turned into a "lurid carnival" without rules or fixed commitments. He was on trend.

We who were actually American girls then may remember watching a fifth grader appear on the morning news to answer

Diane Sawyer's questions about the "sex bracelets" she had been caught selling in her school playground or Oprah warning parents that high schoolers nationwide were throwing "rainbow parties," thus called because the girls who congregated at them applied different shades of lipstick, then fellated boys who tried to collect rings of all the colors you know where. I remember wondering whether Oprah knew how blow jobs worked. My mother grossed me out by implying that she did.

"The idea that girls your age get on their knees for just anyone!" she exclaimed. "I always thought that was something to save for when you're, like, eight months pregnant and feel sorry for your husband." Thank God I was leaving soon for college. Not that parental fretting ended there.

By the time my roommates and I moved into our freshman-year dorm room, a parade of badly behaving undergrads had crossed American screens before us, showing us what to expect. On television, there was *Girls Gone Wild*, where hordes of drunken sorority members lunged at cameras, crying, "We want to go wild!" They kissed one another and lined up to bare their breasts in exchange for *Girls Gone Wild* trucker hats. MTV's *Spring Break* showed a live stream of hard-bodied and bikini-clad students grinding on one another in Cancún.

In movie theaters, the first *American Pie* movie followed the capers of a group of high school friends all desperate to lose their virginity all the way to becoming a huge box office hit. In the sequels, you could watch the gang go to college and return to misbehave at summer beach houses and reunions. Around the same time, a group of actors who some Hollywood reporter dubbed the "Frat Pack" were getting famous by making gross-out college comedies like *Van Wilder* and *Old School*. For anyone with an Internet connection, there was a seemingly infinite variety of both amateur and professional pornography purporting to show "real college sluts."

Surveys in magazines like *Cosmopolitan* suggested that the first generation to arrive at school educated by online pornography had studied up on anal sex, multiple penetration, girl-on-girl action, and were eager to put their theories into practice. I remember a lesbian friend complaining how difficult it was to get her desires taken seriously when so many straight girls were kissing girls just to earn hoots from male onlookers. If you wanted to prove you "really" liked girls, she said, you had to put in a semester sleeping with all the other lesbians on campus.

It was like a teen sex bubble. Plug "hook up" into Google Ngram Viewer—an engine that searches the millions of printed sources available on Google's database, and then generates a graph showing how frequently a word or phrase appears. You'll see that the phrase lurches up around the time of the first tech boom. The hookup rose as unstoppably as real estate and stock market values. It shared the ebullience of an economy that seemed to be disproving the fundamental laws of capitalism.

For a while it looked like kids, at least the kinds of upper-middle-class white kids who showed up on television, really could keep getting *more*.

The average Americans who went to school in the 1990s or early 2000s had around fifteen years between when their bodies hit sexual maturity and when they settled down—if they settled down. As of 2010, the median age of first marriage was over twenty-seven for women, and over twenty-nine for men, and more and more people had no plans of marrying at all.

The spread of high school and college education in the early twentieth century created the ambiguous stage between childhood and work and marriage, where more and more millennials seem to be staying—or stalling, depending on who you ask. By

1910, high school attendance was almost universal in cities, and by 1930, college enrollment was triple what it had been in 1900. Both institutions extended the phase that psychologists call "emerging adulthood."

A period where one had all the freedoms of an adult with none of the responsibilities lent itself to satire. A character in the popular 1912 campus novel *Stover at Yale* delightedly trills the chorus of a popular song: "Oh, father and mother pay all the bills, And we have all the fun!"

Yet to go to college was not just a frivolous self-indulgence. As the United States transitioned from an industrial economy to one based on consumption and services, college offered a new phase of necessary training. Shopgirls and waitresses had to figure out how to conduct themselves in the workplace in order to maximize their chances of success. In the 1920s and '30s, a more privileged group of young people went to school to practice the same skills.

The rise of college and the spread of coeducation in the twentieth century also shaped the history of dating. Young people who moved to four-year institutions and enrolled in classes together started meeting and mixing in new ways. And they started thinking about courtship differently, as a kind of learning process.

Today, friends reassure us that even the most soporific date or apocalyptic breakup teaches us something. Now that many women and men have shaken the stigma formerly attached to premarital sex, we can generally "go the limit" with partners we will not marry without risking arrest or censure. There are few lines you might not cross in order to learn.

For young people lucky enough to spend four years at a residential college, this is especially true during their years on campus. From the outside, campus courtship may look like chaos.

It has, to most onlookers, for as long as students at four-year colleges have dated. In fact it is an extension of the education that such schools offer. The most important learning, the brochures say, takes place outside the classroom. Many students act as if "going out" is the point of going to college.

They are right to sense that going out in college is different from how they will be able to at any other age, or in any other context. The selection process whereby a school chooses students and the relatively homogeneous and predictable environments in which they live and study suggest the opposite of a speakeasy or a wide-open bar. It seems to promise safety, even if that safety is illusory. (According to the most recent statistics, one in four women will be sexually assaulted while attending college.)

Memories of their former dissolution may later console professionals through years of boring desk jobs. *You had to choose adulthood*, they think wistfully. *Your wild youth was too wild to last.* But the most apparently anarchic college courtship rituals in fact train students to follow highly specific scripts. The point of mastering them has less to do with romance than with what might make them successful thereafter. Shopgirls and waitresses had to learn the flirting skills that gave them a chance at professional success on the job. More privileged students can take the time to master them on the quad or at the frat.

The turn of the millennium was not the first time that the American media had been transfixed by young people partying right up to the brink of economic crisis. In the 1920s, national newspapers and magazines reported extensively on the sexual escapades of high school and college students. Before hooking up, there was "petting," and everyone was doing it.

In the 1940s and '50s, Alfred Kinsey defined petting as "deliberately touching body parts above or below the waist" (thus distinguishing it from "necking," or general body contact sustained while making out). In terms of the baseball metaphor, petting covered everything between first base and home plate.

"Mothers Complain That Modern Girls 'Vamp' Their Sons at Petting Parties," *The New York Times* proclaimed in 1922. *The Atlantic* and *The New Republic*, the most prestigious magazines in America, regularly included features on "These Wild Young People" written by "one of them."

At least one audience was guaranteed to take an interest: the petters' parents. Between 1900 and 1930, a dramatic demographic shift changed family dynamics across the United States. Birthrates had been falling since 1800. By 1900, the average American woman was having only half as many children as she would have three generations earlier. Thanks to increased access to birth control, couples in the professional and managerial classes were stopping after their second or third kid. These parents did not have to exercise the kind of severe discipline that had been needed to keep order in households of nine or ten.

Parents lavished affection on children and sought to help them flourish by discovering and developing their interests. The proliferation of advice literature about the new "emotional" family offers evidence of their commitment to this project. By the mid-1930s, 80 percent of women in professional families and nearly 70 percent of women in managerial families read at least one book on child rearing every year. The largest proportion read five. Fathers, too, began buying these books and attending events like teacher conferences.

These were the original helicopter parents. They sent their children to school longer and allowed them a great deal more leisure than they themselves had enjoyed. Ironically, the more they gave their children, the less influence they exerted over them. That role was taken over by their peers. As young people started spending less time with their families and more time with one another, they created their own culture. Petting was part of it, and helped prepare kids for a world that was changing faster than their parents could keep up with.

The process began in high school. By the 1920s, more than three-quarters of American teens attended. A study on child welfare commissioned by the White House in the early 1930s found that outside school activities, the average urban teen spent four nights per week engaging in unsupervised recreation with his or her friends. Their activities included dating—going to watch vaudeville shows or movies, going for ice cream or Coca-Colas ("coking"), going to dances organized by schools or thrown, impromptu, in a classmate's basement, and simply piling into a car together and cruising around.

Parents and schools tried to impose guidelines on these activities. My grandfather, who was a young dater in the 1930s, recalls a schoolteacher admonishing him and his classmates that if they let girls sit in their laps while "joyriding," they had to be sure "to keep at least a magazine between them."

F. Scott Fitzgerald warned that "none of the Victorian mothers . . . had any idea how casually their daughters were accustomed to be kissed." A quick glance at the tables of contents of various editions of Emily Post's *Etiquette* books captures how quickly the shift happened. The 1922 edition contained a chapter on "The Chaperon and Other Conventions"; by 1927 it had been retitled "The Vanishing Chaperone and Other New Conventions"; and by 1937, "The Vanished Chaperone and Other Lost Conventions."

That certain conventions had disappeared did not mean that courtship had devolved into a free-for-all. Rather, having been brought together in schools, young people were developing their own codes. Peer pressure replaced parental discipline.

In 1925, Benjamin Lindsey attempted to explain the changes in attitude that he saw taking place. A judge from Denver, Lindsey had spent decades working in the juvenile justice system. Many of the cases that he describes in *The Revolt of Modern Youth* start with a date gone awry. Take, for instance, fifteen-year-old Helen, who had made plans for a friend of a friend to pick her up at school one afternoon and give her a ride in his new automobile. Though she explicitly stated that she would not let him "make love to" her, she had agreed to give him a kiss.

"That's a fair price," she testified. When Helen's high school principal intercepted her date plans, she had the young man with the car charged with attempted white slave trafficking. But Judge Lindsey marveled at the "strenuous, strict, and self-denying conventions of the strange Flapper-Flipper world she lived in."

Countless cases showed him that Helen was in the new mainstream. "Of all the youth who go to parties, attend dances, and ride together in automobiles, more than 90 percent indulge in hugging and kissing," Lindsey reported. "This does not mean that every girl lets *any* boy hug and kiss her, but that she *is* hugged and kissed."

Lindsey concluded that by the end of high school, 15 to 25 percent of those "who begin with the hugging and kissing eventually 'go the limit.'" The rate among boys was roughly the same as it had been in the late nineteenth century. But whereas previously most middle-class young men said they had their first sexual experiences in the red-light districts, now they petted their female peers on dates. Even if they refused to go "all the way," "nice girls" were no longer insulted by being asked.

In light of these facts, Lindsey argued that it was imperative that parents and educators discard their "wet dishrag morality" and speak openly with children. However, the real revelation was that school, in itself, constituted a kind of sex education. The ways the boys and girls mingled on school premises, and the dating culture that they developed after class, became a key part of what they went there to learn. In the relatively sheltered atmosphere that the school provided, students were willing to take the kinds of risks that only Charity Girls had ventured in dive bars or on boardwalks. When students left for college, they moved into the world of peers and immersed themselves in their rituals full-time.

The rise of coed college education drove the rise of dating. Between 1890 and 1920, the number of students attending college in the United States tripled. By 1927, a majority of colleges had also become coed. Higher education had long interested Americans, because of their belief in self-improvement; coeducation added a dash of sex appeal. In the 1920s and '30s, the growth of the national mass media and entertainment industries fueled a college craze. The new advertising industries used images of well-heeled students to promote new goods. New clothing lines marketed popular articles of clothing as "college style." An army of writers of both fiction and nonfiction told a broader public how to imitate college courtship patterns. They created two archetypal characters: the College Man and the Coed.

Some disciplinarians tried to hold the College Man and the Coed to old standards. Campus YMCAs, YWCAs, and churches offered regular "mixers." Deans exhorted young men to call on the female classmates they met at such events in the parlors of their dormitories or to take them for a stroll. Yet even stubborn traditionalists had to recognize that they were fighting a losing battle.

The College Man and Coed mixed freely. The opening pages of the 1922 short story collection *Town and Gown* show the provincial Peter Warshaw arriving at the unnamed state school where he will study. Peter is frankly overwhelmed.

"The passing and repassing of students was dizzying. Fur-coated co-eds with rouged cheeks; men wearing horn-rimmed glasses; an instructor or two hurrying by with green bags in hand; Chinese students in groups; two colored girls, hesitant and self-effacing; couples who sauntered, gayly glancing about for acquaintances."

The provincial student thrown into this environment had to become accustomed to interacting with far more classmates than he had at home. He also had to master a new, strange language.

The terms that College Men and Coeds tossed around changed fast. Varsity novels devoted a lot of space to slang, dropping terms in scare quotes. In his bestselling debut, *This Side of Paradise*, the young F. Scott Fitzgerald constantly offered definitions. A chapter devoted to "petting" spent less time on love and sex than on how kids gossiped about it.

A riff on the "Popular Daughter" or "P.D." sets a chain of definitions falling like dominoes. "The 'belle' had become the 'flirt,'" Fitzgerald wrote, "the 'flirt' had become the 'baby vamp.'" In the male "fusser," these girls met their match.

Even if you arrived at school sexually experienced, learning to talk the talk constituted a key part of your higher education. The star of *Town and Gown*, Andy Protheroe, was "the champion fusser of a State University that made all of its activities competitive." "Andy kissed a girl when he was fourteen; by sixteen he could 'love em up.'" But during his first year at State University he develops a "new 'line.'" "He learned to use the term 'pet' instead of 'lovin up' and to 'fuss' instead of 'stall.'" He learns to dress the part, too, with "a tiny moustache, shell-rimmed spectacles, tight-fitting, gray coat, and silk gloves."

"Greetings, and all that old rot," he sighs, like he is bored already, when he says hello. Over the course of *Town and Gown*, we see him use this same line on multiple Coeds.

Andy is a "Greek"—a fraternity member. Any College Man worth dating was. A pretty Coed could hope to climb the social ladder on the basis of her looks. But the "barb"—short for "barbarian," or non-Greek—faced steeper odds.

In the 1920s, fraternities were at the center of campus life. For several decades, they had been expanding rapidly. In 1883, there were 505 fraternity chapters and 16 sorority chapters nationwide. In 1912, there were 1,560; by 1930, that number had climbed to 3,900, and 35 percent of all undergraduates were Greeks. Fraternities and sororities became ground zero of college dating.

If the life of the College Man centered on Fraternity Row, the life of the Coed centered on the College Men who lived there. At least it was supposed to, according to the books that College Men wrote about her after graduation. In this, she was very different from her predecessors. The first generation of American women who attended universities in the 1870s and 1880s had inspired an outpouring from experts arguing that education would de-sex them. (The psychologist G. Stanley Hall, for instance, warned that earning a BA would leave a woman "functionally castrated.")

Many of them did indeed remain single. Of those educated at Bryn Mawr between 1889 and 1908, 53 percent never married; at Wellesley and the University of Michigan, the figures were 43 percent and 47 percent. They may not have minded. Women's colleges like Mount Holyoke were described as "hotbeds of special sentimental friendships," where female students "fell in love at first sight" and engaged in "smashing"—cuddling and kissing in their dorm rooms. But many of the new Coeds seemed to have different interests.

In *Town and Gown*, the spinster dean of women feels their differences keenly. "The vulgarity of their dress, their frankness, their cigarettes, their dancing, the things they read, the shows they saw—a mad sex-swirl!" Young women no longer had to choose between men and their studies. The Coed rebelled by putting romantic adventures at the center of her curriculum. Dating dominated social life. Outnumbered by her male classmates by ratios of five or six to one, she could go out with three or four different College Men every week.

What did a college date look like? It could start as a drive. In his 1928 book *The Campus*, Professor Robert Cooley Angell of the University of Michigan argued that "the influence of the automobile on the relations between the sexes" could not be overestimated.

"The ease with which a couple can secure absolute privacy when in possession of a car and the spirit of reckless abandon which high speed and moonlight drives engender have combined to break down the traditional barriers," he sniffed. "What is vulgarly known as 'petting' is the rule rather than the exception."

The College Man with a car often took a Coed *somewhere*. In his "low slung racer," the champion Fusser Andy Protheroe takes girls to the Orph, a vaudeville theater that is the hottest date spot in *Town and Gown*. The entertainment that the College Man and Coed watched together could be salacious. At the Orph, scantily clad shopgirls, topless "Egyptian" dancers, and adulterous vamps take the stage in quick succession, while male members of the audience catcall them with phrases like "sweet papa!" and "hot dog!"

After the show, the College Man took the Coed to eat or drink. The "football joint" Protheroe favors is called the You'll Come Inn. It is "a basement establishment with wooden tables, latticed booths and parchment-shaded lamps," where two chocolate malts cost 50¢. One naïve date of Protheroe's is "thrilled" by it. Her more sophisticated classmates hardly seem to notice the food or jazz music. "The couples in the booths about them were petting whenever the watchful manager, watchful in the fear of an edict from the executive dean would ruin his business, was in another part of the place."

The most important kind of date a College Man and Coed could go on was a dance. Fraternities hosted slews of formals, usually organized around sporting events. Dean Robert Angell estimated that at the University of Michigan in the 1920s, three hundred dances took place every year. At coed and single-sex universities alike, students invited "imports" to attend football games and the parties that surrounded them. More clearly than any other activity, these dances distilled and dramatized the principles that governed college dating.

The first rule was that sex was a secret that young people kept to themselves. Whereas parents had overseen older forms of courtship, now dating took place as far away as possible from watchful adults. On his way into a dance, the College Man would encounter the chaperones, or "shaps," whom university bylaws required to be there. Fraternity hosts became adept at sidetracking them. In the 1924 novel *The Plastic Age*, by Percy Marks, the hero, Hugh Carver, learns how it works as soon as he arrives at his first fraternity dance. "Six men had been delegated to keep the patronesses in the library and adequately entertained."

Second, fraternity dances staged intense competition among peers. Both men and women worked hard to "rate" or merit good dates. Passing the shaps, the College Man joined the stag line at the side of the crowded dance floor and waited for his opportunity to cut in, or steal a Coed from her partner. This system dramatized the idea that courtship was a contest. Even when the College Man invited a Coed to a fraternity party, he accepted that his brothers would take turns dancing with her. Indeed, bringing a girl whose dance card would stay full was taken as a sign of *his* high social status. For the Coed who wanted to impress her date, the best strategy was to flirt with as many others as possible. To do so also cemented her status with her female peers. In *Town and Gown*, the bitter social climber Ellen Pritchett reflects that "men were only the gloves with which one slapped the face of girls. It was women one dueled."

Finally, college dances were explicitly sexual. Your sexuality was the currency you put down to play in this arena, where spending money on clothes and flowers and cars and tickets allowed young people to consume one another conspicuously, too.

In the same way that my parents used to freak out about how children of the 1990s "grinded" to hip-hop, adults in the 1920s panicked about the sexually arousing effects of dancing to jazz music. They fretted about "button shiners" (boys who danced so close to their partners that they appeared to be burnishing their suit or shirt buttons on their dresses), "crumpet munchers" (who danced close enough for, as one young girl told Judge Lindsey, "the kick they get out of it"), and "snuggle pups" (don't ask). And like critics of hip-hop, critics of "unspeakable jazz" expressed their fears in terms that were often racist.

"Anyone who says that 'youth of both sexes can mingle in close embrace'—with limbs intertwined and torsos in close contact—'without suffering harm lies,'" an editorial in *Ladies' Home Journal* declared. "Add to this position the wriggling movement and sensuous stimulation of the abominable jazz orchestra with its voodoo-born minors and its direct appeal to the sensory center, and if you can believe that youth is the same after this experience as before, then God help your child."

Combined with heavy drinking, dances encouraged petting—and more. When Hugh Carver attends his first party in *The Plastic Age*, he is frankly shocked to realize how many of the female imports are hammered. The first girl he cuts in on has breath "redolent with whisky." Another clings to him violently, as they dance, whispering, "Hold me up, kid; I'm ginned." He has to rush another girl to the garden so she can vomit. His fellow Greeks do not behave much better. "A number of the brothers were hilarious; a few had drunk too much and were sick; one had a 'crying jag.'" When the first girl he cut in on accosts Hugh, slurring "Le's—le's pet," and plants a kiss on him, he flees. On his way out, he darts into a friend's room to pick up a shawl for a shap who accidentally left it there, and stumbles in on two strangers having sex.

The way Hugh Carver describes these scenes suggested that a gentleman would not take advantage of a Coed when she was incapacitated. Who knows how many real-life College Men followed this rule? By the end of *The Plastic Age*, even Goody Two-shoes Hugh has fallen into the fray. At the advice of friends, Hugh buys "hooch" to pregame his final prom with his girlfriend, Cynthia. By midnight, "Hugh was aware of nothing but Cynthia's body." When she asks him to "ta-take me somewhere," he leads her to the dorm room of the straitlaced friend who lives nearest to the party. In a deus ex machina move, the friend returns early from his holiday, to find them petting on his carpet. It is only this chance event that keeps the couple from "going the limit." The mutual embarrassment they feel at the extremity of their behavior breaks them up just in time for Hugh's Sanford graduation.

College students may have always misbehaved. In 1752, Yale President Thomas Clap kicked a student out of the university for "sundry riotous and impudent Crimes." The kid had gone on a beer-fueled rampage—yelling and jumping, damaging the walls of the rooms of his tutors and, worst of all, saying that he did not *care* if they expelled him. But in the twentieth century, with the introduction of women into the mix, attitudes toward what constituted acceptable behavior on college campuses dramatically shifted. Increasingly, the kinds of authority figures or disciplinarians who had once been shaps abandoned that supervisory role. They left the kids to work out their own system.

A long legal tradition had argued that colleges had the right to discipline students in loco parentis, or "in place of their parents." The thinking was that by voluntarily entering a university—or, in the case of those under eighteen, being enrolled by one's guardians—a student surrendered many liberties. In 1913, the Supreme Court of Kentucky upheld the right of the private Berea College to expel students for going to a restaurant across the street from campus. In 1928, a New York appellate court upheld the right of Syracuse University to expel a student for not being "a typical Syracuse girl." The opinion argued that if a student harmed the "ideals of scholarship" or "moral atmosphere" of even a public university, she had violated the terms of the contract that she signed in the form of her registration card; the university was therefore entitled to terminate it.

In the 1960s, however, a series of cases brought an end to in loco parentis. Over the course of the decade, judges argued that public universities could no longer expel a student without due process. As more and more undergraduates became active in civil rights protests, courts also defended their rights to freedom of speech and assembly at school.

These decisions had major implications for how college students conducted romantic relationships. Until the 1960s or '70s, "parietal rules" had strictly governed the interactions of men and women at both coed and single-sex universities, imposing curfews and enforcing "intervisitation" policies like "open door, one foot on the floor." Starting in the late 1960s, however, schools dropped these regulations, and more and more dormitories went coed.

In retrospect, it seems clear that the end of in loco parentis was part of a broad shift in how the public viewed higher education. The first American universities were founded to train ministers; the secular schools of the nineteenth and twentieth centuries still were thought to perform a key civic function, preparing young people to be productive democratic citizens. Since the heyday of campus activism in the 1960s and '70s, a new consensus has emerged. Rather than seeing public universities as social goods, with an important moral vocation, more and more public figures speak about them like *businesses.*

By the twenty-first century, corporate universities and defunded state schools were allowing students to conduct their private lives pretty much however they wanted. The new philosophy held that students were customers, and they were always right. One would hope so. Since the mid-1970s, tuition at private colleges has increased at nearly triple the rate of general inflation; at public institutions it has more than doubled. It hardly seems unreasonable for the individual bearing that kind of expense to have a little fun.

And so being an undergrad gives you carte blanche. If that time you had sex with the student council president in the laundry center, then accidentally emailed the entire staff of the student newspaper about it, ever comes up, you can simply shrug. That photo of you making out with three friends in broad daylight on top of a U-Haul truck? *It was college!*

In the 2000s, academic sociologists and university administrators started taking an interest in the growing number of news reports about student promiscuity. It was the first time that many of them had heard that the practice of dating on campus was endangered, and they wanted more than an anecdotal basis to understand the changes taking place. Starting in the mid-2000s, several scholars set up the first large-scale, social scientific studies that aimed to investigate both how undergraduates hooked up and how they felt about it. Like Judge Lindsey in the

1920s, they found that the revolt of modern youth had not created chaos. Rather, it had generated a new set of conventions that peer groups strictly enforced.

While it might have surprised onlookers, undergraduates in the 2000s were in fact having less sex than their predecessors in the 1980s and '90s—if you accepted their definition of sex as vaginal intercourse. (Those of us who grew up during the Clinton years learned from our president that activities other than intercourse do not constitute "sexual relations," however intimate they may be.) Nationally representative studies conducted by the Centers for Disease Control have found that in fact there has been a significant decrease in rates of teen sex over the past twenty years. In 1991, their annual Youth Risk Behavior survey found that half of boys and 37.2 percent of girls age fifteen to seventeen reported having had sex in the past three months. By 2010, the number of boys fell to under 33 percent and girls dropped to 17 percent. The professors who turned to their own campuses found similar patterns.

Paula England, a sociologist at New York University, has carried out the most exhaustive research to date on hookup culture. Over the past ten years, England has interviewed individual students, run focus groups, and conducted an online survey on more than thirteen thousand heterosexual undergraduates at four-year institutions across the United States. England found that on many campuses, the unusually chaste and unusually profligate tend to skew the average number of hookups between matriculating and the time of graduation. However, the median for graduating seniors is between four and seven—hardly a shocking figure, especially when you take into account that only 40 percent of these hookups involve intercourse. Nor were encounters always "random."

The researchers restricted their sample to students who explicitly said that they were not in relationships. Only 50 percent of this group said their last hookup was with someone with whom they had never hooked up before, and 20 percent said it was with someone with whom they had hooked up "ten or more times"—a "repeat" or "serial hookup," aka a "friend with benefits" or a "fuck-buddy." Less than 15 percent of all college hookups took place between strangers.

In sum: Young people today may sleep with more partners over a lifetime than their parents did, because we marry later. But the perception that students are becoming more and more promiscuous is unfounded.

The most significant change in students' sex lives in the Age of the Hookup does not have to do with how much of what kind of sex they are having. What has changed is what sociologists call the "sexual script"—the roles that people feel are available for them to play, and what they think they mean.

Kathleen Bogle, a sociologist who conducted a study of hookup culture at both a secular and a Catholic university on the East Coast, argues that the "dating script" has been replaced. Indeed, it has been reversed. Rather than go out on formal dates, the students she surveyed "hang out" or "party" in large mixed-sex settings. Bogle's informants explain that if two students are interested in each other, they put out "the vibe." If it is reciprocated, they hook up—at the party venue, back at one of the partner's dorm rooms, or somewhere in between. If emotional attachment develops from a series of hookups, partners must "have the conversation" or "DTR" (define the relationship) before things "get weird."

Whereas from the 1920s until at least the 1960s, there was an assumption that a series of dates would lead to sexual intimacy and emotional commitment, students today tend to put sexual activity first. If you want a hookup to lead to "something," you are not supposed to admit it. The defining feature of the hookup is thus an emotional attitude. Lisa Wade and Caroline Heldman of Occidental College have described it as "more than simply casual." After hookups, "students reported a compulsory carelessness."

Donna Freitas, a professor who surveyed several thousand students about hookup culture, agrees. "Hookup culture teaches young people that to become sexually intimate means to become emotionally empty, that in gearing themselves up for sex, they must at the same time drain themselves of feeling."

This reversal of scripts has inspired two major reactions.

Some writers have described hookup culture as a misguided rejection of marriage and monogamy. Susan Patton represents this strain of thinking at its most regressive. Better known as the "Princeton Mom," Patton became an overnight Internet celebrity in the spring of 2013 when she published an open letter in *The Daily Princetonian*. Her goal was to counsel the daughters she never had. Her advice was that female undergraduates at elite institutions should spend most of their time husband-hunting.

"You will never again have this concentration of men who are worthy of you," Patton admonished her imaginary girls. She proceeded to appear on TV show after TV show and, one year later, published a book called *Marry Smart*.

Predictably, *Marry Smart* argues that hooking up is no way to conduct a husband search. Patton admits that it is impossible to compete with "the woman who is easier to make than a peanut butter sandwich" or has "been *around* more times than a laundry drum." The good news is that "worthy" men do not want to marry such women either. Hookup culture is, therefore, a game you had best sit out.

Other writers have argued the opposite. They say that hookup culture is a victory for feminism and precisely what female undergraduates should be doing if they aspire to earn more than an MRS degree.

The *Atlantic* contributor Hanna Rosin claimed in her book *The End of Men* that hookup culture was in fact one of the most important reasons for the gains in educational and professional attainment that women have experienced relative to their male peers during the last decade. In the chapter "Hearts of Steel," Rosin praises hookup culture for letting ambitious young women get sex out of the way, without committing time to relationships that might compromise their career prospects.

A much-discussed *New York Times* article that also appeared in 2013 showed young women at the University of Pennsylvania rationalizing their love lives in explicitly economic and corporate language. The source whom the reporter Kate Taylor quotes in the lead says that she sleeps with a friend she is not dating when she has free time, because "cost-benefit" analyses of the "low risk and low investment costs" of hooking up make this make sense. "I positioned myself in college in such a way that I can't have a meaningful romantic relationship."

Yet this practical stance leaves many problems unaddressed.

It remains unclear how the kind of liberated woman Rosin and Taylor portray is supposed to segue from steely hearted hookups to emotionally meaningful relationships—which almost all of them say they do want, eventually. Can courtship function like a game of musical beds, in which someone turns off the music on your thirtieth birthday, and you have to marry whomever you are lying next to? Does intimacy itself not require any practice? Even if you do not belong to the vast majority (over 80 percent) of millennials who say that they want to get married, hooking up as Rosin describes it—disciplining yourself to resist any tug of emotion so that you can focus on professional advancement—comes at a cost.

Although they draw opposite conclusions about how young

ookup culture, Patton and Rosin
h seem to discount the possibility
worthwhile, or that hooking up
your sexuality if you did it right.
onal television disputing that date
all sex education should be left to
oogle as needed). She is too obvi-
sly. The Rosin and *New York Times*
Yet they, too, seem to be telling
: really enjoy their own capacities
leans wasting precious time.
ort you when you can sell yourself
eir stories often say that they are
nore like perpetual-motion machines programmed to do endless work.

When the College Men and Coeds of the Roaring Twenties graduated and became the ones writing and editing advice columns, they popularized the attitudes that they had learned at school. College had taught these writers to treat dating as a form of recreation, where you used your personality and sex appeal to get the attention and amusement that you wanted from your peers. They had been lucky enough to date during the fat years, when wealthier parents thought nothing of buying their children cars or paying their fraternity dues, and when it was easy to come by part-time jobs to cover incidental expenses that might raise the eyebrows of a mom or dad—to keep themselves in new clothes and flowers, dance cards and movie tickets, chocolate malts and hooch.

"Not even poker played by a man of bad judgment, inept at the game, is more disastrous to an undergraduate's monthly allowance than is the game which the fusser is trying to play,"

Dean Clark of the University of Illinois joked in 1921. Ten years later, even young people who were able to attend four-year colleges could not afford extravagances. And so a shift of emphasis took place. The law governing college dating was still the law that the stag line and cut-in culture had exemplified: the law of competition. But rather than competing through the kinds of conspicuous consumption that daters had indulged in during the 1920s, the College Men and Coeds of the Great Depression competed in the currency of *dates* themselves.

The advice literature of the 1930s is full of tips on how to use dates to increase your popularity, and vice versa. The prestige that you gained by being a popular date offered some consolation for not being able to run up a big tab at the football joint or to update your flapper fashions every other week. Many daters had to content themselves with dating longer, as the bad economy prevented couples from settling down.

Throughout the 1930s, newspapers and women's magazines ran dirge after dirge about the dearth of "marriageable men." Few young men were earning the kind of income that was considered necessary to found a household. Between 1928 and 1932, the number of women marrying between eighteen and thirty-five decreased by nearly 20 percent from the previous five-year period. Students were behaving a lot like today's millennials. Dating prolifically was the one way to keep up their stock, so competition for dates intensified, even as any given date became less likely to lead to a permanent arrangement.

Looking out over the quad, professors started taking notice of their behaviors. In 1937, one scholar lifted a bit of '20s slang and elaborated it into an academic theory. Campus courtship, Willard Waller argued, was controlled by the "rating and dating complex."

———

Waller, who held a PhD from the University of Pennsylvania, may have been predisposed to take a dim view of dating. When he arrived to teach at Penn State University in the early 1930s, he was recently divorced and sorely disappointed by his students' lack of intellectual enthusiasm. When he turned his eye on what did interest them, he was troubled by what he saw.

Waller recognized that the largely middle-class white students he taught had good reasons for putting off marriage. They had come to college because they aspired to "mobility of class." For them, it would be disastrous to actually fall in love: Marrying almost always entailed dropping out. To make good on their investment, they had to wait until they had graduated and landed jobs. It made sense. But Waller believed that the new process of dating without any intention to commit had perverted the functions of courtship.

"Dancing, petting, necking, the automobile, the amusement park, and a whole range of institutions and practices permit or facilitate thrill-seeking behavior," Waller wrote. "Energy is dissipated in thrills which is supposed to do the work of the world."

In addition to diverting resources from the important tasks of forming new couples and families to frivolous entertainment, dating encouraged the development of "exploitative relationships." Specifically, the confusion that arose from rapidly changing courtship protocols allowed young people to take advantage of one another. "According to the old morality a kiss means something, a declaration of love means something, a number of Sunday evening dates in succession means something," Waller wrote. "Under the new morality such things may mean nothing at all . . . So it comes about that one of the persons may exploit the other for thrills."

Unlike the earlier generation of progressive sociologists, who had fixated on the dangers that dating posed to women, Waller believed dating caused moral harm all around. "When a woman exploits, it is usually for the sake of presents and expensive amusements—the common pattern of 'gold-digging.' The male exploiter usually seeks thrills from the body of the woman. The fact that thrills cost money, usually the man's money, often operates to introduce strong elements of suspicion and antagonism into the relationship."

In a sense, Waller was expressing the "prostitution anxiety" that had plagued dating ever since the Charity Girls. The Coed did not actually exchange sexual favors for money. But sometimes she did accept a date from a man she did not truly admire. Not only might she enjoy the cocktail or movie ticket he was offering, she used dates to purchase social prestige—which she could cash in for more dates. Men, meanwhile, took as many physical "thrills" as they could get. Like the stock market, the rating-and-dating complex was a confidence game, which men and women played by different rules.

"Young men are desirable dates according to their rating on the scale of campus values," Waller observed. "In order to have a Class A rating they must belong to one of the better fraternities, be prominent in activities, have a copious supply of spending money, be well-dressed, 'smooth' in manners and appearance, have a 'good line,' dance well, and have access to an automobile . . . The factors which appear to be important for girls are good clothes, a smooth line, ability to dance well and *popularity as a date*."

You had to rate to date, and could rate only by dating. Yet to keep your stock high, you had to seem scarce. In order to be desirable, the main thing a girl had to maintain was a reputation for desirability.

"Here as nowhere else, nothing succeeds like success."

Margaret Mead agreed that the kinds of dating that took place on college campuses were not well suited to creating happy marriages and families. Mead had spent much of the 1920s and '30s in the South Pacific and had opportunities to observe the courtship and mating practices of radically different cultures. Her 1928 book *Coming of Age in Samoa* became a bestseller and made her one of the most famous anthropologists in the world. So in 1946, when Stanford invited her to give a series of lectures on American Courtship Rituals, she brought an unusual perspective. Like Willard Waller, Mead saw dating as "primarily a competitive game." However, she did not believe that this made dating a dysfunctional form of courtship. Instead, she said dating had nothing to do with courtship. Americans had no courtship rituals at all.

"The boy who longs for a date is not longing for a girl," Mead wrote in a chapter of *Male and Female* that she adapted from these lectures. "He is longing to be in a situation, mainly public, where he will be seen by others to have a girl, and the right kind of girl, who dresses well and pays attention." Mead argued that dating taught young people to treat one another as status symbols. A boy wanted the girl he wanted at any given moment because he believed she would improve his image and thus increase his worth. "He takes her out as he takes out his new car, but more impersonally, because the car is his for good, but the girl is his only for the evening."

She may have been the first to anticipate the breakup cliché: *It's not about you.* Petting, Mead said, was not even about sex. Young people learned to "mimic sexual readiness" in order to compete with one another. Your skin and limbs and hair and laugh served you as so many chips in a game. The prize was not love but popularity. The most important lesson from dating in college was to learn to consume and to present yourself correctly: to groom and dress the right way and propose the right activities; to make the right jokes at the right moments. The exercise had less to do with courtship than with job training.

Colleges themselves were shifting their priorities in this direction. In the early twentieth century, American universities were changing. Under the influence of figures like John Dewey, who advocated "learning by doing," administrators started allowing and even encouraging students to develop their own organizations. In addition to fraternities, campuses saw the proliferation of activities from student newspapers and theater companies to intercollegiate sports teams. Along with rating and dating, these clubs prepared students to succeed in the corporations they often resembled.

In 1915, the Yale English professor Henry Seidel Canby wrote that "it is mere pedagogery to suppose that all effort not directed toward intellectual development is wasted." Yale, Seidel said, was "graduating 'good mixers' by the hundred."

Like rating and dating and fraternity culture, contemporary hooking up sorts students. The Princeton Mom took a frankly elitist approach to dating in *Marry Smart*, telling young women that nowhere but at Princeton would they find "men worthy of them." All the social scientific data on hooking up suggests that that practice, too, is overwhelmingly white, straight, and upper middle class. It is not nearly as universal as the articles in places like *The Atlantic* and *The New York Times* suggest. Lisa Wade's research has shown that African American students, perhaps wary of a long history of stereotypes that accuse African Americans of being hypersexual and then punish them for it, are far less likely to participate than their white peers. Students who commute to college, or work to support themselves, do not have the time or disposable income to join the party scene. Queer students have their own reasons for avoiding fraternities, and although gay men have a reputation for being more promiscuous than their straight peers, sociologists and school counselors and psychologists have suggested that they do not earn it. In fact, they are generally better at defining and demanding what they want from relationships, which often includes abstaining from sex.

Why does the media pay so much attention to hooking up? At one level, the answer is obvious: As a shopgirl could have told you, sex sells. The people writing the articles and the people reading them are also mostly white, straight, and middle class. These are the people who get to set the terms of what is seen as "mainstream" culture, even when what they are describing is, in fact, exceptional. At another level, reports of hooking up spread the idea that working all the time and using others indifferently is desirable and glamorous.

What kind of education does hooking up provide? And what happens to the people who pursue continuing hookup education after they have graduated? Are we investing in experiences that will qualify us for a dream position someday? Or does every year of hooking up simply put us in the emotional equivalent of more student debt?

An app like Tinder presents a mirage of precisely the kind of endless sexual possibility that young people, dispersed over cities, miss from their undergrad years. The average user opens it ten times a day. It does not, however, seem terribly effective as a matchmaker. As their use of the verb "play" suggests, many treat the app more like a video game. The most valuable service it provides may be the jet of endorphins you get when you are reminded that there are singles who would be willing to swipe you into their "right" pile—that someone, somewhere would consider hooking up with you.

One friend based in Los Angeles confesses that he does most of his Tindering to pass the time in traffic. "There"—he hesitates—"and on the pot." After eighteen months of playing addictively, he has gone out on a total of three dates. Yet the app helps him keep faith that he will find his Tinderella someday. And maybe this—to be content sitting alone, pants bunched around our ankles; to look for our opening while creating free money for the tech industry—was what hooking up was prepping us for all along.

Margaret Mead looked at American courtship rituals and saw that by mixing courtship and competition, they sent young people deeply confusing messages. Go ahead, girls, said America. Work hard to win as many dates as you can. Go out with them and pet! But God help you if you ever actually *give in* to the urges that petting awakens in your partner. This way of thinking assumed that any warm-blooded boy was always trying to "go farther." It could not countenance the possibility that the flutter a girl felt in the floor of her stomach when being kissed might make her want to steal the next "base," too. That is, it gave women no way to understand their own desires, much less express them.

In the 1930s, sex was something a girl had to lose. A nice girl gave as little as she could get away with. Then, as soon as she married, America about-faced. Not only should a young wife have sex, it told her, she should have lots of sex, and she should like it. If you do not like sex as much as your husband, your marriage will not be "well-adjusted."

Mead recognized that rating and dating was not great preparation for long-term relationships. Neither is hooking up today. If petting left a nice girl no way to feel pleasure, except as a failure of will, hooking up teaches people to feel the same way about their feelings. The fact that "hookup" can refer to almost anything indicates that its defining feature is *not* a particular set of sexual activities. The only thing that all the intimate acts called hookups share is that the participants are not supposed to care about, or harbor any expectations of, the other. To hook up is to make no promises. Hence the weird way we can break off with someone we have been hooking up with for months, without offering an explanation.

In the age when college students are told they must be endlessly adaptable and prepare themselves for an economy where they cannot count on anything, of course this is how they relate—and how many of them continue to act after graduation. As rating and dating taught young people then to be captains of industry and good career girls and housewives, hooking up teaches us the flexibility that the contemporary economy requires.

Today, the average millennial spends no more than three years at any job, and more than 30 percent of the workforce is freelance. Hooking up gives you the steely heart you need to live with these odds. Like a degree in media studies, it prepares you for anything and nothing in particular.

CHAPTER 5. **STEADIES**

Over the course of nine seasons, the character that Jerry Seinfeld played on *Seinfeld* had sixty-six girlfriends. Something was wrong with every one of them. They were all attractive enough to appear on network television. Yet each had some fatal flaw, which became shorthand for the episodes in which she was featured.

"Two Face." "The Loud Laugher." In the show about nothing, no reason was too trivial to end a romantic relationship. In one episode, an exasperated blonde whom Jerry has been seeing demands that he choose between her and mimicking a voice that he imagines yodeling *Helloooo* out of her belly button, and Jerry chooses The Voice. Why not? He never seems to doubt that for a man with a job, New York contains an infinite supply of potential dating partners. Even the fat, bald, and hapless George Costanza regularly finds good-looking women who are willing to sleep with him.

"Of course he does," a friend groans when I bring it up. "George was to the '90s what the beer-bellied hipster is today. Those guys get laid *constantly*." Yet it does not seem as if Jerry or George is motivated by a strong desire for sex per se. Their profligacy has more to do with a need for story. It is what the show needs in order to keep going.

It takes a particular kind of dating to drive a sitcom. A date can introduce novelty into a format that is essentially repetitive. But the number of characters and plotlines must not multiply beyond what viewers can keep track of, and no relationship should become so serious as to eclipse the original premise. It was fine that Jerry and Elaine had dated before *Seinfeld* started. And it was fine that they sometimes fell back into bed together. But if they had ever really gotten together, the show would have changed beyond recognition.

Irksome postmen and surly deli managers can linger in the backgrounds of our lives for years. But usually, someone you are dating will either assume a larger and larger role or drop out of the picture. And so on *Seinfeld*, one dater after another came and went. Same thing on *Friends*. The characters were less frankly misanthropic than Jerry, George, Elaine, and Kramer, but they, too, tended to put off making romantic commitments. *Would they or wouldn't they?* became a key strategy the show used to sustain our interest over the seasons. Would Chandler and Monica tie the knot? Would Ross and Rachel? How about Pam and Jim on *The Office*?

As long as NBC kept us wondering, millions of Americans kept tuning in. Yet Jerry Seinfeld and Jennifer Aniston did not invent the style of romance they practiced. Young people who started dating around the beginning of World War II did. We now call it "serial monogamy." They called it "going steady." Their slang may sound quaint today, but many singles still follow the patterns that they pioneered.

The writing started to show up on the walls of high school gymnasiums around 1940. Rather than rating and dating, young people were pairing off. High school and even middle school students were going out to dances and movies and pharmacy counters, where they bought Cokes and root beer floats. They parked and petted like college students of the Roaring Twenties, but always with the same person. They professed themselves to be "going out" with that person, even if they mostly stayed in.

The "steady" part of the expression came from the Era of Calling. Back then, "keeping steady company" implied a serious commitment. A boy and girl who consistently spent time alone together were expected to marry soon. Steadies revived some aspects of calling. Couples often visited each other at their family homes, where they chatted and ate snacks or listened to a record or watched television. Steadies might refer to themselves as "Tom's girl" or "Bob's girl." Male steadies gave "their" girls tokens in order to let them display the bond they shared. A girl who had been "pinned" wore her beau's varsity pin on her blouse or sweater. She might wind tape or yarn around his class ring, so that it fit her finger.

Some couples exchanged "pre-engagement" rings. In practice, however, few of them were seriously considering marriage. For one thing, most of them were far too young. By the mid-1950s, one in ten middle school students would go steady at least once before he or she turned eleven. Rather than a step toward marriage, going steady became an important coming-of-age ritual in itself.

In 1942, a young Midwesterner named Maureen Daly captured how exhilarating going steady could feel, and how dramatically it could change you. The Daly family had emigrated from Northern Ireland to the Midwest when Maureen was a young child. By the time she graduated from high school in Fond du Lac, Wisconsin, Maureen had already published several short stories that were establishing her as an authority on people her age. The media were just starting to call them "teenagers."

When her debut novel, *Seventeenth Summer*, came out, Daly was still an undergraduate at Rosary College in River Forest, Illinois. The publicity around the book stressed that it was based on Daly's personal experiences. The photo that appeared with reviews shows a serious-looking young woman with a heart-shaped face and concentrated features; her dark hair is side-parted into a soft schoolgirl bob, but her eyes look sharp and quick. It is easy to imagine her in the place of her narrator, Angeline Morrow.

Seventeenth Summer tells the story of a three-month relationship from Angie's perspective. At the beginning of June, Angie has just graduated from high school. When Jack Duluth, the son of the local baker, asks her out on a date to a popular soda fountain, she feels anxious.

"It was almost like making my debut or something," she remarks. "I had never been out to Pete's on a date before, and in our town that is a crucial test."

Afterward, she is sure that she has flunked. "I had acted all wrong . . . It made me squirm inside to think of it."

Not only is Angie awkward, she also is naïve. When she notices the rows of cars parked outside Pete's, she feels puzzled.

"There don't seem to be nearly as many people inside as there are cars parked out here," she says. Jack assumes she must be joking: The cars are clearly full of couples. Yet within three days, Angie is urging Jack to lead her out of a country club dance onto the darkened golf course for her first kiss.

"In the loveliness of the next moment," Angie remembers, "I think I grew up."

Soon, professors at several institutions were confirming that their students favored going steady, too. In 1948, researchers at Bucknell University asked 484 undergraduates about their love lives; 105 said that at that time, they were seeing one partner exclusively.

By 1955, the sociologist Robert Herman declared that Willard Waller's "campus rating complex" had become obsolete; a new "going steady complex" had replaced it. When Herman surveyed nearly two hundred students at the University of Wisconsin, they told him that going steady was the most common way that they and their peers dated. Seventy-seven percent of them said they themselves had gone steady. And more than half of the ones who had, had done so more than once.

"Going steady was the thing to do in my high school," one of Herman's students wrote.

"The fad in my school was going steady," another corroborated. "You either went steady or you never went."

That was basically how it worked at my high school, too. A handful of boys and girls were known to hook up with each other without committing to any one boyfriend or girlfriend; the rest of us whispered about their liaisons with disapproving fascination. But most of my friends passed through cycles of being celibate, then being coupled, and back. They seemed to assume, as I did, that we would each go through a string of partners until by some mysterious mechanism, one of them turned into The One. Then we would stand side by side, in pairs, as the screen faded to black.

Such a simple trajectory seemed natural when I was fifteen; now my faith in it strikes me as naïve. But the first adults who noticed that teens were beginning to date this way found their behavior strange and scandalous. Columns offering personal and romantic advice were becoming a common feature of American newspapers during the 1940s and '50s, and the new class of nationally syndicated experts seemed to agree: Going steady was a terrible idea.

Elizabeth Meriwether Gilmer was the most strident. Writing under the pen name Dorothy Dix, Gilmer became one of the highest-paid female journalists in the United States. At the peak of her popularity, she had millions of regular readers around the world. And as early as 1939, Dix was warning young women against the "insane folly of 'keeping company.'" "The custom has all of the worst features of marriage and none of its advantages," she wrote.

Doris Blake agreed. Blake was another pseudonym, for a woman named Antoinette Donnelly; her column was syndicated in forty-five daily papers nationwide. In 1942, Blake published a lament for the good old days of high school and college dances, where young men cut in on girls and girls filled up their dance cards.

"It's simply a pernicious habit grown out of we-don't-know-what that has fostered this ridiculous custom of a couple of 16, 17, or 18 year olds pairing off to the exclusion of everyone else on the dance floor," Blake fumed.

The advice from the *Baltimore Afro-American* was more measured. The largest black-owned paper in the country, the *Afro* featured a weekly column called "Date Data" signed simply by "the Chaperone." It offered thoughtful advice to steadies experiencing a wide range of problems. But at the end of the day, the Chaperone agreed that young people would be better off dating around.

When one girl wrote in, despairing because her boyfriend had joined the army, the Chaperone reproached her: "Just remember that you are not married to him, and he has a life to live."

When a fourteen-year-old pleaded for advice on how to save a steady relationship with a boy she knew "talked sweet" to others, the Chaperone was blunt. "Seems as though he's already given you up. However, don't feel too badly about it. When you're as young as you are, it's healthy to be interested in lots of boyfriends/girlfriends, rather than settling down to one steady."

What were the skeptics so worried about? For one thing, going steady seemed to deprive young people of the pleasures of courting and being courted. In the era of rating and dating, you had to make plans to see a partner. In the 1920s, if a Fusser had wanted to take out a Flapper, convention said he had to call her. If a College Man wanted to see a Coed, he had to propose some activity—a walk around campus, a joyride, or a trip to the movies. Going steady changed this. For the first time in history, it was possible for daters to take one another for granted.

In 1951, the education branch at RCA-Victor made a short film that was used in high school classrooms to teach students about the danger of falling into exclusive relationships. It featured two forlorn steadies, Jeff and Marie. They look like children but already they are feeling bored and trapped. In the opening scene, Marie's mother asks her whether Jeff will take her to the school dance that night, and she wrings her hands in anguish.

"Oh Mother, that's the trouble. Jeff doesn't ask me, he just shows up!"

We then cut to Jeff. He turns out to be equally distressed.

"We haven't agreed on anything," he sighs to his wiser, older brother. "We haven't even *talked* about going steady. We just sort of . . . go steady."

He pauses. "How did I get into this?"

If you were foolish enough to rush into a steady relationship, the fishbowl quality of high school could make it difficult to get out. Peers conspired to enforce the Steady Code. In *Seventeenth*

Summer, a clique of boys called "The Checkers" spends evenings loitering in front of the town's most popular date spot. "They watch to see who is having a Coke with whom and to report any violations on the part of the girls who are supposed to be going steady," Angie, the narrator, explains.

One popular textbook for college "marriage and family" courses claimed that young people who wanted to see more than one person had to resort to "late dating"—sneaking out for a second dinner or Coke or beer after their steadies had brought them home. Was this cheating? Is it possible to betray someone to whom you have sworn to be true for a semester or a summer? It certainly seemed to be possible to feel guilty about it.

If going steady made for less fun before marriage, the authorities worried that it could also harm your marriage prospects. Dorothy Dix warned that it was a lose-lose. A girl could squander her best years on a boy who ultimately left her in the lurch. Even worse, a couple could end up drifting down the aisle out of habit.

Dix was too delicate to point out another likely possibility: that Steadies would find themselves in need of a shotgun wedding. The Catholic Church was not. On Ash Wednesday 1957, the archbishop of Chicago, Cardinal Samuel Alphonsus Stritch, publicly denounced the practice as a trap that would lure children into sex: "Too much familiarity between the adolescent girl and the adolescent boy is dangerous and sinful," he said.

That year, Catholic schools across the country began expelling students who were discovered to be "seeing one other student to the exclusion of all others," and a Catholic magazine issued a warning to its readers: "It is impossible for a boy and a girl to be alone together in an intimate and exclusive companionship for any length of time without serious sin."

————

Cardinal Stritch was not wrong. In the United States, a long tradition gave courting couples tacit permission to engage in sexual behavior so long as they stopped short of intercourse. One familiar custom in Colonial America was "bundling," sometimes called "tarrying." Two young people were allowed to sleep side by side in a bed, partially clothed or enclosed in a sack that shut with a drawstring at the neck. Sometimes a piece of wood called a "bundling board" was placed between them.

In his autobiography, Benjamin Franklin reminisces about how the parents of his first marriage prospect encouraged him to fool around with their daughter. They would invite him over and leave the two of them in the parlor alone. Versions of this wink-winking permissiveness toward serious couples persisted up through the Calling Era.

By the time urban vice squads were breaking up the first daters, many working-class parents had accepted the fact that their children would have premarital sex with their future spouses. In the 1910s, several fathers in New York State successfully sued men who had slept with, then spurned, their daughters, for "seduction under promise of marriage." The courts that ruled in favor of these fathers implicitly decreed that sleeping with your fiancé was a reasonable thing to do.

In the 1940s, Alfred Kinsey had discovered that most of the students he interviewed at the University of Indiana engaged in "heavy petting," which often included stimulating each other to orgasm. The Kelly Longitudinal Study, a survey of three hundred white couples who started families in the 1950s, found that only 7 to 10 percent of them had only hugged and kissed before marriage. All others had "gone farther."

But if premarital sex had become common well before the Steady Era, going steady increased the odds that kids would have *pre*-premarital sex with partners they did not intend to marry. Studies conducted throughout the 1950s found again and again that teens believed going steady sufficed to make even the heaviest petting respectable, so long as you did not "go the limit." In 1961, the sociologist Ira Reiss coined a phrase for the new moral code. He called it "petting with affection."

It was not all bad. Becoming emotionally intimate with one partner created opportunities to explore that felt safer than casual dates or "petting parties" had. It still does. I remember the long afternoons my high school boyfriend and I spent in the apartment his working parents never came home to before six or seven. Having exhausted the obvious things, we spent hours searching for the body part that could not be made erogenous. Where had we learned that word? The search became a game. We would leave for sports practices and come back saltier. Forced to fumble in the bathroom at some party, I would never have learned the important lesson that *basically nothing is not A Thing*.

For young women especially, going steady provided reputation protection. It limited your overall number of partners and let you "neck" with someone who cared about you. The fact that his public image was tied to yours discouraged kissing and telling. Having a boyfriend could also shield you from unwanted advances. In 1963, the girl group the Angels gleefully repeated a steady's threat to an aggressive admirer: *My boyfriend's back and you're gonna be in trouble*. Any woman who has been hit on hard can relate. Sometimes, telegraphing or even outright stating that you have no interest in a man will not cut it. You have to drop the "B" bomb—bring up a boyfriend real or imagined—to make him back off.

Still, petting with affection placed a heavy burden on young women. It conscripted them into a kind of police force, tasked with guarding sex. In surveys and studies, teenagers continued to profess that nice girls did not go all the way. Yet they also asserted that most boys would go as far as their girlfriends would let them. The outcome was a setup that subjected girls to constant stress, self-blame, and regret. And the games of brinksmanship that couples played often blew up in their faces.

In the 1950s, rates of teen pregnancy soared. In 1957, 97 out of every 1,000 girls age fifteen to nineteen gave birth. (In 2013, by contrast, that figure was 26.) Between 1944 and 1955, the number of babies born out of wedlock who were put up for adoption also increased by 80 percent. If a girl got pregnant, the parents often simply handed her and her boyfriend wedding rings. There is no reliable data on African Americans for the decade, but over its course, the proportion of pregnant white brides—brides who gave birth less than nine months after their weddings—more than doubled.

The 1958 movie *Going Steady* turned this peril into a source of comedy. In the theme song, the young star Molly Bee breathily conflated going steady with marriage. *I will marry the dream that I adore, the boy that I've been getting ready for*, she murmured. *And we'll be going steady evermore. . . .*

Bee plays a chipper high school senior who elopes with the classmate she has been dating for all of six weeks, when her parents let her accompany him to an "away" basketball game. The couple finds a justice of the peace, who also happens to own an inn and is willing to marry them after hours. They use a class ring as a token of their vows. Because their marriage looks basically identical to steady dating, they plan to conceal it until after they graduate. Their plot takes an unexpected twist, however, when they realize that their wedding night tryst got her pregnant. He moves into her parents' house, and both immediately realize how unprepared they are to start a family. Hilarity ensues.

In real life, however, most young Steadies did not end up going steady forever unless they had to. Instead, they let relationships run their course. Then they did something else that an earlier generation could not have imagined. They broke up.

Steadies invented the Breakup. Going steady was a prerequisite
for that specific kind of heartache. In the 1920s and '30s, a College Man might have stopped calling a Coed for dates without
offering any explanation. However, she was likely to have other
dates lined up. If he privately felt disappointed when she declined
his invitation to a dance, he could seize the first chance to cut in
on her sorority sister.

For Steadies, however, things were different. A Steady was
likely to mean more to you than any given person you went out
with. And because so much of high school social life revolved
around coupling off, a split meant more than losing a boyfriend or
girlfriend; it meant getting left out. The first lovers who *forgot to
remember to forget* their exes learned that *breaking up is hard to do.*

After a breakup, most people I know make a point of trying
to stay friends. When they run into someone who knows an ex,
they say, *Oh, X was one of my best friends in college!* And yet
when she calls out of the blue and asks whether you will meet her
for dinner, because she is having family problems that only you
will understand, you have to admit that dinner is awkward. If he
writes, years after you moved out of a place you shared into two
tiny, separate places, to ask whether there's any chance you ended
up with his college diploma, you say *Sure*, of course he can come
over to search the boxes in your basement storage unit. You two
grew up together. Yet when my first love does this, I cannot help
wondering what he still has of mine.

I don't mean boxes. Looking over faces of which we once had
every inch memorized, we realize that our exes must have
stashed the selves we were with them somewhere. "Love's monu-
ments like tombstones on our lives," the young poet James Mer-
rill wrote, heartbroken, in the 1940s. To pick through memories
of old love can feel like wandering through a ruin whose intact

image haunts your dreams. Scenes from our past lives drift around the Internet.

In the weeks after a breakup, you reread old messages and emails. Cringe fondly at the first overthought flirtations. Follow the banalities that show you becoming comfortable to the vanishing point of intimacy where your tracks disappear. Keep scrolling, and soon a fight pops up. Then comes a long apology and counterapology, and so the end begins.

Detagging your old photos, you cannot be sure whether you are protecting a past or making room for a future. You become a stranger to yourself. Who was that, at that party, on my vacation? *Delete, delete* until you, as you are now, are all that you have left.

Given the risks, it was difficult for onlookers to understand how dating culture had changed so much so quickly. The man shortage that World War II created clearly had something to do with it. On the college dance floors where Coeds had been swarmed by stags trying to cut in on them, there had been far more men than women. When American troops deployed, however, the gender ratios reversed.

"Army or Navy or just plain civvies!—there aren't enough men around to date," *Newsday* exclaimed in 1945.

When the "Roving Reporter" who wrote the story approached a young personnel worker on her lunch break and asked her about the problem, she interrupted him: "Did you say civilian? Where can I find one?"

In this environment, a Popular Daughter could not hope to establish her status by dating many different boys. Instead, women competed to lock down a partner. The romance of your beloved being shipped out, and the desire to be there for him as a pen pal, also encouraged women to stay faithful to soldiers overseas. Even naysayers of going steady allowed that it would be unkind not to keep responding to letters you received from European battlefields or the South Pacific.

This explanation made some sense, and historians have since repeated it. But it was incomplete. It had to be, because the practice of going steady did not end with V-day. On the contrary, it was only after our boys came home that going steady really started to take off among a younger set. The course it took demonstrated that this dating style was not fundamentally about the scarcity of men. Rather, it had to do with previously unimaginable forms of abundance.

The end of World War II ushered in a period of prosperity unlike anything that our country has seen before or since. During the war, the United States had rapidly recovered from the Great Depression, but there had been nothing to buy. When peace arrived, people had money they were eager to spend. At the same time, the government was enacting a number of laws that encouraged upward mobility—for white people, anyway. The GI Bill covered college tuition for veterans and provided housing loans at low interest rates. Between 1945 and 1960, per capita income increased by 35 percent. In the 1920s, only 31 percent of the country had been middle class. By the 1950s, the proportion doubled.

The economic boom that dramatically expanded the white middle class did far less for everyone else. The idylls that the 1950s created of itself were so whitewashed that the gardener on *Father Knows Best*, played by the (clearly Latino) character actor Natividad Vacío, was called "Frank Smith." The millions of people who came to the United States from Mexico and Puerto Rico between 1945 and 1960 gained little from the growth of national GDP, and the economic position of native-born blacks actually worsened.

In the North, black families were systematically shut out of the suburbs that were becoming symbols of the American dream and a cornerstone of wealth accumulation in the form of real estate. In the South, in addition to legal segregation, they faced rampant violence.

In August 1955, the farmer and civil rights activist Lamar Smith was shot dead in broad daylight, outside the county courthouse in Brookhaven, Mississippi, where he had been registering black voters. Ten days later, in the nearby town of Money, two white men heard rumors that a fourteen-year-old boy visiting from Chicago had made a pass at a local white woman. They dragged Emmett Till from his bed in the middle of the night, beat and tortured him for hours, finally shot him in the head, tied a seventy-four-pound cotton gin fan to his leg, and threw him in the Tallahatchie River. When the child's body was found, it was so badly disfigured that the uncle who had been hosting Emmett could identify him only by a ring that he recognized on one of his fingers.

Till's was just one of an untold number of murders of black men supposedly based on white fears of miscegenation. Though popular culture was encouraging children to start pursuing romance younger and younger, an innocent crush—real, imagined, or maliciously invented—could prove deadly for a black teen in the South. But like their parents, white teenagers were flush, and the images of dating that we have inherited from that era focus on them.

By 1956, there were thirteen million teens with an average income of $10.55 per week. Fifteen years earlier, that amount would have represented the total disposable income of an average family, and children who worked outside their homes would have been expected to hand over their earnings to their parents.

But kids who came of age during the Eisenhower presidency had no memory of the Great Depression and little inclination to save. Together, they spent more than $7 billion per year.

Companies fell over themselves to cater to their tastes. Novelties like mass-market paperbacks, 45 rpm record singles, and cheap transistor radios allowed teens to live increasingly on their own wavelength. In order to continue growing, companies created products targeting younger and younger buyers. Take the training bra. Through the 1940s, young girls had usually worn undershirts until their breasts were developed enough to warrant a brassiere. But at the end of the decade, Maidenform and other lingerie companies began marketing "bralettes" or "Bobbie bras" to girls as young as nine or ten. Experts reassured parents that going steady was simply like wearing a training relationship.

If the privileged students of the 1920s and '30s had made dating a respectable activity, it was the Steadies of the 1950s who made it middle class. In their world, dating no longer involved the competition of a selling floor or stag line. It was based on a promise of mass production and mass consumption in which everyone was supposed to be able to partake. The wealthy Fussers and Popular Daughters of the 1920s and '30s had vied with one another to rate as many dates as they could. However, by the 1950s, many more young people could afford to go out dancing, or for burgers, or to the movies. And so the battle for survival of the fittest that had dominated fraternity dance floors gave way to a kind of romantic full employment.

Democratized dating was one of the many fruits of the booming economy. If everyone was going to enjoy it, six boys could not fight to cut in on each single girl. They had to pair off.

We can see how closely steady dating was tied to the new culture of consumerism by how often authorities compared dating to shopping. By the 1950s, shopping had become the go-to metaphor to explain courtship.

In his popular textbook *Modern Courtship and Marriage*, the family expert E. E. LeMasters wrote that "random dating can best be compared to American shopping practices." He likened the casual dating of the College Man and Coed era to window-shopping. "The couple take a superficial look at each other with no obligation to buy."

In 1968, the psychologist Tom McGinnis argued in his popular book *A Girl's Guide to Dating and Going Steady* that going steady could be a good way to try on partners, too. "Deciding what kind of marriage you want is something like choosing a dress in a store," McGinnis wrote. "The fact that only one dress seems right for you out of perhaps a hundred that you look at does not mean that the ninety-nine others are poorly made or in horrible taste. They just are not for you."

Few Americans are likely to remember LeMasters or McGinnis now. But I bet you know the advice that Smokey Robinson handed down from his mother: *You better shop around.*

Shop, the Miracles chirp behind him. *Shop around!*

When I think about it, every single one of the Motown hits that have been etched into my memory since childhood is about serial monogamy. They all evoke the ecstasy of falling hard for someone, the agony of losing him or her, and the excitement of starting the process all over again. The Temptations topped the charts with "My Girl," and the Four Tops did the same with "Sugar Pie Honey Bunch." Both songs open with swells of infectious celebration. Diana Ross and the Supremes tended to sing about the sad parts. *Where did our love go?* they plead in their song of that title. "Stop in the Name of Love" forgives a faithless man and says that he should stay. "Baby Love" laments the pain of breaking up. But even when mourning, Motown hits sounded joyful. "Same Old Song" evokes the sense of disorienting empti-ness that follows losing a lover in a doggedly bright key. The soaring scales of the Jackson 5 made being desperate to get back an ex sound irrepressibly fun.

No wonder these became the anthems of the Steady Era. They were like advertisements for that dating pattern. Motown hits captured the power of exclusive passion followed by a healthy breakup. For the millions of teens who heard them, their rhymes and rhythms must have reinforced the sense that *breaking up* and then *making up* was just the way things went.

With their cheap radios and phonographs and the money to buy records, teens developed listening patterns that followed the same cadence. You went out and bought your favorite single and then listened to it to death. Once you got sick of it, you went out and bought another. You fell in love with purchases, spent time with them, and then parted ways. Later you recalled them fondly.

This model of cyclical consumption is a very particular kind of shopping around, and in the 1950s it was new. It, too, was in-vented in Detroit.

It is not clear who coined the phrase "dynamic obsolescence." In *The Fifties*, the journalist David Halberstam cited Harley Earl, a flamboyant designer from Hollywood, who had built a career custom-making cars for Hollywood celebrities, before the GM CEO Alfred P. Sloan hired him to start an Art and Color depart-ment. Other sources credit Sloan himself. In any case, the prob-lem that GM had on their hands in the Era of the Steady was clear: The market for cars was saturated. How can you get people to keep buying new versions of a product that they already have? Dynamic obsolescence was the solution that Sloan and Earl came up with.

Before the war, there had been a joke that anyone could afford to buy a Ford in any color that he wanted—as long as it was black. After the war, however, GM started making cars in many colors, releasing new versions of the popular models with minor changes to their sizes, shapes, and outlines every year. Some colleagues and competitors denounced this strategy. "Planned obsolescence," they sneered. But it worked. Hype around the GM cars created the idea that a man's ride was a key sign of his character. The look of your car was supposed to signal your personality and aspirations.

For the Steady who tried on relationships, dating performed a similar function. The shopping around that it involved no longer meant looking for one night's entertainment. Instead, dating became a bigger investment in someone who would define you over a longer period. You could buy into a relationship even if you ultimately intended to trade it for a newer and better one.

It was the promise of affluence that had made the spread of going steady possible. But an undercurrent of anxiety came with it. There was something slightly panicked about the eagerness of teenagers to throw themselves at one another. The Norman Rockwell years of soda fountains and high school dances were also an era when a huge proportion of Americans believed that their world was about to end soon.

In the 1950s, the prominent psychiatrist Robert Jay Lifton wrote that a silent stress disorder was afflicting the entire country. He called it "nuclear numbing." In 1950, 53 percent of Americans believed that there was a "good" or "fair" chance that their community would be bombed during the next world war. By 1956, two-thirds of those polled believed that in the event of another war, the Russians would use an H-bomb against the United States. By consuming clothes and loves, Americans of all ages attempted to compensate for the feelings of insecurity and incipient disaster that the Atomic Age created. Families afraid of being nuked walled their houses with consumer goods as if they were bomb shelters. Their children watched and learned.

Teens, who could now afford movie tickets, Cokes, and hamburgers, did not want to die alone on doomsday. Even if you would not go steady for good, it felt good to have a Steady for now, especially if now might turn out to be the closest thing to forever. Anyone would want someone to do it with at their side right before the bomb dropped.

Today, we are in fact living at the end of the world order that the Golden Age of Going Steady created, if not the world itself. Our endtimes feel less dramatic than the nuclear blasts that the Steadies feared. Average temperatures are climbing. Ice caps are melting. The rich grow richer, while everyone else grows poorer around them, all down with the long slide into what economists call "secular stagnation." In an age when so much feels precarious, serial monogamists cling to their partners for comfort. But in our version of the apocalypse, it seems less clear what going steady is for. No bomb fell, and everyone did it anyway. Whatever is coming now, how is it that we hope the people we love might protect us?

The postwar dream of a detached house, a happy housewife, and a full-time working husband was feasible only for a brief window of history. Even then, it was feasible only for a limited segment of the population. Since wages stagnated in the late 1970s, working-class families of the *Ozzie and Harriet* type have collapsed under the strain. Cohabiting relationships without marriage and single-parent households have long since become a norm.

The cultural conservatives who call for a revival of "The Family"—as if there has ever been any one kind of family—ignore the fact that the choices many people make about marriage are not just cultural or moral. They also are influenced by money. Studies show that many members of the working classes feel that they simply cannot afford to marry. Either they cannot afford a wedding, or they cannot afford other markers of adulthood that feel like prerequisites for marriage (paying off student loans, buying a house, etc.). Many of those who give marriage a go learn the hard way that living hounded by financial worries with no end in sight is not the greatest aphrodisiac.

More and more evidence suggests that today marriage has become a privilege of the middle class. In the United States, the middle class is shrinking quickly. Since the 2008 financial crisis, even college-educated people have faced falling wages, waning job security, and a lack of benefits. Increasingly, we have no choice but to resort to part-time and contract work. The dream of "settling down" forever—or of *anything* being steady forever—is fast fading. For more and more people, the future feels impossible to predict.

Young people today are told that if we want to stand a chance, we must be mobile. We must be ready to move across the country in order to take a job, or to move in with family members after we lose one. We should chase promotions and freelance gigs where we can. Professional pressures often force people to make tough choices regarding their relationships. With the possibility of a break looming constantly on the horizon, it can be difficult to feel sure enough about someone to commit. And when both members of almost any couple have to work, the prospect of the commitment always comes with the question of what professional opportunities you would be willing to give up later.

In a world of uncertain prospects, having a partner can be a source of joy and support not unlike that of having a Steady. To be part of a couple can provide a sense of security and companionship. Even if we know it is probably not for good, to have someone who cares for us, for now, feels stabilizing. It creates a small oasis.

Despite the many gains that women have made since the 1950s, the double standards that punish us for acting on our sexual desires still exist. If you are a woman who has been raised to believe in such standards, serial monogamy may seem like an attractive compromise. An urban legend says that if a woman hopes to marry, as the vast majority of all young Americans still do, she must not let her "number"—her lifetime tally of partners—get too high.

As a teenage virgin, I remember reading in a well-worn magazine in some hair salon that the outer limit had been statistically proved to be five. The 2011 Anna Faris rom-com *What's Your Number?* put it at twenty. If you become sexually active around seventeen, as the average American woman does, and do not marry until nearly thirty, as she also does, you either have to spend long dry spells celibate or go steady if you want to stay in bounds.

What's Your Number? had a happy ending. After a misguided quest to reconnect with each of the twenty men she believes she has slept with, in order to convince one of them to marry her, the goofy party girl played by Anna Faris ends up falling in love. By the end, she seems to be headed into Happily Ever After with Mr. Twenty-One. But in the final scene, she and her new beau receive a surprise answering machine message from one of the men she had been counting. To fans, the voice of "Jay from Club Med Turkoise" immediately gives him away as the comedian Aziz Ansari.

"Hey, um," Jay says. "I got a weird message from your assistant, and I just wanted to let you know . . . we never had sex. You did this awkward striptease, involving maracas, and then gave me a shitty hand job. It was something you like to do called dry style. You vomited in my suitcase, and then you passed out in the shower."

Anna Faris's character is elated. The One is her Number Twenty, after all!

What's Your Number? got to have it both ways. Mostly, it poked fun at a piece of advice whose rigidity is clearly absurd. But it also hinted that an anachronistic-sounding rule might hold true after all. It was like a *Wizard of Oz* about female sexual liberation. Like Dorothy, its heroine wakes up in a narrow, tidy bed she thought she had lost forever. Her misadventures with the men hovering around were just a dream!

Still, many people do take their numbers seriously. In 2014, researchers at the National Marriage Project reported that the more sexual partners a woman had before marriage, the more likely her marriage was to fail. Academic sociologists have pointed out myriad problems with the institute's data, but the press widely reported it as fact.

"Women who don't sleep around before their wedding have happier marriages—but men can play the field without worry, study finds," the headline in the British newspaper the *Daily Mail* declared. I had to read a few paragraphs to realize that the editors did not intend this as a parody.

Despite the benefits of serial monogamy, members of many couples end up feeling entrapped, bored, or taken for granted. Like Jeff and Marie, the Steadies of the RCA social hygiene video, you can become desperate to get out of something you are not sure how you got into. Some speak of the casual drift into pre-marital cohabitation that has become the norm among my peers, the way Dorothy Dix wrote about going steady back in 1939: *The custom has all the worst features of marriage and none of its advantages.*

Moreover, they say, the risks and long-term costs of such an arrangement will be borne disproportionately by women. Like girls who were expected to resist any urge they felt to give in and "go all the way" with their boyfriends, women who are serially monogamous today often hear that they must be careful. Experts say that It is our responsibility to manage how a relationship proceeds.

Today, most authorities accept that women may want premarital sex. Not all men are presumed to be aggressors whose lust a good girl must parry. More often, popular culture seems to suspect them of being George Costanza–like man-children. At the same time, there is a consensus that men have all their lives ahead of them to fumble relationship after relationship. But women are assumed to have a limited window of time in which to find a partner before their attractiveness and their fertility wane. According to this logic, the risk you take by drifting into serial monogamy has less to do with compromising your virtue than letting your value fall.

Every day, the mother of a friend who has been living happily with a nice boyfriend for two years sends her a text message: *No ring on the finger, you must not linger!* I know her mother, and she is not joking. My friend has just turned twenty-six. This kind of threat assumes that, to reverse Jane Austen's famous phrase, a single woman in possession of good sense, must be in want of a husband. It can go the other way, too. A man wants to marry his girlfriend; she wants to continue exploring. I have known more than one gay couple that split for similar reasons. If one partner wants more and the other does not, heartbreak follows. The greatest liability may be this: Many times, nobody can be sure.

There are plenty of reasons a person might not be interested in marrying. The Steadies may already have seen them. Popular culture during the Steady Era idealized family life. But it was an open secret that many husbands and housewives were desperately unhappy. Across the country, Freudian psychiatrists told patients that their discontent was a sickness. Churches swelled their numbers by assuring parishioners that they could pray away their boredom and fretfulness. But many children must have seen that their parents were suffering. In 1960, when the editors of *Redbook* magazine issued a call for letters from readers on the subject of "Why Young Mothers Feel Trapped," they received twenty-four thousand replies. Advice experts thought that Steadies were blindly ruining their marriage prospects. They might have simply been putting marriage off.

Today, Americans seem to have an almost hysterical ambivalence about marriage. On the one hand, we spend obscene sums on weddings and binge-watch episodes of wedding-related shows like *Say Yes to the Dress*. We accept laws that incentivize people to marry by offering tax breaks and tying access to health care, other benefits, and visitation rights to the institution; we celebrate the triumph of gay couples who have gained the same privileges. More than 80 percent of never-married Americans still say that they want to marry. Yet many of us live in ways that seem incompatible with the institution. We work too long, we move too often, we may remain ambivalent about monogamy or children. Serial monogamy is a way of putting marriage off. Does it also call into question its place as a central value in our culture?

With the apocalypse forestalled, the contemporary equivalent of going steady can easily turn into a recipe for indecision. We stay in relationships out of convenience, long after our infatuation has passed. Now that marriage is no longer the obligatory conclusion of a serious relationship, we can feel comfortable merging lives with people we may not want to be with for life. We introduce them to our families; we go on vacations together. We learn everything about their friends and jobs and still remain unsure. We drift in and out of relationships.

You claim you might not want to spend your lives together. But you wake up and realize you already have.

CHAPTER 6. FREEDOM

Linda LeClair was an unlikely sex symbol. The Barnard sophomore had grown up going to Sunday school in Hudson, New Hampshire. At twenty, she wore her lank dirty-blond hair tucked behind her ears. For press photos, she favored cardigans and pastel-colored shift dresses that fell at her knees. She had been living with her boyfriend, Peter Behr, in an apartment on Riverside Drive for around two years.

He was a junior at Columbia; they had met in a seminar. It is difficult to imagine that either of them anticipated the uproar that they would cause when they agreed to give an interview to a *New York Times* reporter in March 1968. The trends piece that appeared, quoting them, made Linda into a national celebrity—and scapegoat—overnight.

"An Arrangement: Living Together for Convenience, Security, Sex," the headline read. The article called Peter only by his first name, and it called Linda "Susan." But she had identified herself as a sophomore at Barnard, and the college quickly tracked her down. Almost as soon as they did, calls and letters started inundating the office of the president, Martha Peterson. Some men wrote in saying that LeClair was living proof that women were ruined by higher education. Prominent Barnard alumnae, including Iphigene Ochs Sulzberger, an heiress to the *New York Times* fortune, threatened to cut off donations to the school if she was not expelled immediately.

Officially, LeClair was in trouble for lying on her housing forms. According to Barnard regulations, students could live off campus only with family or an employer. She had claimed to be working as an au pair on the Upper West Side and provided the address of a married friend who agreed to cover for her. But the hate mail that poured in made it clear that she had violated a more serious, unspoken rule.

As disciplinary proceedings against LeClair began and the national media picked up the story, letters arrived at Barnard from all over the country. They called LeClair a "whore" and an "alleycat"; they called Barnard "Barnyard." In his widely syndicated column, the conservative pundit William F. Buckley Jr. denounced this undergraduate student as an "unemployed concubine" who was "gluttonous for sex and publicity."

When *Life* magazine put her on their April cover, LeClair said the opposite. All the attention was exhausting. "I find it hard to think of myself as a person any more." She shook her head. "I have ceased to exist. I am Linda LeClair, the issue."

What exactly was the issue? It could not be only that a young woman was having premarital sex; statistics had long shown that most young women did. Nor was LeClair a "whore" by any stretch. She had been in a monogamous relationship for years. What rankled was that she felt no need to hide it. Again and again the hate mail Barnard received used the verb "flaunt." LeClair and Behr were "openly flaunting their disregard for moral codes." They were "flaunting their dereliction."

LeClair and Behr rallied fellow students to support Linda.

They had a mimeograph machine in their apartment, and they printed hundreds of pamphlets and questionnaires. Three hundred Barnard students anonymously admitted that they had lied on their own housing forms; sixty sent the college signed letters attesting that they had done so.

LeClair and her defenders argued that the Barnard regulations constituted a form of sex discrimination, since Columbia placed no equivalent restrictions on male students. And they argued that all students, male or female, had a right to date however they wished.

"Is the purpose of Barnard College to teach students or to control their private lives?" LeClair asked an interviewer at *Time* magazine. "I believe that it is the former. Barnard has no right to control personal behavior." President Peterson soon pressured her into dropping out, and Peter Behr left Columbia in solidarity. But they had made their point, and those who shared their point of view would win in the long run. They already were winning. By the late 1960s, the belief that everyone has a right to love without outside interference was becoming widespread.

We are all heirs to the sexual revolution. Whatever our sexual preferences, we now live and date in the world that revolution created, and we do so freer from fears of ostracism, persecution, or unwanted pregnancy than we would be if it had not taken place. But the expression came to refer to such a wide range of phenomena that it can be difficult to know what exactly we mean when we say it.

It is also easy to forget that the 1960s marked its second coming. The term "sexual revolution" was first used to describe the antics of the Flappers and Fussers of the Roaring Twenties. Two young and then unknown *New Yorker* writers, James Thurber and E. B. White, coined it in 1929, in a book that they wrote together and Thurber illustrated. *Is Sex Necessary? Or, Why You Feel the Way You Do* parodied the kinds of advice manuals that had become popular over the previous decade, which used Freudian vocabulary to explain to readers their own sex lives and psychological "adjustment."

In the chapter titled "The Sexual Revolution," the authors described the changes taking place in the language of rights. Specifically, they said that the revolution began when young women discovered that they had "the right to be sexual." When the archetypal New Woman went to college, and then took a paying job, they said, she began to discover that she could do many things that only men had done before. The New Woman rented her own apartment. She smoked and drank and bobbed her hair. Sometimes she even *wanted* sex.

On January 24, 1964, *Time* magazine announced that "The Second Sexual Revolution" had arrived. The cover story observed that "champagne parties for teenagers, padded brassières for twelve-year-olds, and 'going steady' at ever younger ages" had resulted in an "orgy of open-mindedness."

There have always been rebels and libertines. Plenty of statistics show that turn-of-the-century shopgirls and dykes, Greeks and fairies, could be just as promiscuous as the hippies who succeeded them. The difference was that the first group had often described their own activities as unnatural, or at least exceptional. Their sex was sexy because it felt illicit.

By contrast, the soldiers of the second sexual revolution declared that no desire could be unnatural. If prior generations had winked that rules were made to be broken, more and more young people seemed to believe that no rules should exist. They agreed with the Flappers that everyone had a "right to be sexual." However, they did not stress the equality that this right gave them.

Instead, they argued that having sex was a way to express another inalienable right: freedom.

The 1960s' most important philosopher of freedom was a Jewish Marxist named Herbert Marcuse. Often hailed as the "father of the New Left," he fled Nazi Germany and eventually took a position as a professor at Berkeley, where his teaching and writing made him a hero to the student radicals.

Marcuse's 1955 book *Eros and Civilization* anticipated the second sexual revolution, saying that technological progress would soon make sexual repression obsolete. Following Marx, Marcuse argued that increasing automation would eliminate the need for work and expand the opportunities for leisure. Freed from labor, people would soon escape what Marx called the "realm of necessity" and enter the "realm of freedom." This meant that everyone would have more time to do what he or she wanted—including experimenting with sex.

To make the most of this new freedom, Marcuse wanted people to unlearn the Freudian psychology that had become so popular in the preceding decades. For Freud, sexual repression was an essential ingredient of human civilization. If we all had as much sex as we wanted all the time, Freud said, our species would never have discovered fire or made the wheel or figured out how to grow food or build houses or develop medicines.

Although this may have been true at an earlier stage of human history, Marcuse argued that sexual repression was no longer necessary. The new leisure would liberate sexuality, and transform society in the process. Laws governing sexual behavior would be repealed. Traditional institutions like marriage and monogamy would be overthrown.

Marcuse's message resonated with the partisans of the second sexual revolution. In his 1965 book *The Erotic Revolution*, the Beat poet Lawrence Lipton hailed the emancipation of sexual pleasure that technology and prosperity would soon make possible. "'The New Leisure' is already presenting new opportunities for orgiastic recharging of the life-force," he wrote.

Like other figures of the counterculture, Lipton demanded an end to all legal restraints on sexual behavior: "Repeal all the laws and statutes regulating premarital sex. Repeal all laws making homosexuality, male or female, illegal . . . Repeal all laws making any sexual act, the so-called 'unnatural acts,' illegal."

These laws had tried to contain sexuality within the conventions of marriage. They said that individuals should be allowed to invest their sexual energy only in particular kinds of relationships—the ones that would create new nuclear families and produce children. Lipton disagreed. He said that private relationships were like private property. Individuals should be able to spend their own sexual desires, and whatever desire they attracted from others, however they saw fit.

The ways that sexual revolutionaries spoke about sex often echoed the ways that free-market advocates were beginning to speak about the economy. Both wanted to maximize individual liberty. Both agreed that a laissez-faire approach was best.

While Marcuse was in Berkeley demanding sexual liberation, the economist Milton Friedman was in Chicago arguing for market liberalization. Friedman wanted to make markets as "free" as possible, by shrinking the state and slashing social protections. He believed that removing all barriers to economic activity was the fastest way to create a wealthy society.

The sexual revolutionaries said the same things about sexuality. Even though Friedman and Marcuse came from opposite ends of the political spectrum, each wanted to liberate individuals from all external restraints. The second sexual revolution is often cited as the moment when dating died. Dating did not die;

it was simply deregulated. "Free love" turned the meet market of dating into a free market.

Laissez-Faire Love took many different guises. Before Marcuse and Lipton wrote about eros and the orgiastic life force, Hugh Hefner launched *Playboy* magazine. The first issue hit the newsstands in 1953. The centerfold showed a stark-naked Marilyn Monroe, sitting on folded knees and tilting back with one arm crossed behind her head. A wall of scarlet fabric is unfurled behind her. Her eyes are closed but her ruby lips are parted. They match the fabric.

Alongside nudes, *Playboy* brimmed with photos of "bachelor pads," well appointed with barware and stereo equipment. The magazine allowed readers to enjoy a fantasy life of pure leisure, where having sex would be just like drinking a cocktail or listening to a record. Afterward, a man could smoke a cigarette and forget about the whole thing as quickly as he would the details of a James Bond paperback.

The life of ease that *Playboy* promised not only freed men from the constraints of marriage or monogamy. By turning female bodies into consumer objects, it also freed men from the burden of having to have feelings about the women they slept with. The editors promised readers that in the new age of abundance, they could "enjoy the pleasures that the female has to offer without becoming emotionally involved." The architectural spreads promised men that they, too, could have rooms of their own.

Playboy said that sex was ideally a form of recreation. The vision clearly appealed to people. At least, some people. The first issue sold out in two weeks, and *Playboy* quickly became a cultural fixture. By the early 1970s, each issue sold millions of copies and one in four male college students in the United States subscribed. By then, the Food and Drug Administration had approved the oral contraceptive pill for use. The availability of reliable birth control seemed to make it possible for women as well as men to at least daydream about treating sex as harmless fun.

When *Cosmopolitan* hired Helen Gurley Brown to rebrand it in 1965, after a decade of falling circulation, they created a national spokeswoman for the *Playboy* point of view. With Brown as editor, *Cosmopolitan* became a *Playboy* for girls—sort of. Like *Playboy*, the magazine was all about consumer pleasures, of which sex was the most important. Like *Playboy*, the covers featured scantily clad, conventionally beautiful white women. But while *Playboy* presented its readers with images of women they could enjoy and then dispose of, *Cosmo* told women how to make themselves enjoyable and disposable—the kinds of girls playboys desired.

The magazine called the ideal reader it imagined the Fun Fearless Female. Fun Fearless Feminism promised young women that they could have the same freedoms that their brothers and boyfriends did when it came to enjoying sex. It said that all these pleasures would come to them along with the other formerly masculine privilege they were suddenly claiming: the right to work outside their homes.

When a census taker arrived at the front door of the Friedan household in 1960, Betty was having a coffee with her friend and neighbor Gertie. Gertie overheard the man asking Betty what her occupation was, and Betty answering "housewife."

Gertie interrupted. "You should take yourself more seriously."

Betty corrected herself. "Actually, I'm a writer."

It took her two more years to finish the book she was then struggling to finish, *The Feminine Mystique*. By the time it came out in 1963, Friedan was already used to giving interviews and appearing on television; the excerpts she had been publishing were garnering widespread attention. Over the next few years, she would be widely hailed for having helped launch the second-wave feminist movement in the United States.

The Feminine Mystique opened with a chapter describing the sense of entrapment and discontentment that Friedan herself experienced as a full-time housewife during the 1940s and '50s, despite leading a life that closely resembled the ideals she saw on television, in movies, and in women's magazines. Friedan attested that her peers were suffering, too. She called what afflicted them "the problem that has no name." By the end of the first chapter, she had diagnosed it. The housewives suffering from anxiety and depression and the alcohol they used to self-medicate were all struggling to come to terms with a voice in their head that said: "I want something more than my husband and my children and my home."

For hundreds of pages, *The Feminine Mystique* investigates the forces that conspired to convince American women that they should want this life—and that if they were unhappy in it, there was something wrong with them. In the final chapter, Friedan laid out the necessary steps women could take to emancipate themselves.

The first thing they needed was work. Women, Friedan said, must make a "lifetime commitment . . . to a field of thought, to work of serious importance to society. Call it a 'life plan,' a 'vocation,' a 'life purpose' if that dirty word *career* has too many celibate connotations," she joked.

Friedan devoted many pages to the importance of systematic reforms in order to help women meet these goals. She called for a national program similar to the GI Bill for women who wanted to continue their education, which would cover tuition fees, books, travel expenses, and even household help, while they pursued higher degrees that might enable them to reenter the workforce.

She was optimistic that the first lucky women who broke through into male professions would help their sisters. "When enough women make life plans geared toward their real abilities, and speak out for maternity leaves or even maternity sabbaticals . . . they will [not] have to sacrifice the right to honorable competition and contribution any more than they will have to sacrifice marriage and motherhood."

Yet in the popular version of the call to women to develop life plans, the serious and systematic elements of Friedan's argument faded out. The popular feminism Helen Gurley Brown pioneered at *Cosmo* sold well because it turned the life plan of the Career Girl into another glossy product.

Before she took over *Cosmo*, Brown had become a national celebrity for her advice book *Sex and the Single Girl*. It was hugely successful. One point of comparison: To date, *The Feminine Mystique* has sold three million copies. *Sex and the Single Girl* sold two million within the first three weeks. *Sex and the Single Girl* told female readers that they should feel just as free as the men they worked with to date around. They should ignore all the concerned friends and relatives urging them to get married and enjoy casual sex while focusing on their careers.

Like *Playboy*, Helen Gurley Brown constantly described sex as a form of "play" and "fun." In her bestselling follow-up book *Sex and the Office*, Brown even refers to her male coworkers as "playmates." Yet if a Single Girl could collect lovers, just as a playboy would, a big difference remained between them. Hugh Hefner constantly appeared in photographs in his bathrobe. He presented a vision of the life of *Playboy* as a life of leisure. Helen Gurley Brown, always pictured in neatly tailored skirt suits, knew that the women she wrote for could expect no such luck.

"There is a catch to achieving single bliss," she warned. "You have to work like a son of a bitch."

Despite her breezy prose, Brown's descriptions of the life of the Single Girl make it sound exhausting. "Why else is the single woman attractive?" she asked. "She has more time and often more money to spend on herself. She has the extra twenty minutes to exercise every day, an hour to make her face up for their date."

At the dawn of dating, Charity Girls had turned to men to treat them because the pittances they earned hardly allowed them to support themselves otherwise, much less afford any leisure. But Helen Gurley Brown's Single Girl does not aspire to rest.

"Your most prodigious work will be on *you*—at home," Brown instructed. "You can't afford to leave any facet of you unpolished."

In asides that are no doubt meant to be endearing, she hints at the rigors of her own beauty routine. "When I got married, I moved in with six-pound dumbbells, slant board, an electronic device for erasing wrinkles, several pounds of soy lecithin, powdered calcium and yeast-liver concentrate, for Serenity Cocktails and enough high-powered vitamins to generate life in a statue," she says.

Brown encourages Single Girls to treat their jobs as opportunities to meet men, just as the working-class Shopgirls who came before them did. However, Brown tells readers that ideally they perform this work with no end in sight. Shopgirls aspired to find husbands to save them from the sales floor. But the ambitious Single Girl reverses their priorities. She sees her desire for men as a kind of engine to make herself work harder.

"Managements who think that romances lower the work output are right out of their skulls," Brown exclaimed. "A girl in love with her boss will knock herself out seven days a week and wish there were more days."

Sex and the Office also extolled work as the highest moral virtue. It is through work on her person, as well as her professional image, that a Single Girl comes to deserve the delights that come her way. "Your goal is a sexy office life with marvelous things happening to you," Brown says, "and these don't accrue to girls who are *slugs*."

In an earlier era, Shopgirls had aspired to attain the glamour of a life of ease. Brown made doing endless labor look like the most glamorous thing imaginable. The highest goal, in this worldview, is not actual companionship but *desirability*. The Single Girls Brown writes about work hard to accrue the attraction of men like currency. The men themselves seem interchangeable.

"Use them," Brown exhorts her reader, "in a perfectly nice way just as they use you."

Playboy was all for it. Hugh Hefner ended up being one of Brown's biggest advocates. Her insistence that regular gals were interested in sex encouraged *Playboy* readers that "the pulchritudinous Playmates" they admired were not "a world apart." They were everywhere.

"Potential Playmates are all around you," the editors wrote. "The new secretary at your office, the doe-eyed beauty who sat opposite you at lunch yesterday, the girl who sells you shirts and ties at your favorite store. We found Miss July in our circulation department, processing subscriptions, renewals, and back copy orders."

Brown promised that if you just worked hard enough, you might be the girl lucky enough to get plucked up by the powers that were, to become the ultimate *Sex and the Office* success story—a nationally recognizable pornographic star.

———

It is easy to imagine why a young woman facing down a lifetime spent making beds and sandwiches and grocery shopping and watching the light change until dinner and then getting drubbed nightly by the same man in missionary position might find the life Helen Gurley Brown described appealing. But as a solution to the problems that Friedan had diagnosed, it was short-sighted.

On the surface, *The Feminine Mystique* and *Sex and the Single Girl* seem like very different books. One is set in suburbia; the other takes place in the city. The narrator of one is a bored housewife; the heroine of the other is a sexually liberated career girl. Yet the two books share more in common than it seems. Both embraced the idea that once individual women took paid work outside their homes, all women's problems would be solved.

Both also shared the same blind spot. They imagined that "allowing" women to work would eliminate gender inequality.

The opportunities that certain women gained in the 1960s to work outside their homes and earn money did give them choices. As Brown emphasized, Single Girls could now support themselves. They had the income to buy all kinds of things—particularly if they opted not to have children. But this freedom to choose how they spent their time and money did not end gender inequality. It simply gave women a chance to work harder trying to break even in a system that was rigged against them.

Ginger Rogers did everything Fred Astaire did, but she did it backward and in high heels, the saying goes. The Single Girl was told to do everything a Playboy did while making herself into a Playmate as well.

To put it slightly differently, the sexually liberated woman whom Brown describes does not get out of the predicament of having her worth defined by men. In the end, the *Cosmo* girl was not so different from the Steady who desperately fended off her boyfriend in the backseat of his car. The one was told that she had to parry male desire. The other was told that she had to attract it constantly. Neither convention produced any model of what a woman who was an *agent* of desire might look like.

Black feminists and working-class feminists tended to be much more perceptive than their white middle-class counterparts about the limitations of Fun Fearless Feminism. Because African American women had always worked outside their homes, ever since their ancestors were brought to the United States as slaves, they did not mistake the "opportunity" to work as an adequate solution to all the problems that women had to deal with.

To work or not to work had only ever been a choice for a very limited part of the population. The rest knew that earning a wage was not a fix-all. In fact, many black feminists attested that *in* their homes was the only place that they felt respite from a racist world.

When the young black writer Gloria Watkins published her first book, *Feminist Theory*, in 1984 under the pen name bell hooks, she faulted Betty Friedan's school of feminism for its obliviousness of the majority of American women.

"Friedan's famous phrase, 'the problem that has no name,' . . . actually referred to the plight of a select group of college-educated, middle- and upper-class, married white women—housewives bored with leisure, with the home, with children, with buying products, who wanted more out of life," hooks wrote. "The one-dimensional perspective on women's reality presented in her book became a marked feature of the contemporary feminist movement."

The new feminine mystique that Brown hyped has also persisted. Cultural icons from Britney Spears to Sheryl Sandberg still tell young women that, for them, the prerequisite to a good life is an insatiable appetite for effort.

As a teen, the pop star entreated an imaginary boyfriend to "hit her one more time" and panted that she was "a slave 4 him." But after marriage, children, divorce, and a very public nervous breakdown, her comeback album celebrated Single Girl self-reliance. "You'd better work . . . work . . . work . . . work . . . ," she intoned in her hit single "Work, B*tch." Sandberg offers the same advice to young female professionals in *Lean In*. When the going gets tough, she says, "keep a foot on the gas pedal." If working does not work, work harder. A worthy girl always has more to give.

If Fun Fearless Feminism failed to address the concerns of so many women, then what explains its success? It was market-friendly. This brand of feminism can be used to sell almost anything.

During the 1960s and '70s, Virginia Slims turned feminism into an advertising slogan. *You've come a long way, baby!* meant: You have come far enough to be able to buy the gender you were assigned at birth back in the form of special cigarettes. Companies fell over themselves to capture the earnings of the Fun Fearless Female. They sold her back her labor as liberation. Today we can thank them for ads that brand everything from pens to dildos to political candidates who oppose reproductive rights as "empowered."

Cosmopolitan continues to speak as if having choices were the same thing as having power. Its signature feature is the list. Every single issue lists dozens of Ways You Can Please Your Man. That the same tips show up, worded slightly differently each month, should tip us off that our choices may not be as infinite as the constant updates imply, and that they may have less to do with fulfilling our needs than with fulfilling those of the magazine to sell issues. Read one, and you will find that there are fewer choices than the cover led you to believe. Almost invariably, many are rewordings of the last month's choices. At least three will involve applying pressure to the prostate.

Most important, *your* pleasure rarely makes the list. *Cosmo* not infrequently lists, as one of the main reasons to enjoy sex, the fact that *men like women who like having it.*

Brown was progressive in her positivity about sex. But she did not challenge a view of the world in which women were there to offer recreation to men. Part of the ways they were supposed to make things easy was by performing the familiar role of the woman-as-object. Brown did not call the power structures that enforced sexism into question. On the contrary, she directly told her readers that it was morally imperative, as well as profession-ally strategic, to accept these structures and work them to her advantage.

"I don't feel there's any justifiable cause to criticize a boss ever," she declared in *Sex and the Office*. "You must love him like crazy. Denying love and devotion to a good boss who spends eight hours a day with you would be like a yellow-breasted mother swamp finch denying worms to her yellow-breasted swamp-finch babies."

The opening pages of *Sex and the Single Girl* belie that al-though Brown encourages her readers to revel in their sexual freedoms, these freedoms do not make them independent. The book begins with a boast.

"I married for the first time at thirty-seven," Brown writes. "It *could* be construed as something of a miracle considering how old *I* was and how eligible *he* was." She goes on to tell us that her husband is a successful Hollywood producer and that she herself did not start out with any unfair advantages. She was not unusually pretty and did not grow up with money; she did not go to college.

"But *I* don't think it's a miracle that I married my husband. I think I deserve him! For seventeen years I worked hard to be-come the kind of woman who might interest him," she exclaims.

Before we embark on the adventure of single girlhood with her as our guide, she wants us to know why we should trust her: In the end, she did get her prince.

Given the choice between housework and working like a son of a bitch, it becomes easy to understand why a young woman might say "Fuck it," toss her Valium and soy lecithin, and head for the West Coast.

The second version of the sexual revolution was more radical than the one *Playboy* and *Cosmo* developed. The hippies of the 1960s were not the first Americans to call themselves free lovers. The country has a long history of countercultural movements gathering forces beneath that banner. The white abolitionist Frances Wright established its first "free love" commune in 1825. She invited freed slaves and abolitionists to live and work together in a community that had no marriage and no expectation of monogamy.

Many nineteenth-century Marxists, anarchists, and feminists denounced marriage as a form of "sexual slavery" or prostitution. They rejected the idea of private romantic contracts that, they said, led men and women to treat one another like property. These critics recognized the fundamental inequality on which marriage rested: economic conventions and divorce laws that heavily favored men. The fact that many wives had no means of earning money outside the home meant that they had to sit tight while their husbands screwed around. If a man left a woman, he lost only her. But if she left him, her livelihood dried up.

In the 1870s, Victoria Woodhull, an activist who became the first female candidate to run for president of the United States, campaigned on a free love platform.

"Yes, I am a Free Lover," Woodhull told her audience in an 1871 speech. "I have an inalienable, constitutional and natural right to love whom I may, to love as long or as short a period as I can; to change that love every day if I please, and with that right neither you nor any law you can frame have any right to interfere."

By this, Woodhull meant that women should have rights to marry and divorce freely. She argued that instead of economic needs and social obligations, affection and choice should govern loving relationships. But she recognized that in order for free love to flourish, the individuals who wanted to practice it would have to build new institutions to replace marriages and families.

She told her listeners in 1871 that she had a "right to demand a free and unrestricted exercise" of her right to love. "It is your duty not only to accord it, but, as a community, to see that I am protected in it."

The mistrust of institutions felt by many young Americans during the aftermath of the Civil War made a powerful comeback during the Vietnam War. Once again young people turned toward free love in order to express their dissatisfaction with the world of their parents. But in contrast to Woodhull, they focused on what they wanted to destroy rather than what they wanted to build.

Young radicals in New York and San Francisco knew that they wanted something very different from the "sexy . . . successful life" that glossy magazines of the era promised. They did not want to grow up to be like their hypocritical fathers who pored over *Playboy*, or their stay-at-home mothers who sniffled when they found sticky issues stashed under the mattress. They did not want a more fun, fearless version of the society they had grown up in. They wanted a new world altogether. They were just not sure exactly how it should look.

One of the most influential free lovers was Jefferson Poland (at various points in his career, he went by Jefferson Fuck and Jefferson

Clitlick). Together with the gay activist Randy Wicker and the poet and musician Tuli Kupferberg, Poland founded the Sexual Freedom League in New York. Members met weekly to debate just how many sexual taboos one could violate. Gender roles, they unanimously agreed, should be abolished. Bisexuality and group sex were in. Monogamy was out. Bestiality, they decided, was okay as long as the animal did not resist.

The rallying cry of the Sexual Freedom League was "no rape, no regulation." Consent, or the absence of it, was the only factor they believed ought to restrict anyone from engaging in any sex act he or she wanted. In 1965, Poland moved to San Francisco and founded a chapter of the Sexual Freedom League there. He held a highly publicized "nude wade-in" at a city beach and participated in the vibrant street culture of the Haight-Ashbury neighborhood.

Student protests at Berkeley, which had paralyzed the campus during the previous school year, produced an environment receptive to these ideas.

The spiritualist Richard Thorne had been using the *Berkeley Barb*, an underground paper that started on campus, as a platform to argue that in the absence of monogamy, copulation was "holy." "We must abstain from selfishness, jealousy, possessiveness," he wrote, "but not copulation."

At the beginning of 1967, thousands of young people flooded Golden Gate Park for the "Human Be-In," a public festival presenting Beat poetry, radical leftist speeches, and performances by hippie bands. The audience openly took drugs and sunbathed nude as reporters and photographers gawked and snapped pictures. The psychologist–turned–LSD evangelist Timothy Leary called on them to "turn on, tune in, drop out."

It was the image of freedom, but some worried it wouldn't last. Standing onstage waiting to read his poetry, Allen Ginsberg turned to his friend Lawrence Ferlinghetti and asked him a question below his breath: "What if we're wrong?"

Images of the activities in San Francisco kept drawing more and more runaways and seekers. Many of them had no idea what they were looking for. They knew only what they were *not* looking for.

Julie Ann Schrader remembered seeing a series of photos of San Francisco in *Life* magazine when she was still a teenager living in suburban Wisconsin. They showed "a group of people wearing big smiles and little else at a love-in," she reminisced to an interviewer in 2013. The moment she saw it, she said, she realized that she had to flee.

"If I remained in Wisconsin, I would marry my college sweetheart, teach Sunday school, have a family, and live the life my parents lived," she wrote. "My future was locked in. The thought of it terrorized my spirit." Schrader dropped out of school, ditched her middle-class life plan, and hitched a ride west. Many others did the same, eager to find love and romance outside the narrow possibilities that traditional marriage offered.

In San Francisco, couples dispensed with the formalities of dating. They met, mated, and drifted apart at incredible speeds. This is not to say that their relationships did not involve drama. Sex in San Francisco could mean many things. A one-night stand might lead to a spontaneous common-law marriage. A whirlwind romance might ensnare you in a life of hard drugs.

By the end of 1967, the Haight was flooded with runaways. The new world the hippies were trying to create was difficult to sustain. When they had repealed all the laws, they had not clearly established who would do the things that still needed to be done. In the absence of a plan, they often fell back onto highly stereotyped gender roles.

In her essay about the Summer of Love, "Slouching Towards Bethlehem," Joan Didion described her encounter with "Max," a young man who earnestly insists to her that it is possible to have loving relationships without any responsibilities or constraints.

"Max is telling me how he lives free of all the old middle-class Freudian hang-ups. 'I've had this old lady for a couple of months now, maybe she makes something special for my dinner and I come in three days late and tell her I've been balling some other chick, well, maybe she shouts a little but then I say 'That's me, baby' and she laughs and says 'That's you, Max.'"

"Max," Didion concludes, "sees his life as a triumph over 'don'ts.'"

Max may have rejected the repressive laws that had governed the lives of his parents. But what is striking about the relationship between Max and his "old lady" is how traditional it sounds. Max mentions his partner's cooking offhand; he takes it for granted that she should make him meals and love him unconditionally. After the destruction of the institutions of marriage and family, it was unclear how else things would ever run.

The Haight did have one rogue group of volunteers who attempted to respond to the mounting disorder that was taking over the streets: the Diggers. The core members of this semianonymous group of artists and radicals had met performing in the San Francisco Mime Troupe. Their guiding star was the concept of "free."

With a doctor named David Smith, the group established the Haight-Ashbury Free Clinic, which treated the rampant spread of venereal disease and drug-related illness. They founded a "free store," full of donated goods that anyone was allowed to take. They staged several "eat-ins," serving free meals to runaways and municipal employees. They supported free street concerts by Big Brother and the Grateful Dead. They protested every for-profit, commercialized music event.

"Suckers buy what lovers get for free," their protest signs declared. "It's yours. You want to dance—dance in the street."

The greatest ambition of the Diggers had been to teach by personal example.

The actor Peter Coyote, one of the founding members of the group, later explained their philosophy: "Our hope was that if we were skillful enough in creating concrete examples of existence as free people, the example would be infectious."

Yet this process did not take place quite as spontaneously as they expected. Gathering clothes for the free store, cooking and distributing food—it all got to be a drag. And so, while the men planned spectacles to draw attention to the group, the women did the grunt work to keep things going.

They woke up at five in the morning, got the old truck running, stole or charmed meat and vegetables from grocers, cooked up hearty stews, lugged them, steaming, out to the Panhandle in massive steel milk containers, and ladled them out. Susan Keese, one of the female Diggers, later helped found the Black Bear commune north of San Francisco. She recalled what it took to keep the philosophy of "free" going.

"We would go collect free food from the San Francisco produce market a couple of days per week," she told a reporter in 2007. "The guys at the market would give us food because of how we looked. We traded on that." It turned out that free wasn't free. Like Charity Girls of the 1890s and 1900s, these activists had to flirt for food; once they had it, they handed it over to boyfriends and strangers. The ethos that the Diggers promoted depended on being able to take advantage of female work.

Even the most politically radical men often sought traditional romantic relationships. In her autobiography, the activist and scholar Angela Davis expressed frustration and exhaustion at the sexism that she encountered while organizing with the Black Panther Party. "I was criticized very heavily, especially by male members . . . for doing 'a man's job.' Women should not play leadership roles, they said. A woman was supposed to 'inspire' her man and educate his children."

The activist and writer Toni Cade Bambara reported that the men she worked with in the Panthers justified their disregard for the concerns of female members by appealing to their shared ambitions to win racial justice. "Invariably I hear from some dude that Black women must be supportive and patient so that Black men can regain their manhood," she recalled. "So the shit goes on."

It made sense that many of the "dudes" Bambara worked with felt unmanned by the legacy of slavery. Systematic racism harshly punished black men for any show of sexuality and made it almost impossible for them to earn a living wage. Still, the fact was that the macho culture of the Black Panthers told its female members that they had to put their desires and aspirations second. Like the female Diggers, and like Max's "old lady," they should work and wait.

The Black Power leader Stokely Carmichael famously dissed the sisters who were trying to assist his cause. In 1964, he heard about a position paper that female volunteers were circulating about the role of women in the Student Nonviolent Coordinating Committee, the civil rights organization he would later lead. "What is the position of women in SNCC?" Carmichael joked. "The position of women in SNCC is prone."

Many "hippie chicks" ended up paying for "free" with more than shopping and washing dishes. They endured a culture of rampant sexual violence—of rape or sex they forced themselves to endure. "If It's Their Thing," the *Berkeley Barb* advised women in 1967, "Just Let 'em Leer." Pity the women who did not feel so nonchalant.

In 1967, a member of the Diggers named Chester Anderson left the group in disgust and started publishing public communiqués on his mimeograph machine. Some of the bulletins that he posted around the Haight criticized the hypocrisy and racism of what he called "segregated bohemia." Others criticized its misogyny. One announced that the streets had become dangerous for women.

"Pretty little sixteen-year-old middle-class chick comes to the Haight to see what it's all about & gets picked up by a seventeen-year-old street dealer who spends all day shooting her full of speed again & again, then feeds her 3000 mikes [micrograms of LSD, twelve times the standard dose] & raffles off her temporarily unemployed body for the biggest Haight Street gang bang since the night before last. The politics & ethics of ecstasy. Rape is as common as bullshit on Haight Street."

The policeman Colin Barker claimed in 1968 that rapes were so common in and around Golden Gate Park that they were "hardly ever reported." The poet Ed Sanders described the neighborhood during those years as "a valley of thousands of plump white rabbits surrounded by wounded coyotes."

Even when they were not drugged and "raffled off," women in the counterculture often strained to live up to the ideal that they should always want sex. Susan Keese recalled her fears of seeming counter–sexual revolutionary. "There was this ethic that it was good for you to have as much sex as possible . . . and you were uptight and hung up if you did not. Some women seemed to be comfortable with that, but I was not."

Within the counterculture, gameness for any sexual adventure was seen as proof of sophistication. Women felt enormous pressure to act on the principle of "free love," even when their desires told them to act otherwise.

"It became the personal responsibility of women in the 1960s to work at removing their inhibitions," the feminist Sheila Jeffreys recalled in her memoir *Anticlimax*. "To be accused by a man of having inhibitions was a serious matter, the implication being that the woman was old-fashioned, narrow-minded and somehow psychologically damaged."

According to this logic, psychological health meant having to embrace a form of sexuality much like the one that *Playboy* purveyed. That is, sex understood strictly as (physical) "pleasure . . . without becoming emotionally involved."

The sexual revolution did encourage many women to do what they wanted, when they wanted, despite any cultural inhibitions they inherited. But when free lovers described the revolution as the freedom from *all* inhibition, they failed to acknowledge that individuals should also have the freedom to remain as inhibited as they like. Most of us feel inhibited when we feel unsafe. Many of us feel inhibited when we are with strangers. We may suddenly rediscover inhibitions and "hang-ups" after losing trust or interest in a partner.

Like Jeffreys, many women in the counterculture struggled to overcome creeping sensations of reluctance and fear. Often, they had good reasons to feel them. A woman was far more likely to experience sexual violence than her male counterpart. If a pregnancy or sexually transmitted infection resulted, she would almost always suffer worse consequences. The Summer of Love took place five years before she could legally seek an abortion.

Advocates of free love proposed to remove the obstacles that convention put in the way of the free exchange of affection. Yet in some cases, rather than liberating sex, sexual revolutionaries simply seemed to take it from people who were most vulnerable to being exploited.

Despite the great hopes that this era had placed on freedom, it could not bring the utopia that some had hoped for. In an unequal society, being freed from formal legal restrictions will not immediately make individuals equally free to pursue their ambitions. Freedom to start a business, for example, is not much use if you have no start-up capital. Freedom without food may mean only freedom to starve.

The free love that promised to liberate individuals from social conventions took a very particular model of male individuality for granted. It was based on a fantasy of manliness that media like *Playboy* sold. Freedom from having to feel certain ways about sex turned into an imperative not to feel anything about sex. This free love could start to look a lot like freedom from love.

Today, conservatives often say that the sexual revolution duped women into seizing freedoms they did not actually want. The opposite is true. The sexual revolution did not take things too far. It did not take things far enough. It did not change gender roles and romantic relationships as dramatically as they would need to be changed in order to make everyone as free as the idealists promised. It tore down walls, but it did not build a new world.

CHAPTER 7. **NICHES**

G reed is all right," the legendary stock trader Ivan Boesky told the graduating class at Berkeley's School of Business Administration. "I think greed is healthy. You can be greedy and still feel good about yourself." This was in May 1985. A lot had changed since protestors paralyzed the campus twenty years earlier. The student radicals of the 1960s had insisted that they had a right to conduct their private lives as they saw fit. By the 1980s, however, Berkeley students took for granted that they could sleep with whom they wanted, when they wanted. They were less interested in free love than in high finance.

The screenwriters for Oliver Stone's movie *Wall Street* lifted the most famous lines of the antihero Gordon Gekko directly from Boesky's Berkeley commencement speech. Gekko, played by Michael Douglas, is engineering a hostile takeover of a family-owned paper company.

"Greed, for lack of a better word, is good," he tells a room of wavering shareholders. "Greed, in all of its forms; greed for life, for money, for love, knowledge, has marked the upward surge of mankind."

By the time *Wall Street* came out in December 1987, the stock market had collapsed, and Boesky had been convicted of insider trading. He would pay $100 million in penalties, serve a three-and-a-half-year prison sentence, and be barred from working in securities for life. But his mantra *Greed is good* has stayed in the American lexicon. The more surprising phrase that Gordon Gekko coined, *greed for love*, never caught on the same way.

There was always something a little tongue-in-cheek about the decadents who crooned, as Madonna did, that *the boy with the cold hard cash is always Mr. Right*. But in the late 1970s and early '80s, shifts in the American economy did begin to turn marriage into a luxury good. The sense that only upper-middle-class and wealthier, college-educated people could manage to get and stay married dramatically changed the landscape of dating. So, too, did another important idea that the '80s bequeathed us. If greed was good, desire works best when it is specific.

Romantics tend to associate love with serendipity. They wait for what the French call the *coup de foudre*, to be stricken by a lightning bolt of attraction. But realists recognize the advantage of strategically cornering the dating market. In order to do it, you have to know your niche. All algorithm-driven dating services rely on the premise that with good enough data, they can match anyone to his or her soul mate. But in order to use these services effectively you must first narrow your search terms.

Since the era of the Shopgirl, the "likes" that daters use to telegraph their personalities have multiplied and become more precise. A friend recently admitted that he had found his last girlfriend by searching OkCupid for W4M in the New York area who had liked Alice Munro. He had planned to go on dates with each of the five results but then hit it off with the second; they were together for four years. I was surprised that the Munro search turned up only five straight women. After all, she is a Nobel laureate. "Oh yeah," the friend said, and then confessed that he had started with other authors, whose names had not culled his prospects as effectively. "I like David Foster Wallace. But if you type David Foster Wallace into OkCupid, it's a shitshow."

In order to appeal to prospective lovers, you must know where to look. You must learn to brand yourself so that you will be searchable by the right people, too. The dating website How about we . . . relies on the idea that you will get along well with someone to whom your spontaneous flights of fancy appeal. Users propose dates, which then appear in the feeds of other users; if you want to do something someone proposes, it puts you in touch. Successful daters, on this site, must master a push-pull between quirkiness and conformity. You won't get many bites by posting, *How about we go to a movie?* But neither will *How about we play* Mario Kart *at my place while eating leftover Ethiopian takeout and then laugh at how flatulent it makes us?* Even though, with the right person, doing either of those things sounds fun.

Scott Kominers, a visiting scholar at Harvard Business School who teaches about online dating in his courses on market design, explains why the signals that singles send to one another through dating sites and apps tend to diverge. The push-pull effect between suggesting a movie and *Mario Kart* is the result of competing tendencies toward "pooling equilibrium" and "skewing," or "polarization."

The first effect explains why so many dating profiles look so boring. For instance, why does almost everyone profess to love travel?

"When there are high costs associated with providing a certain response that is perceived as unusual, people will tend toward giving answers that they see other users give—answers that are average," Kominers says. For instance, someone who puts down "math rap" under interests can immediately turn off many other users on that basis.

"If I'm a heterosexual man who has listed one of the high-cost responses and not many women I am interested in are responding to my messages, I go and try to find out what other guys are putting. And I see that they said 'travel' and that they did not mention anything as nerdy as math rap. And I think to myself, 'Well, travel's okay. I don't *dislike* traveling.' So I add travel to my interests in the hopes of having greater success."

Eventually, however, the pooled equilibrium can inspire the opposite effect. Users who find themselves flooded with average profiles or feel lost in the sea look for signals to differentiate themselves. According to Kominers, "skewing is an effect of the site, a consequence of and reaction to the fact that everyone looks the same." Over time, the process leads to the multiplication of niche services like FarmersOnly.

The dream of finding your other half, the one custom-made just for you, is an old one. In Roman mythology, the lonely sculptor Pygmalion spends his days creating a statue of his ideal woman. The goddess Venus eventually takes pity on Pygmalion and brings his marble girl to life. They get married and live happily ever after. The 1980s version of this story is the John Hughes movie *Weird Science*, about two high school geeks who conjure up their dream girl. They are inspired not by Venus but by watching the 1931 movie *Frankenstein* on cable. Instead of stone and chisel, they use a desktop computer, which they connect with wires to a bunch of magazine cutouts. The Frankenbabe who emerges is a little grown-up for them. But by conjuring a cool car out of thin air, and helping them throw wild parties, she raises their social stock to the point where they can score cute human girlfriends.

Weird Science was science fiction, and it was meant to be funny. But today the Internet dangles out the tantalizing prospect that any man or woman could actually almost do this. Now any of us might dream of becoming Pygmalion 2.0.

On the surface, the beginning of the Era of the Niche looked very different from the free love years that preceded it. When Ronald Reagan first ran for governor of California in 1966, he had promised to get rid of the "Berkeley bums." During his first campaign for president, in 1980, he scored points with conservative supporters by expressing contempt for hippies who (he said) "act like Tarzan, look like Jane, and smell like Cheetah" and indulge in "orgies so vile I cannot describe them to you."

Most Americans seemed to agree that the free-for-all of the sexual revolution had gone on long enough: Reagan won by a landslide. But however eager conservatives were to return to the "traditional" values of the 1950s, they could not simply undo the real changes that had taken place since then. The thriving manufacturing economy had collapsed. With it, the wages that had let millions of working men support stay-at-home wives, and keep their going-steady kids flush with spare cash for gas, milk shakes, and dances, had plummeted. So, as it happened, the Reagan Revolution did not erase the central tenets of the counterculture. Instead, it spread them.

The press loved to lampoon former radicals who switched teams during the 1980s. They could take their pick. Bobby Seale, the cofounder of the Black Panther Party who had appeared on television during the Watts riots in 1965 chanting "Burn, baby, burn," rebranded himself as a gourmet chef. Jane

Fonda went from being a protest icon to building a fitness empire based on aerobics videos.

It was not just cynicism or disillusionment that drove radicals from rioting to retail. While free-market evangelists dressed differently from free lovers, they shared certain deep similarities. The philosophies of personal freedom espoused by writers like Lawrence Lipton or activists like Timothy Leary laid the groundwork for the worldview in which, as Boesky put it, being "all right" meant being "healthy," and being "healthy" meant "feeling good about yourself." Where the point of living in the free world was to pursue happiness, as you defined it, without interference.

Like the Steadies who preceded them, the young people who flocked to Haight-Ashbury during the Summer of Love believed that the goal of life was well-being, and that you achieved it by consuming. The difference was that they refused to accept the limited range of goods and lifestyles on offer. They did not want to go for root beer floats with "one certain boy." They did not want to marry the first or second girl they parked with and petted, or spend their days working nine to five to pay off the mortgage on a prefabricated house that she could grow old washing their dishes in. They wanted *experience*. This could mean consuming drugs or taking lovers or both.

The radicals who grew up to be yuppies added this twist. Not only should social institutions, like marriage, not stop an individual from pursuing any desire he feels; a well-functioning economy should be able to deliver any kind of love you can imagine. The core principle remained: *greed was good.* You are free to want what you want, whether it is a tab of LSD and an "old lady" to cook dinner for your commune in the Haight, or a Rolex and a fellow law associate to make a quick detour to pick up tuna sashimi takeout on her way home to your co-op. As the Berlin Wall fell and the Soviet Union fell apart, it seemed like the Material Girls had it right. The benefits of deregulated desire would trickle down.

"Niche" became a business buzzword in the early 1980s. In the Era of the Steady, GM pioneered the strategy of using "dynamic obsolescence" to stimulate demand in markets that were already saturated. By introducing new models of their cars annually, and offering payment and leasing plans that made it possible to trade your older model up, car companies convinced middle-class car owners to keep shopping around for new rides, even after they had found them.

By the 1970s, however, marketers started adopting a different tactic: divide and conquer. Whether your goal was to introduce a new product, or to expand demand for something that already existed, the best strategy was to identify a narrow demographic and shape the product to appeal to it.

Some marketing experts had recognized as early as the 1950s that the economic growth based on mass consumption that took place after World War II could not last long. An article that appeared in the *Journal of Marketing* in 1956 proposed that the future lay elsewhere: in what the economist Wendell Smith called "market segmentation." Soon, more and more managers were saying that it made sense to appeal to people with very different desires rather than try to capture a large swath of all consumers. By the early 1980s, technological advances made it seem as if there might in fact be no limit to how finely a good company could slice its market segments.

In 1983, an article in the academic journal *Management Review* predicted that the advent of computer-aided design (CAD) and manufacturing (CAM) would soon allow single companies to cater to a potentially infinite number of niches. The robots that worked in the "factory of the future" could be programmed to turn out variations on products for a fraction of what it would have cost to train and keep human workers to do the same. The rise of a single bar code system across manufacturing industries helped. Making it possible to tag and track components, along the entire supply chain, "Code 39" allowed consumers to specify what they wanted in advance. Not only could you get this year's Buick, you could get it with whatever color, upholstery, and paneling you liked.

Meanwhile, new media technologies were making it possible to advertise to niche audiences more efficiently than ever before, too. In 1980, there were five television networks in the United States, and the big four, ABC, CBS, FOX, and NBC, commanded 90 percent of the attention of TV viewers. By 1990, there were hundreds of cable channels and none of them had anything like the market share that the big four had enjoyed. A similar sea change had taken place in radio broadcasting, and the Internet was already beginning to amplify its effects. Soon there would be more channels of communication than the advertisers of the *Mad Men* era could have imagined.

During this time, dating also became more targeted. Businesses aimed to attract a particular kind of dater. Like Madonna, they wanted the ones with the most cold, hard cash.

It is not clear who coined the term "yuppie," but credit usually goes to Bob Greene. The *Chicago Tribune* columnist used it in an article about the Jerry Rubin Business Networking Salon in March 1983. Rubin, the erstwhile radical who had led the Youth International Party with Abbie Hoffman and stood trial with the Chicago Eight, was now hosting weekly "networking sessions" at the legendary Studio 54 disco in New York.

"When you're ambitious in the business world, your day does not end at 5 o'clock," Rubin told Greene. His parties were invitation only. Guests had to pay $8 and deposit their business cards at the door, to be sorted later and ranked on a scale of networking value that ranged from A to D. The lights stayed on, and the sound track was soft classical music.

"This is not a singles bar," Rubin emphasized. "It's a way for businesspeople to meet other businesspeople. It's an extension of the business day." In March 1983, he had plans to franchise in thirty-six cities. Someone at the party that Greene attended quipped that Rubin had gone from being leader of the *yippies* to spokesman for the *yuppies*—young urban professionals. In the process, he had also converted one of America's most famously debauched places to go out to into a place to network.

Rubin was not the only one who recognized that yuppies presented an enormous opportunity. In the early 1980s, political pollsters and market research firms became fixated on the emerging demographic. A study conducted by the California think tank SRI International in 1984 found that there were four million Americans between the ages of twenty-five and thirty-nine who earned at least $40,000 per year in professional or management positions. Between 1979 and 1983, 1.2 million of them had moved to the cities that their parents had fled for the suburbs. They bought up Victorian brownstones and co-ops in factories and warehouses, which had fallen into dereliction as America deindustrialized, and developers were now racing to renovate.

One million–plus was not enough to command serious attention from national politicians. But when pollsters lumped together all baby boomers with college degrees who were working in white-collar or technical professions, the number came to more than twenty million. As the companies aimed to capture the growing incomes of this market segment, the media obsessed about them, producing taxonomy after taxonomy of their peculiar traits.

The main mythology that grew up around yuppies concerned not how much they bought, but *what* they bought. Armed with credit cards, they spent high sums on things that would have seemed absurd even five years earlier. Gourmet mustard. Espresso machines. Gym memberships. They did not want it all. They wanted very specific things. To train their triceps, not their deltoids. Not a Labrador, but an Akita.

When the bestselling satire *The Yuppie Handbook* came out in January 1984, it established that the foremost trait of a yuppie was an obsession with *particular* products. The cover depicts a white couple standing side by side, with each item they are wearing and holding clearly labeled, as in a high school physiology diagram. He has a pinstripe suit, in the pocket of which there is a Cross pen; a Rolex watch; and L. L. Bean Maine Hunting Duck boots. He is carrying a Gucci briefcase and a Burberry trench coat is slung over his forearm. She sports a Ralph Lauren suit, a Cartier Tank Watch, and white running shoes. With a Coach bag on one arm, and a bag of gourmet fresh pasta on the other, she is listening to her Sony Walkman.

Name checking became a common feature of serious writing about yuppies, too. In one scene of Don DeLillo's 1985 breakout novel, *White Noise*, the narrator overhears his young daughter murmuring the names of car models in her sleep. "She uttered two clearly audible words, familiar and elusive at the same time, words that seemed to have a ritual meaning, part of a verbal spell or ecstatic chant. *Toyota Celica*."

Jerry Rubin not only inspired a label for a generation obsessed with labeling. His Business Networking Salon also captured an important shift in how young professionals were approaching their careers. That was the rise of the idea that everyone should work—and should *love* working—nonstop. If shopgirls of the 1920s had tried to flirt, and even date, on the job, yuppies continued to hustle well after the office closed.

The complicated financial instruments and maneuvers that Wall Street bankers and their lawyers cooked up inspired many a pun. "Corporate marriage" could refer either to a corporate merger—the consolidation of companies that was generating so much of the new wealth on Wall Street—or to a romantic partnership in which both lovers were lawyers or bankers, too busy to have much sex and therefore tolerant of affairs conducted on business trips. Consider the possibilities for double entendre afforded by "horizontal mergers," "profit squeezes," "position limits," "extension swaps," "rollovers," "interlocking directorates," and "tender offers," and you get a rough idea of what passed for flirtation at an MBA cocktail hour.

The famous speech that Steve Jobs gave at Stanford's commencement in 2005 was tame by comparison. However, Jobs, too, exhorted college graduates to mix business and pleasure. Jobs insisted that the best thing that ever happened to him was being fired from his own company in 1985, because it taught him how important passion was for professional success.

"I'm convinced that the only thing that kept me going was that I loved what I did." What he said next was widely reprinted and reblogged. "You've got to find what you love. And that is as true for your work as it is for your lovers . . . The only way to do great work is to love what you do. If you haven't found it yet, keep looking. Don't settle. As with all matters of the heart, you'll know when you find it."

Do what you love. Love what you do. By the 1990s, versions of this exhortation had become ubiquitous. Still, they could not quite cover up the fact that the career prospects of many Americans were getting worse.

In the Year of the Yuppie, the Research Institute of America found that overall, young Americans were experiencing downward mobility. Between 1979 and 1983, the median annual income for households in the twenty-five-to-thirty-four age range decreased by 14 percent in constant dollars. For the relatively unskilled, $12/hr union jobs manufacturing cars were disappearing and being replaced by $5/hr gigs flipping burgers.

Today *do what you love, and you'll never work a day in your life* no longer sounds very reassuring. Since the 1970s, falling wages have meant that everyone has to work more and more, whether they love it or not.

With the stakes of staying upper middle class so high, the yuppie who would consider dating anyone other than another yuppie would be out of his or her mind. And indeed in the 1980s, for the first time since the dawn of dating, America experienced a trend toward *assortative mating.*

In biology, assortative mating is "a nonrandom mating pattern in which individuals with similar genotypes and/or phenotypes mate with one another more frequently than would be expected under a random mating pattern." Textbook example: Animals with similar body sizes tend to reproduce with each other. Although it might theoretically be possible, one rarely sees a Yorkshire terrier attempt to mount a Great Dane, or (God forbid) vice versa.

Before the rise of dating, courtship rituals like calling and church socials or Jewish settlement dances encouraged and even enforced similar mating patterns among humans. Parents and communities collaborated to ensure that young people paired off with partners who came from similar backgrounds.

Dating did not entirely break down these old biases and barriers. The middle- and upper-class men who frequented saloons and speakeasies did not all marry the Charity Girls they treated. Institutions like schools sorted young people by educational attainment, which strongly correlated with family background and future earnings. Still, the migration of courtship from the privacy of the household, or the closed ranks of community centers, into public places where daters roamed unsupervised introduced an element of unpredictability. People who went out and hit it off with a stranger might actually fall in love.

Moreover, workplaces offered opportunities for people from different classes and backgrounds to mix. At least until the early 1960s, a young woman in a professional workplace usually came from a lower socioeconomic bracket than the men she worked for. Until the 1980s, it was far from unheard of for a manager to marry a shopgirl, a boss to marry his secretary, or a doctor to marry a nurse. However, as women gained opportunities to enter corporations as associates and partners, as well as secretaries and stenographers, the office dating pool grew. It made sense that young men and women who came from similar backgrounds, had attended the same colleges and graduate schools, and spent twelve-hour-plus days working closely together would hit it off.

It is difficult to find reliable government data on how much and what kinds of people date in any given period. But it is clear that in the final decades of the twentieth century, the highly educated women climbing the corporate ladder started *marrying* men who were their professional peers.

A 2014 study by the National Bureau of Economic Research showed that, whereas in 1960 only 25 percent of men with university degrees married women with them, in 2005, 48 percent did. Moreover, most highly paid women loved what they did. Or at least they faced huge opportunity costs for any time they spent off the job. If and when they had children, most promptly returned to work. Amplifying the growing economic inequality among

American households, assortative mating patterns reinforced themselves.

Yuppies wanted to date other yuppies. The thing was, who had time? They may have been the first elite in human history to boast, as a mark of their status, that they could not afford a moment's leisure. The leisure goods that yuppies did consume, they described as necessary to their work—as conveniences that made nonstop work possible (like eating out) or as part of a lifelong effort to work on themselves (like diets).

Marketers soon discovered that you could sell yuppies anything if you promised that it would make them better. In New York, in 1982, a line of fitness studios called Definitions opened, offering $600 monthly memberships to young professionals who already belonged to a gym but wanted more targeted personal training. Today you can still buy sessions with a personal trainer in packages of twenty-five, for $2,800, at any one of a dozen locations.

A sense of anxiety and precariousness lay not far below the well-toned surface of the yuppie, urging him or her to improve harder, better, faster. In 1984, Kellogg ran an ad campaign with the tagline *It's not "Are Grape Nuts good enough for you," but "Are you good enough for Grape Nuts?"* *If you're not the predator, you're the prey,* billboards for Puma sneakers warned.

No wonder people were stressed! How could you know who was good enough to date? And where could you take them out, to prove you might be worthy of them?

Yuppie daters were very particular about the restaurants they went to. Local newspapers of the 1980s are full of reviews of hot spots coming in and going out of fashion faster than the writers can keep up with. The *Washington Post* food editor Phyllis

Richman told *Newsweek* in 1984 that whenever she went somewhere, "I inevitably find the same crowd of people have discovered it already." She said that she could also sense when the yuppies would ditch a place, or taste—basically, as soon as the plebs caught on.

"When I saw white-chocolate mousse being served in a Hot Shoppe," Richman recalled, "I knew."

Luckily for daters who got restless so quickly, yuppies themselves came in many flavors. The press and pollsters sometimes talked about yappies ("young aspiring professionals") and yumpies ("young, upwardly mobile professionals"). *The Yuppie Handbook* included a three-page spread listing the traits of Buppies ("black urban professionals"), Huppies ("Hispanic urban professionals"), Guppies ("gay urban professionals"), Juppies ("Japanese urban professionals"), and Puppies ("pregnant urban professionals").

Each subspecies had its own defining characteristics, but all were presented as customizations you might choose on a single yuppie model. Bullet points under "Buppie" included *Greater familiarity with Reggae music. Preference for custom-made business suits. Tendency to name their daughters Keesha instead of Rebecca. If female, the inclination to wear a second pair of pierced earrings with their diamond studs.* Guppies, by contrast, were distinguished by *summer holidays on Fire Island instead of in the Hamptons* and *use of free weights instead of Nautilus equipment.*

These rhyming labels caught on with newspapers and magazines that carried stories about dating. The pun "yuppie love" became inescapable; "buppie" and "guppie" made good showings, too. The aural proximity of these jingling acronyms reinforced deeply held beliefs of the Reagan era: politics were passé; everyone started out the same; it was this equality of opportunity, not outcomes, that mattered.

By this logic, a yuppie might choose his mate as freely as

he chose a blue or tan or silver paint job for his Saab. Indeed, satirists described yuppies as treating their love lives like any other consumer or career choice. Only, if anything, a little *less* important.

The section of *The Yuppie Handbook* devoted to dating and marriage is called "Personal Interfacing." "Yuppies don't love their lovers," the preamble begins. "They love Vivaldi, their new apartments, and the color of the ocean off St. Thomas in January. They have *relationships* with their lovers." According to the *Handbook*, yuppies broke relationships, like business deals, into three stages: (1) getting into, (2) working on, and (3) getting out.

In an article on "Yuppie Love" in its 1984 *Year of the Yuppie* issue, *Newsweek* adopted a similarly arch tone. "It can happen anywhere, anytime. You're sitting at a sales meeting, and this fabulous looking guy stands up and gives this really tremendous presentation, and all of a sudden you know, you've just got to have him in your division."

All joking aside, many yuppie daters felt despair. In 1985, the Associated Press interviewed a Boston social worker who taught a free course on "Spouse Hunting" at the city's Adult Education Center. She recalled that ten years earlier, most of her students had found being single glamorous. Now, they all seemed miserable. "Urban life is so anonymous," she said, "everyone is dying to know how to meet somebody."

Spending long days at the office, and one or two hours a day besides in the gym and personal-training sessions, many yuppies found that they had little of themselves left over to invest in romance.

What could you do if doing what you loved took so much time and energy that you had none left for dating? One 1980s dating advice manual suggested buying an eye-catching breed of dog to meet other singles. The fitness addict could kill two birds with one stone by taking his or her canine conversation piece for a jog.

"That's still a thing!" my friend exclaims when I read this tip aloud to him.

A more efficient approach was figuring out what you wanted in a partner *before* you started shopping. Just as businesses developed to cater to yuppies who were too busy to cook, or wanted to target their trapezius muscles without wasting time on, say, rowing, so did new services promise to help you date. To have highly specific taste was a plus: It helped you speed up your search by narrowing it down.

Cookie Silver was short. But she wanted tall.

"I want tall," she kept telling her matchmaker. "When I'm with a short man we look like Munchkins."

"But this one's a doctor," the matchmaker protested, of one of her prospects. "When he stands on his wallet, he's over six feet!"

Cookie recounted her story to the *Chicago Tribune* in 1985. By then, she and the tall man she held out for—an entrepreneur by the name of Howard Feldstein—had met, married, and acquired the local franchise of the video-dating service that introduced them. IntroLens was growing at a quick clip, adding hundreds of users every month and opening several new offices across the Midwest. It was only one of a spate of new businesses offering dating services to yuppie lonelyhearts. These promised to help daters find what they wanted in what little time they had.

Dating services had been around since the 1960s. The first primitive forms of computer dating debuted during that decade. Like Facebook, Operation Match was designed by three students at Harvard. It allowed curious singles to submit several pieces of information about themselves and what they wanted, have these cross-referenced in a database, and receive a handful of recommended partners.

In 1964, an accountant and an IBM programmer in New

York unveiled a similar prototype that they called Project TACT (for "Technical Automated Compatibility Testing"). It catered to singles on New York's Upper East Side. But these were novelties. The first "introduction services" to develop viable business models were low-tech.

You would sign up, usually after a phone call, and then make an appointment to do an in-person interview with one of the "counselors" who worked in the office. The counselor would ask you a long list of personal questions—about your childhood, romantic history, job, hobbies, and religious preferences—and then whether you yourself had any deal breakers. Would you date a smoker? Would you date a divorcé? Within a few weeks you would start receiving cards in the mail with the names and phone numbers of dating prospects. These would continue arriving as long as you paid your membership fee. If you liked someone after talking on the phone, you could meet in person. The whole thing was basically like outsourcing the role of a meddlesome aunt who sets you up on blind dates to a stranger who had a bigger Rolodex.

The personals sections that proliferated in the backs of many newspapers and magazines in the 1970s seemed less enticing to yuppie daters of the 1980s. Dating services that required so little investment up front were generally suspected of delivering low returns. For singles who wanted more selectivity, video dating offered an alternative.

The first video-dating services started appearing in the 1970s, as the prices of video cameras, cassettes, and players fell. At most companies, when you signed up, you would be paired with a counselor. After you filled out some of the usual questionnaires—with basics like race, age, education level, occupation, and religious beliefs—the counselor interviewed you on camera, hiding herself offscreen. At IntroLens, Cookie Silver called this part "the talk show." When you had finished, she allowed you to view your tape. You could ask to reshoot and edit, if you wanted. She labeled the finished product with your first name and filed it in a video library. At the best companies, these libraries were large.

After you had made your recording, your matchmaker ran the answers you had put on your questionnaire through a computer database, which generated a list of prospective matches for you. You could make an appointment to pull the videos these singles had made, so that you could screen them in a private room. If you liked what you saw, you told the service; the service contacted the person on the tape and offered to show him your video. If you both were interested, you would be introduced. At most companies, these services would run you between $500 and $1,000 per year. Some also offered more expensive "lifetime" memberships, which were valid as long as you remained unmarried.

The first video-dating company in the United States, Great Expectations, was founded in Los Angeles in 1975 by a mother and son team, Estelle and Jeff Ullman. It expanded quickly, franchising all over California and the West; in 1990, Jeff claimed that Great Expectations was responsible for six thousand marriages. (A current Facebook page for couples who met through the service fondly remembers Estelle as "everyone's Jewish mother.") In the meantime, the company had inspired a lot of copycats. The first IntroLens office opened in 1979. Between 1980 and 1983, similar services rapidly started multiplying in cities across America.

Eventually, video-dating services would cater to daters at almost every price point and in every demographic. There was Soul Mates Unlimited (for Jews in California) and Soul Date a Mate (for African Americans in or around Framingham, Massachusetts). In Boston there was Partners (for gays and lesbians) and Mazel Dating (for Jewish singles). Washington, D.C., had Today For Singles Inc., which served daters with herpes.

In 1988, an exhibition at the Chicago Zoo called ZooArk even let visitors play a video-dating game on behalf of animals that belonged to endangered species. Using a computer connected to the International Species Information System—the resource that professional zookeepers use to do this—the exhibit let visitors browse prospective mates for one of the zoo's "bachelors" and two "bachelorettes." These were a white, black, and Asian rhinoceros.

In personal ads, computer databases, and video-dating tapes of the 1980s we can see contemporary online dating technologies struggling to emerge from their analog chrysalis. If yuppies had not invented the Internet, their personal assistants would have had to invent it for them. These text and VHS predecessors of online dating prepared us. For one thing, they taught busy singles to focus their romantic expectations—to spell out what they had to offer, what they were looking for, and where they might be likely to find it.

Print classified ads already required daters to do this. They forced you to boil down yourself and your desires into sound bites—and to know your audience. You could expect different people to read the personals at the backs of *The New York Review of Books* versus *New York* magazine, in the African American paper the *Los Angeles Sentinel* versus the beefcake glossy *Exercise for Men Only*. You had only a few words to catch the right eyes. Jeff Ullman, the Great Expectations founder, traveled the United States offering motivational lectures and seminars to anxious singles. When I reach him at his home in Colorado, he recounts how he used to boost the confidence of attendees by telling them they should not feel ashamed to be selling themselves.

"'What is advertising?' I would ask. 'Let's look it up in the dictionary.'" Then he would pull out a dictionary.

"'*Advertising.* Taking a product or a service and promoting it.' I believe that is what you're doing. You're a product, you're a service, you're a thing—you're a bag of carbon and water—and you're here because you want to mate, date, procreate. Every one of you is advertising for yourself."

As more and more dating services began using computers—creating databases of clients and cross-listing them—the imperative to *go niche* would turn from being a good strategy to a technical requirement. You had to be able to express your personality in *exactly* the right keystrokes. Daters quickly learned to convert themselves to code.

Until the early 1980s, dating services had been seen as slightly pathetic. You can tell by how adamantly the pioneers of video dating insisted that their customers were *not* pathetic. Jeff Ullman, the Great Expectations owner, actually sued a local bank in Southern California whose billboards joked that its generous interest rates offered clients "more zeros than a dating service." "When I saw it," Ullman fumed to the *Los Angeles Times*, "I almost drove off the road!"

"These aren't losers, you understand," Joan Hendrickson assured *The Washington Post* of the clients she served at the branches of her upscale D.C. service, Georgetown Connection. "On the contrary, these are people who are confident and willing to take a risk." In a business piece on the spectacular growth of the People Network and several other New England video-dating companies between 1981 and 1983, *The Boston Globe* concurred. "Once viewed as the alternative for love's losers, they appear to be gaining a new image of respectability, especially among singles who are busy career professionals.

Yuppies had made work itself glamorous. In doing so, they had made it admirable (rather than pitiful) to be too busy to have a social or romantic life.

The way people talked about video dating reflected a new

level of comfort with the idea that courtship was simply another part of the economy. Today, controversial dating services frequently invoke the existence of demand for their services as a moral justification that needs no further explanation. Before the August 2015 data breach that made Ashley Madison, the dating site for cheating spouses, infamous, the founder, Noel Biderman, defended it by saying that it simply facilitated interactions that would take place anyway. SeekingArrangement describes the "sugar dating" it brokers as "relationships on your terms." It promises convenience—"find a relationship anywhere, anytime on any device"—and advertises "ideal relationships" that are "upfront and honest arrangements with someone who will cater to your needs."

Of course, the market does not always offer happiness. The idea that new technologies could create a perfect delivery system for human desire set many daters up for disappointment. For some, it inspired unrealistic expectations.

In a video-dating tape that is still floating around on YouTube, a thin man with a mullet describes what he is hoping for: "a figure that is sexy . . . slim, tight, excellent legs." He pauses to look up into the camera and literally smacks his lips. "Mmmm." His was the problem that still confronts daters on many apps and services: The specter of infinite possibility and choice creates hopes that only can be dashed, again and again, in a search that never ends.

Article after article related how brutal video dating was on women. A headline in the *Chicago Tribune* joked drily that "For a 4-Figure Fee, You Get Rejected Regularly." The story focused on the plight of an attractive, professional forty-something-year-old woman, recently divorced, who was roped into paying $1,450 for a membership from which she never got one single date. "Video dating services are great," the authors joked. "Just as long as you're either (a) A gorgeous woman, under 35, with a glamorous career, or (b) An average-looking man, under 65, with an ordinary job."

Even the proprietors of dating services admitted that it was hard for them to help female clients who had passed middle age. Bob Greene, the columnist who had coined "yuppie," told the heartbreaking story of a seventy-year-old widow named Nancy who drove in from the Chicago suburb of Berwyn to sign up for a service called Sneak Previews Inc.

"My husband died seven years ago," Nancy told the owner, Joseph De Bartolo. "You get so lonely when that happens. Every year you get lonelier."

De Bartolo told Greene that he had not wanted to take her money. He warned the septuagenarian, "We really don't have a lot of people who it might be appropriate for you to choose."

"That's okay," she replied. "I don't expect to walk out with a date today." When Greene followed up several months later, he found Nancy at home, alone.

Like the bars, speakeasies, and school dances that came before them, computer-dating services were platforms. Only the technology of courtship was supposed to have improved. Computers promised to rationalize the dating market—to clear up inefficiencies that kept the supply of yuppie singles from finding its demand. When online-dating companies began to take off in the mid-1990s, they assembled larger and larger databases and deployed automated processing power. As more Americans got online, and it became possible to delegate the work of a Cookie Silver to algorithms and a webcam, dating services would become affordable and available to virtually anyone who wanted to use them. You could belong to two or three dating services at once. By the turn of the millennium, the numbers of members of sites like Match .com and PlentyOfFish had climbed into the tens of millions.

In an article that appeared in *Wired* magazine in 2002, Nerve .com's founder Rufus Griscom declared that the ascendancy of online dating was inevitable.

"Twenty years from now, the idea that someone looking for love won't look for it online will be silly, akin to skipping the card catalog to instead wander the stacks because 'the right books are found only by accident,'" Griscom wrote. "We have a collective investment in the idea that love is a chance event, and often it is. But serendipity is the hallmark of inefficient markets, and the marketplace of love, like it or not, is becoming more and more efficient."

Had we come *Back to the Future*? At the dawn of dating, all sorts of people had decried the fact that courtship was moving out of the home and into an anonymous, public world where money changed hands. Policemen worried that making dates was equivalent to turning tricks. Love was supposed to lie outside the economy; women could only give it away. By the 1980s and '90s, however, respectable people were celebrating the possibility that courtship might be made to behave as rationally as the market was supposed to, via technologies that let you "do comparison shopping of potential dates from the comfort and privacy of your own home."

The undercover vice investigators who stalked Charity Girls in the 1900s and 1910s were horrified by their transactional approach to romance. However, an odd couple that appears all over Hollywood comedies of the 1980s suggests that by then, mass audiences embraced it. The couple consisted of a prostitute and an entrepreneur.

It started with *Risky Business* (1983).

In *Risky Business*, when his wealthy parents leave him alone for a weekend, the high school senior played by Tom Cruise phones a call girl, Lana, on a dare. After their night together leaves him in her debt, and her pimp steals his parents' chichi furniture, Tom Cruise must go into business with Lana to earn the money he needs to buy his heirlooms back. They team up to run a prostitution ring out of his family home for one night.

"My name is Joel Goodson," Cruise announces after it has all worked out. "I deal in human fulfillment. I grossed over eight thousand dollars in one night." Today, the portrait of the entrepreneur as a young pimp—or, rather, teen male madam—feels prescient. Had Joel Goodson been born two decades later, he might have founded Facebook. Like Mark Zuckerberg, he uses his parents' capital to create a platform where others can exchange attention and emotions so that he can skim off the surplus.

In the Calling Era, the parlor, watched over by the lady of the house, was the inner sanctum of a female world entrusted with taming male tendencies toward aggression, greed, and lust. By the time of *Risky Business*, the parlor had become a living room and then a pop-up brothel. No parents were home.

The mythology of the 1980s and early '90s glorified the escort and the entrepreneur as a perfect match because neither had anything he or she would not be willing to sell. In *Pretty Woman*, Richard Gere puts this bluntly. "You and I are such similar creatures," his suave businessman tells the streetwalker played by Julia Roberts. "We both screw people for money."

There was a lot embedded in this crude pun. For one, the idea that at the bottom, the escort and the entrepreneur did the same kind of work. In the late 1970s, the United States continued to deindustrialize, and the country experienced a trade deficit. Unable to keep up with increased competition from Japan and Germany or to afford the increasingly expensive oil that had once powered industrial production, the United States grew its service sector. Both the streetwalker and the stockbroker belonged to it.

In this sense, Richard Gere was right: They were not so different. Yet this service sector itself continued to split into two increasingly unequal groups. On the one side was the precarious and poorly paid majority; on the other were finance aristocrats. The kind of work the first did tended to be thought of as female—cleaning, serving food, handling customers, and so on. The kind the second did was quantitative and competitive; in their broad-shouldered suits, its icons projected masculinity. So while they had their similarities, these lovers were also opposites. They both screwed people. But they had very different power relationships with them and received different rewards.

Pretty Woman became the highest-grossing love story of this era, because it turned the disappearance of the American middle class into a fairy tale.

Many other romantic comedies told tales of class mobility, where humble, honorable people manage to marry out of dead-end positions into yuppiedom. The 1988 classic *Working Girl*, for instance. The title wink-winks, yet again, at the fundamental similarity of the businessperson and the sex worker. In the beginning, the "working girl" secretary played by Melanie Griffith must commute from Staten Island to work in a Wall Street office as a personal assistant to the pantsuited megabitch played by Sigourney Weaver. However, when an improbable series of events lead Melanie to impersonate her boss, she ends up landing a big deal. She also manages to steal her boss's fiancé, Harrison Ford.

The final scene shows what happily ever after in a yuppie household looks like. Getting ready to leave for work in the morning, Melanie and Harrison wolf down their low-cal breakfast in a wordless ballet. As she pours his coffee, he pops the toast out of the gleaming toaster, and sticks it in her open mouth.

Calling and old-fashioned courtship, the scenery and setting of the parlor, encouraged the fiction that love had nothing to do with the economy. For bourgeois people, marriage was supposed to be a matter of spontaneous, spiritual affinity; for others, it was supposed to propagate a community or bloodline. But as dating neared its centennial, the situation reversed. Dating came to be seen as just another kind of transaction. Many people struggled to reconcile their desire to live efficiently with their desire to feel sexual desire itself.

Shortly after the 1987 stock market crash, *Newsweek* reported that a new disorder was troubling the yuppie population. "Psychiatrists and psychologists say they are seeing a growing proportion of patients . . . whose main response to the sexual revolution has been some equivalent of 'Not tonight, dear.'" The Viennese psychiatrist Helen Singer Kaplan, who had established the first academically accredited sex therapy institute in the United States, in New York in the 1970s, diagnosed this. She called the problem "inhibited sexual desire" (ISD). It entered the *DSM-III* in 1988.

"Over the past decade ISD has emerged as the most common of all sexual complaints. By varying estimates, anywhere from 20 to 50 percent of the general population may experience it at some time, to some degree," *Newsweek* reported. "One clinician goes so far as to call it 'the plague of the '80s.'" Against this backdrop, the sex worker starts to look like the prototype for a new woman who is expert in managing feelings—inspiring particular feelings in others and repressing her own—until the time when revealing them might be advantageous. This expertise allowed her to convert the desires of others into money, which was what any yuppie lover most wanted. She made feelings economically productive.

In *Pretty Woman*, Julia Roberts lands Richard Gere by doing precisely this. Richard Gere admits to being a commitment-phobe who has never felt capable of falling in love; friends Julia Roberts meets when he takes her to a horse race emphasize that he is universally desired. No one seems struck by the fact that his professed inability to have feelings qualifies him as a textbook sociopath.

Richard Gere is handsome and eligible, and Julia seduces him by masterfully turning her own body into a commodity. "Did I mention, my leg is 44 inches from hip to toe?" she asks, in an early scene when she embraces him in the bathtub in his swank suite at the Beverly Wilshire Hotel. "So basically we are talking about 88 inches of therapy, wrapped around you for the bargain price of $3,000."

When Richard returns a necklace that he had borrowed for her to wear to the opera, after failing to man up and become her boyfriend, the jeweler sighs. "It must be hard," he says, as he accepts it back, "to give up something so beautiful."

It is these words *equating Julia Roberts with the necklace* that make Richard realize that he has made a terrible mistake. He sprints away to get her back, scrambling up her fire escape just in time for the happy ending.

Bret Easton Ellis's novel *American Psycho* came out several months after *Pretty Woman*. Whereas *Pretty Woman* was instantly beloved, *American Psycho* was and remains highly controversial. Several publishers dropped the manuscript before Vintage finally published it. But *American Psycho* basically tells the same story as *Pretty Woman* in another genre: horror.

Like Richard Gere, the protagonist Patrick Bateman is a wildly successful, handsome finance guy with a good pedigree who cannot feel anything without engaging the services of sex workers. Richard Gere consumes Julia Roberts figuratively. By letting him treat her body like a beautiful object, she helps him find it in himself to feel love. Patrick Bateman literally murders and eats the prostitutes he sleeps with.

"When I see a pretty girl walking down the street," he jokes to a colleague, "I think two things. One part wants me to take her out and talk to her and be real nice and sweet and treat her right."

"What does the other part of him think?" the colleague asks.

"What her head would look like on a stick."

Over the course of the novel, Bateman gnaws girls' pussies off with his teeth and rips their limbs apart. He stuffs their orifices with Brie and prods a pet rat to eat their bodies from the inside out. He tries to cook girls into sausages and meat loaf. He fails. The matronly apron he wears is a joke. He is no good at cooking; he has clearly never had to do any housework for himself.

Bret Easton Ellis leaves his narrator unreliable. But the fact that we cannot be quite sure whether Patrick Bateman really kills anyone or is just hallucinating the whole thing should not reassure us for a minute. It is just another symptom of a terrifying kind of feelinglessness, the total devaluation of emotion in his world.

American Psycho highlighted the dark underside of a dating market that said that anything anyone wanted and could pay for was fair game. It exposed the yuppie as more than dysfunctional. He was satanic.

Meanwhile, downtown, a real-life nightmare was unfolding.

CHAPTER 8. PROTOCOL

N o wonder Africans called it 'The Horror,'" Andrew Holleran wrote in 1988, in the introduction to *Ground Zero*.
The collection of essays and articles documented the
early years of AIDS in New York City, where Holleran, who had
recently published his first novel, was writing columns for the
gay magazine *Christopher Street*. At first, his "New York Note-
book" mostly covered gallery openings, clubs, and the music
that played at them. Then, in 1982, Holleran's friends and lovers
started falling sick.

Week by week, Holleran watched healthy young men go
blind and grow emaciated. Lesions appeared on their faces and
limbs; they lost their hair to chemotherapy. Holleran recorded
his experiences visiting friends in the hospital. He brought them
magazines. He searched for places on their bodies with no tubes
running in or out, where he might lay a hand.

"Living in New York," he recalled, felt like "attending a dinner party at which some of the guests were being taken out and

shot, while the rest of us were expected to continue eating and make small talk."

In November 1986, the lesbian artist and activist Jane Rosett attended a party at the home of her friend David Summers. In 1997, she would describe it in a eulogy for *POZ*, a magazine for people living with HIV. David had full-blown AIDS. His partner, Sal Licata, had organized the gathering to celebrate their seventh anniversary. He invited friends over to their apartment to "hang out in bed and hold David while he pukes." Despite his suffering, David projected warmth and wit.

"It was a party," Rosett wrote. "David held court and stressed how honored he was to have lured a lesbian into his king-size bed." When his guests relayed gossip of who was sleeping with whom, he cheered. "More people are in love than in the hospital!" Within a few days, however, David died. Rosett returned to keep Sal company as he waited for movers to arrive and empty the apartment. He played the piano and taught her a song as they waited. *Miss the touch, the touch of your hand, my buddy* it went. During World War II, gay men in the armed forces had used it as a code. The next year, Sal passed away in a hallway of St. Vincent's Hospital.

"Within a few years," Rosett recalled, "everyone else in David's bed that day—except me—was also dead."

The Centers for Disease Control had noticed the first signs in the summer of 1981. In June of that year, the CDC's *Morbidity and Mortality Weekly Report* noted a strange outbreak of *Pneumocystis carinii* pneumonia in Los Angeles. Between October 1980 and May 1981, five young men had been diagnosed with the disease. The article speculated that it might have to do with "some aspect of the homosexual lifestyle." The next month, the *MMWR* reported that in the prior thirty months, twenty-six young gay men in New York City and California had been diagnosed with Kaposi's sarcoma, a cancer that was extremely rare in the United States and all but unheard of except among the elderly. By June 1982, 355 Americans were known to be suffering from KS and other opportunistic infections. Doctors and the press had started calling what afflicted them GRID, for "gay-related immuno deficiency." In July 1982, the CDC would rename GRID "AIDS" and identify four populations that were especially at risk: homosexuals, heroin users, hemophiliacs, and Haitians. As shorthand, doctors called them the "4 H's."

Of course, AIDS dramatically changed how gay men dated. "A profound panic has crept over men in the major centers of the outbreak," *The Advocate* reported in 1982. "Few know what to do or not to do." But the disease was not striking only gay men.

As early as 1983, *Essence* magazine reported on CDC findings that 4 percent of HIV-positive patients were not 4 H, and that many new infections were occurring among African American women. By 1996, the number of African Americans with AIDS would surpass the number of whites who had it. At first, many magazines that aimed at black middle-class readers seemed inclined to blame drug users and black men who engaged in homosexual or bisexual activity, despite leading straight-looking lives. "MSM," the CDC called them, for "men who have sex with men."

An article that appeared in *Ebony* in April 1987 warned: "Not only is it killing 'them,' but many of 'us' as well." The author of an article that appeared in *Essence* later that year warned black women to be careful whom they dated. "If I find a guy who's a little swishy," the author confided, "I stay away."

With brutal speed, throughout the 1980s, AIDS would divide daters into Positives and Negatives, straights and swishes.

Us and *them*. For yuppies, niche dating may have been a matter of preference. For those trying to live and love where AIDS struck, it was not snobbery at stake. It was survival.

The communities struggling to cope with AIDS had to re-write the rules regarding how people talked about sex. For decades, euphemisms like "necking" and "petting" had sufficed to cover everything short of "going all the way." No more. The AIDS crisis compelled Americans to speak about sex at great length and in great detail. It forced even conservative politicians to do so in public.

AIDS raised the stakes of dating: There had been crises be-fore, but never one with such deadly consequences. It required daters to develop new protocols for how to interact. Combined with new technologies, the new precision about desire that activ-ists invented would change how everyone went about looking for love.

For six years after the "gay cancer" appeared in California and New York, the Reagan administration did almost nothing about it. The right-wing Christians on whose support Reagan depended saw it as a disease of "junkies and queers." In their eyes, the people who were dying were more than expendable: They deserved it. In 1983, the conservative TV host Pat Buchanan remarked in a moment of faux-compassion: "The poor homosexuals. They have declared war upon nature, and now nature is exacting an awful retribution."

In 1984, researchers at the National Institutes of Health iso-lated the virus that caused AIDS. But even after his close friend Rock Hudson died of AIDS-related causes in 1985, the president remained silent. He would not address the public on the subject until 1987. By then, it was known to have killed more than twenty thousand Americans. In the face of this indifference, the communities suffering from AIDS had to activate and expand existing social networks in order to bring care to those who needed it. They had to develop strategies for delivering information about how to protect yourself to the people who were at greatest risk.

Well before the first cases of GRID were recorded, LGBT activists in many cities had created their own public health institutions. In 1971, the Fenway Health Community Center in Boston was founded with the mission of providing care to gays and lesbians; the Gay Men's Collective at Fenway developed a strong track record treating hepatitis B and other STDs. At the University of Chicago, a group of gay medical students founded the Howard Brown Health Center in 1974. They hired the well-known drag performer Stephen Jones, aka Nurse Wanda Lust, to help with community outreach. Donning her signature wig, nurse's outfit, and round spectacles, Wanda drove around Chicago in a brightly painted "VD van," giving lectures about sexual health. On Easter Sunday 1979, a group of drag performers based in the Castro neighborhood of San Francisco began making public appearances in nuns' habits and dramatic makeup in order to evangelize similar information. They called themselves the Sisters of Perpetual Indulgence.

In 1980, a New Yorker named Richard Edwards created a "discreet fraternity" of "fuckbuddies" called Meridian. Meridian required prospective members to undergo an STD screening. After receiving a clean bill of health, you got a membership pin. In a series of letters that he wrote to the gay newspaper the *New York Native*, Edwards—or "Mr. Rick," as he signed them— explained his thinking: "Buddies care about buddies. It is naturally masculine." Camaraderie, the fuckbuddies reasoned, was the best protection.

When news of GRID broke, networks like Meridian sprang into action. The problem was that nobody was sure what exactly the "gay plague" was or how it was transmitted. Some CDC researchers thought that GRID might be a reaction to a toxic substance that gay men used in greater numbers than the population in general. Others, like the prominent Greenwich Village doctor Joseph Sonnabend, thought that GRID was caused by repeated exposure to less devastating infections, like syphilis.

Facing so many unknowns, some activists preached monogamy and even abstinence. The writer Larry Kramer became infamous for taking this position. In 1983, Kramer wrote a furious screed for the *New York Native*, "1,112 and Counting."

"If this article doesn't scare the shit out of you, we're in real trouble," it began. Kramer aimed to inflame his readers to demand action from the mainstream press and from the government. But he also expressed rage at gay men who put themselves at risk. "I am sick of guys who moan that giving up careless sex until this blows over is worse than death," Kramer wrote. "I am sick of guys who can only think with their cocks."

To many gay men this attitude seemed to come dangerously close to blaming people with AIDS for their disease. Besides, pragmatists realized that the abstinence Kramer preached was impracticable. The best method of prevention was to teach people how to continue to enjoy sex while minimizing its risks.

In 1983, the young gay writers Michael Callen and Richard Berkowitz collaborated with Joseph Sonnabend to produce a forty-page booklet titled *How to Have Sex in an Epidemic*. The five thousand copies they printed got snatched up in a flash. The opening chapters urged gay men to treat one another not as conquests but as *partners*. This required placing a high value on the health of your lovers and speaking truthfully with them.

In a section called "Staying in Control," the authors recommended discussing sexual health ahead of time with any prospective partner and even treating such conversations as foreplay. "Discussing precautions before you have sex might seem like a turn off, but if you enjoy staying healthy, you may eventually come to eroticize whatever precautions you require prior to the sexual encounter."

In addition to openness, Callen and Berkowitz insisted on precision. *How to Have Sex* breaks down gay sex into a menu of discrete safe and unsafe acts, and provides very clear instructions about the difference. For instance, the section "No Risk Sex" makes the following suggestions:

> *Creative Masturbation* offers alternatives to jerking off alone at home. These include: mutual masturbation, group J/O, body contact, fantasy, dirty talk (verbal), voyeurism, exhibitionism, touching, fingers (not fists), titplay, toys, etc. (See section on "Jerk Off Clubs" on page 31.)
>
> *Creative Penetration* includes the use of condoms, fingers (not hands) and "toys." (For a discussion of safe dildo practices, see page 24.)

Other chapters offered equally frank practical advice on "Sucking," "Getting Sucked," "Fucking," "Getting Fucked," "Kissing," "Rimming," "Water Sports," "Dildoes," "Sadism & Masochism (S&M)," "Fist Fucking," "Washing Up," "Closed Circle of Fuck Buddies," "Jerk Off Clubs," and so on.

In the years that followed, AIDS service organizations across the country would produce educational material that presented similar terms in similar menu formats. Rather than telling readers to "Just Say No," these pamphlets offered a wide range of options. The checklist format encouraged readers to mark off new fancies, the way they might dog-ear items in a catalog. It assured them that they could still enjoy an almost infinite variety of sexual experiences as long as they followed the right protocols.

The condition was learning to recognize and name what they wanted.

In order to survive the plague, gay men had to become comfortable talking openly about their histories, diseases, and desires, and seek out partners who shared their attitudes. They would have to break sex down into constituent parts and determine which were safe and which were dangerous. These efforts produced descriptions of sexual behavior that were at once explicit and specific.

Individuals and subcultures had surely come up with terms for activities like "rimming" and "fist-fucking" before. But now these terms were being deliberately codified and disseminated. Different descriptions were needed for each act and target audience.

"Safe sex" promised to save many aspects of gay liberation for a frightening new era. But there was a problem: A lot of the people at risk did not think of themselves as part of that movement. Many black and Hispanic men who had sex with men did not call themselves "gay"; some took offense when others did.

In many cities, communities of Men who had Sex with Men were highly segregated. Bouncers at bars and bathhouses would turn away black men by demanding multiple forms of identification when they did not block them outright. This meant that the viral marketing campaigns launched by organizations like the Gay Men's Health Crisis in New York and the Harvey Milk Foundation in San Francisco reached only a limited demographic.

The techniques that the San Francisco AIDS Foundation used to distribute tens of thousands of condoms every month in the Castro did not put them in the hands of African Americans and Latinos who lived in the Mission District or the Tenderloin. And to the women contracting HIV in these poor neighborhoods, risqué pamphlets and posters would have felt irrelevant.

Billy Jones, the African American activist who founded the San Francisco organization Black and White Men Together (BWMT) warned that most of the people he served thought AIDS was a "white boy disease" that could not strike them.

Different populations needed their own leaders to speak to them in their own language. In San Francisco, a group of non-white community leaders called the Third World AIDS Advisory Task Force stepped in. In 1985, TWAATF started designing and disseminating educational materials. "AIDS is striking people of color," their first brochure warned readers. In 1989, the San Francisco AIDS Foundation and BWMT conducted a series of focus groups with blacks and Latinos in order to try to determine what kinds of ad campaigns might reach them.

SFAF learned, among other things, that the sexually explicit language and images that appealed to gay white men often offended and alienated nonwhites. They realized that to reach recent immigrants from Latin America, the best bet was to go not through bars but through churches. The result was two ad campaigns aimed specifically at each of these populations: "Get Carried Away" and "Listo para la acción."

Not all daters found it easy to adopt new safe sex measures. Yet a growing number of Americans recognized that it was imperative that they talk about sex. *Don't decoy, avoid, or make void the topic / Cuz that ain't gonna stop it*, the hip-hop trio Salt-N-Pepa warned. By the late 1980s, even the Reagan administration was realizing they were right.

In late 1986, Surgeon General C. Everett Koop enraged his fellow Christian conservatives by issuing a public report on AIDS that called for franker discussions of sex and for distributing condoms in public schools. "Education about AIDS should start at an early age so that children can grow up knowing the behaviors to avoid to protect themselves," Koop recommended.

Over protests from the secretary of education, Koop printed twenty million copies and had fifty-five thousand sent to the National Parent Teacher Association. He followed up with a detailed brochure titled *Understanding AIDS*.

The CDC started mailing *Understanding AIDS* to American households in January 1988. By June, one hundred million copies had gone out. Koop did not use the kinds of explicit images or sexual slang featured in GMHC pamphlets and posters. But he studied them carefully. Like gay activists, he instructed couples to talk about their desires and the dangers they might entail.

"Some of the issues involved in this brochure may not be things you are used to discussing openly," Koop warned in a short note that ran on the front page. "I can easily understand that. But now you must discuss them." The brochure described safe and unsafe behaviors directly and in detail. A section called "What About Dating?" emphasized to readers that they had an obligation to initiate conversations about these subjects with their partners.

"You are going to have to be careful about the person you become sexually involved with, making your own decision based on your own best judgment," Koop wrote. "That can be difficult. Has this person had any sexually transmitted diseases? How many people have they been to bed with? Have they experimented with drugs? All these are sensitive, but important, questions. But you have a personal responsibility to ask."

Indeed, in the context of the AIDS crisis, even a conservative like Koop emphasized that being able to *talk* with each other was the single most important test of whether two daters should take their intimacies to the next level. "Think of it this way," he admonished. "If you know someone well enough to have sex, you should be able to talk about AIDS. If someone is unwilling to talk, you shouldn't have sex."

Communication was paramount. Not formal commitment or community approval. Marriage itself provided no guarantees. Wedding bells did not toll the end of talking about sex. "Do Married People Get AIDS?" an insert on the page dedicated to dating asked. Of course they did. "If you feel your spouse may be putting you at risk, talk to him or her. It's your life."

The country had been through a lot since Reagan smirked to voters that free lovers at Berkeley engaged in "orgies so vile I cannot describe them." Public health officials now spoke with a degree of frankness that would have been unthinkable during the wildest years of the freedom era.

In 1994, Bill Clinton was forced by Republicans to fire his surgeon general, Joycelyn Elders, for saying—at a UN conference on AIDS—that perhaps schools should teach young students to masturbate. But two years later, her replacement, Audrey F. Manley, went on television to talk about "outercourse"—all the sexually pleasurable activities that one could enjoy without exchanging bodily fluids. And in January 1998, when the Monica Lewinsky scandal broke and everyone in America started obsessing over whether or not penetrating someone with a cigar or fellating him in the highest office in the nation constituted "sexual relations," even those of us who were still children had opinions. Sure, it may have felt a little cringeworthy to debate the ins and outs over family dinner. But we had already discussed them in sex ed.

American public schools began offering classes in sex education precisely during the years when dating first became mainstream: the 1910s. As courtship moved out of family living rooms and church basements into public settings, progressive educators recognized that young people might no longer be able to rely on their parents and pastors to tell them what they needed to know, when they needed to know it.

What exactly should be included in the curriculum of sex ed courses had always been controversial. The Chicago teachers who developed pilot programs for the city in the 1920s, for instance, hotly debated whether information about puberty, sex, and family planning should simply be added to existing biology and home economics courses or whether the school should invite doctors and nurses to speak to students during dedicated sessions. Educators bounced back and forth between versions of these two approaches for years. But in the 1980s and '90s, sex education became a political battlefield.

The effects were paradoxical. During these years, the absolute number of programs grew dramatically. Between 1980 and 1989, the number of states that mandated public schools to teach sex ed went from six to seventeen, plus the District of Columbia. But the fact that federal law left it up to local school boards to set the curriculum meant that students from different parts of the country learned very different things. In many places, conservatives managed to restrict what they were taught to "abstinence only."

Between 1999 and 2009, states received nearly $1 billion of federal funding to support abstinence-only programs, and as of 2009, 86 percent of schools in the country mandated that the sex ed classes advocate abstinence. Not mine. In the liberal public high school that I went to in New York around the turn of the millennium, we talked about sex early and often.

I still remember my fifth-grade gym teacher crowding us into a room to play a warm-up game. She would throw out a word or phrase that we might have heard around, and then cold-call on someone, who then had to tell the class what he or she thought it meant. "Boner?" the gym teacher would ask. "Wet dream?" She had one lazy eye. The entire room would squirm trying to avoid catching the Eye, while also trying to look like we were not avoiding it, because *that* would get you called on for sure.

I humiliated myself when I guessed that "oral sex" meant

talking about sex, maybe using a tape recorder? (I had just interviewed my grandfather about his experiences in the Korean War for an oral history project.) My ignominy lasted for weeks. But soon even nerds like me became fluent. We learned about anatomy. We learned words like "fallopian" and "frenulum." In later years, we learned what "crowning" looked like from the childbirth scene in the movie *The Miracle of Life*. We learned what a pain it would be to have a child in high school from the Baby Project. The New York Board of Ed sent a box of rubber babies to our school, which would wail and wet themselves at all hours; they contained computer chips that kept track of how responsive you were to them. When one of our babies started howling tinnily on the subway, a group of fellow teen passengers snatched it and beat it against the pole. The "father" explained what had happened and argued his failing Baby Project grade up to a B-minus.

The point was mostly to scare us. Classroom slides showed HPV warts sprouting over genitalia like cauliflower blossoms and aching slits that our teacher said were "syphilitic chancres." They showed us all kinds of discharge. Another teacher taught us that *extra-large condoms are for extra-large egos* by unwrapping a Trojan Magnum over her fist and yanking it down until it covered her entire fleshy forearm.

The main goal seemed to be instilling terror, and the cure for terror was supposed to be *talk*. Pleasure was secondary. Still, fear can edge its way toward desire, and wanting to know more becomes its own perversion. It was not as if the abstinence-only line that other kids got at school was keeping them from seeking out information about sex. More and more of us across the United States could find out what we wanted from cable television—from documentary shows like *Real Sex* and *Sex in the Nineties*, explicit fiction shows like *Sex and the City*, or pay-per-view pornography. Otherwise, we could try to learn for free, from the Internet.

Online, we all become autodidacts.

AIDS forced Americans to develop a shared, detailed language for talking about sex. Programs like my health class institutionalized it. The Internet made it possible for anyone to join the conversation. As a searchable repository of information about sexual practices, it helped further standardize the ways they were described. And it served as an infrastructure over which new subcultures could develop.

The computer dating pioneered in the 1960s, and the video dating that followed it, harnessed the power of machines to match people who lived near a particular database. These services were limited by geography. Project TACT could connect only daters who both lived on the Upper East Side. Today For Singles could connect only daters with herpes to other daters with herpes in the D.C. area. The reach of any of these services was limited.

In the 1970s, sociologists reported that one of the main reasons that couples formerly committed to free love had retired from swinging was that it took so much time and effort to find other couples who were game. Swingers had to place personals, send and sort letters, take and send photographs, then spend weekends driving to meet one another for coffee, before they decided whether to go ahead with a liaison. A decade later, if you knew how to use the right discussion pages and Listservs, you could arrange real-life meetings with umpteen other couples without ever having to leave your desk.

In addition to providing a way for people to find each other, the Internet created new models for romantic relationships. You might say that it turned sexual and romantic energy into *connectivity* and relationships into *interactions*.

In the Eras of the Petting Party and the Steady, national advertising campaigns and nationally distributed magazines, books, and movies created archetypes for all daters to follow. Greek and

Coed. Boyfriend and Girlfriend. Daters who did not conform to these types were clearly recognizable as deviating from them. They were either not dating, or they were "juvenile delinquents." But in an age of protocols, there were suddenly infinitely many ways that one might date. The curious dater must simply learn how to communicate his or her desires, and find someone who is receptive to the things he or she wants.

Under these arrangements, a lot of the work of dating becomes the process of setting, testing, and resetting your own limits. I meet a woman at an academic conference who has been dating someone steadily for four years. They moved across oceans and continents to be together, then spent a year and a half "opening" their relationship. She says that it took nearly a year of discussing their fantasies and fears, and speculating about how they might react to certain situations, before either of them felt comfortable actually being with anyone else. They both took for granted that an open relationship—where each partner was allowed to sleep with others, and even to bring new lovers back to their shared home—was possible. They simply had to invest the time in articulating how these interactions would work. Eight months into opening her relationship, a younger acquaintance confesses to me that so far all she and her partner have done is talk.

Today, dating protocols seem to change so quickly that the end of even a medium-term relationship can leave you feeling like a Rip van Winkle. To be *back on the market!* is supposed to be exciting. And yet, like so many other dating phases, it often inspires anxiety and bewilderment.

"What do the kids do these days?" an old friend wants to know. He is only half joking. We are at a party, sometime in our midtwenties, and he has just broken up with the girl he had been with since we all went to high school together. "Do we just have sex now?" "Does who just have sex?" the rest of us ask. "Like, on what date is it normal to have sex at our age? The first? The fifth?"

Having gone to bed with his prom date as a virgin geek and risen to find himself transformed into a well-dressed investment banker, the friend feels bewildered by the sheer number of his dating options. We can sympathize. Everyone agrees that there is no agreement on this subject.

To be adult today is to become responsible for determining the rules under which you will date. "I never lied to you" is a fair defense against many charges of misconduct, not that it makes having been not lied to feel much better. We must each spell out the terms of our own sexual and romantic encounters. *Caveat dater.* Many people my age first learned how to online.

I cannot have been the only child of the Clinton era to have stumbled on the porn site www.whitehouse.com while doing social studies homework. I remember furtively clicking on thumbnail after thumbnail in an "Interns of the Month" gallery, watching spray-tanned haunches and balloon-taut breasts of girls posed around a faux Oval Office materialize, bit by bit. When my sister, searching for images of her favorite British pop stars, accidentally typed "Spicy Girls" into Yahoo, the search results made her run, shrieking, from the family computer.

Still, cybering was the safest sex around.

"It is probably no coincidence that this sea change comes on us at a time when AIDS lurks in the alleyways of our lives," a writer for *The Nation* mused in 1993. Months later, *The New York Times* reiterated the point. "Computer erotica appears to provide many people with a 'safe' alternative to real, personal relationships in a world where HIV is deadlier than computer viruses." This was in a book review. The book, *The Joy of Cybersex*, argued that the World Wide Web was a godsend for this reason.

The author of *The Joy of Cybersex*, Deborah Levine, had spent several years counseling college undergraduates at the Columbia University Health Education program. Levine encouraged them to use their computers to flirt, start online relationships, and explore their farthest-fetched fantasies without taking real-world risk. "The driving source behind sex in the 1990s, whether you're partnered or single, is the human imagination," Levine declared. "Enter the world of cybersex. The place where imaginations go wild, anonymity is the rule, and desire runs amok."

Like earlier safe sex educators, Levine used multiple-choice and fill-in-the-blank questionnaires to help readers take stock of what they wanted. She placed more emphasis on expanding your horizons than on safety. Online you had no body to protect. But the format looked almost the same. The chapter "Overcoming Sexual Inhibitions," for instance, started with a quiz intended to help you assess how uptight you were.

"Are you ready to embark on a mission to learn about the expansive range of sexual expression?" Levine asked. "Answer a few questions and find out:

"1. *If your best friend started unexpectedly talking about his or her sex life over coffee one day, you would:*
    a. Start choking and try not to spit up your drink.
    b. Nod enthusiastically, and change the subject.
    c. Ask lots of questions.
    d. Feel relieved, and share your own experiences.
2. *If a partner asked you (while undressed in the bedroom) to pretend to be something you're not, say a cashier at a grocery store or a famous astronaut, you would:*
    a. Say: 'Sure, honey, but I'd actually rather be a rocket scientist, okay?'
    b. Hop to it, and get into role.
    c. Think he or she had totally lost his or her mind, and suggest a visit to the therapist.

d. Think about it for a few minutes, fix yourself a drink, and succumb to the unknown."

Like earlier safe sex activists, Levine used bullet point lists to introduce the sites her readers should know and to teach them the language that they would need to thrive there. The pages she cited ran the gamut from tutorials for geeks, like www.getgirls .com, to resources for free lovers like the Open Hearts Project and www.lovemore.com. A service called Tri Ess connected heterosexual couples who were into cross-dressing.

The chat abbreviations that Levine lists—like ASAP and LOL—now seem so obvious that it is hard to remember that they once needed defining. But mastering them was critical. Decent webcam technology and the bandwidth needed to transmit high-quality images were still a few years off. In the interim, using the right expression at the right time was the only way to flirt and bond.

Like *The Joy of Cybersex*, the first issue of *Wired* magazine came out in 1993. It contained an article about a woman whose prolific activity in "hot chats" transformed her from a "paragon of shy and retiring womanhood" into a bona fide "man-eater." The author describes a female friend who spent hours a day in the 1980s on a service called the Source. He calls her by her handle: "This Is A Naked Lady."

"The Naked Lady egged on her digital admirers with leading questions larded with copious amounts of double entendre," the piece began. "When I first asked her about this, she initially put it down to 'just fooling around on the wires.'"

"'It's just a hobby,' she said. 'Maybe I'll get some dates out of it.'"

Yet under the spell of her dirty-talking alter ego, the Naked Lady began to undergo a metamorphosis. She ceased to be "a rather mousy person—the type who favored gray clothing of a conservative cut . . . She became (through the dint of her blazing typing speed) the kind of person that could keep a dozen or more online sessions of hot chat going at a time." The effects carried over into real life. "She began regaling me with descriptions of her expanding lingerie collection. Her speech became bawdier, her jokes naughtier. In short, she was becoming her online personality."

Surfing was the new cruising, and it could change lives. In "health" class, the point of our endless discussions was to scare us off of sex for at least a few years. But the safer substitutes for sex to be found online offered whole new kinds of titillation. To talk (or type) about sex constituted its own kind of intimacy.

As more and more Americans got online in the early 1990s, they learned how to enjoy relationships that were text only. Pioneering "cyber citizens" developed forms of dating that were all talk.

In 1990, only 200,000 households in the United States had Internet connections. By 1993, that number was 5 million. (The upward climb has continued to 43 million in 2000 and 85 million in 2013.) When the price of personal computers dropped dramatically in the mid-1990s, many families acquired more computers and moved them out of their living rooms into bedrooms and private places. There, the experimentation could really begin.

In many ways, the liaisons between early online boyfriends or girlfriends followed the pattern set by earlier generations of daters. You met by chance. After crossing paths in a chat room, if you hit it off, you could start making appointments to come online at the same time and talk together.

This opportunity could be life-changing. In some chat rooms, disabled singles who found it physically challenging to go out or hook up in real life, connected and fell in love. In others, queer teens who felt isolated in the homes they were growing up in could do the same. This was no small thing. By the time he graduated, one in six gay kids who went to high school in the late 1990s would get beaten up so badly he needed medical attention at least once. But the ambiguous setting of these cyberdates made many people nervous.

At the turn of the twentieth century, "tough girls," "charity cunts," and other early daters upset their parents and the police by taking a process that had always been conducted in private to the streets. For the first time in history, dating let young people seek mates and life partners on their own behalf, in public places. Spaces like bars and boardwalks shared many features in common with chat rooms. Both were enticing despite being slightly dangerous. Or was it because they were dangerous? Risk was part of their appeal.

Sure, people worried about other people misrepresenting themselves. A cyberlover might say he was tall and strong when in fact he was short and skinny, or thin when she was fat. This was the price of freedom. Back in the day, in your parents' parlor, or at a church- or synagogue-sponsored dance, any other young person you met would have been screened in advance. A penny arcade or nickelodeon was anonymous. The man who held your hand as you shuddered through the dark of the Tunnel of Love might be anyone. But daters soon discovered that the anonymity of being out in public offered its own kind of intimacy. Without family and friends hovering over you, you could be yourself and frankly express your feelings. It was the strangers-on-a-train thing. If she wasn't into it, who cared? You never had to see a girl you had picked up at the dance hall again.

Early on, mental health professionals started observing that meeting strangers online often had a similar effect. The psychiatrist Esther Gwinnell decided to write a book about "computer love" after a string of patients came to her office reporting that they or their partners had fallen for a stranger online. In *Online Seductions*, she coined a phrase for the kinds of relationships that her patients struck up. They were "uniquely intimate" because they "grew from the inside out."

Gwinnell's patients said some version of the same thing again and again. "The relationship is all about what is happening inside of the soul and the mind, and the body doesn't get in the way." "We met our souls first." This was the benefit of cyber-dating, especially for singles who felt insecure in the flesh. The downside was that in the absence of visual cues or social context, it was often difficult to tell your interlocutor from the person you hoped he or she might be. The cyberlove of your life could turn out to be little more than a mirage or a private psychosis.

"When internet lovers leave the computer to go to other activities," Gwinnell reported, "they may feel as though the other person is 'inside' them."

Finding your soul mate online could also leave you feeling dissatisfied in real life. The psychiatrists warned that cybersex addiction would mess up your preexisting relationships by giving you unrealistic standards and stimulating insatiable appetites. Your husband will never understand you as well as your online husband understands you, if the online one lives mostly in your head. Even the lithest and gamest wife will not be able to help you realize *all* the pornographic scenarios that alt.sex .bondage.golden.show-ers.sheep offers at a glance.

What's more, the rapid-fire pace of online love raises the stakes of every communication. Gwinnell observed that her patients who were in computer love seemed to vacillate between paralyzing anxiety (when waiting to hear from their online lovers) and exuberance beyond all proportion (when they did hear back). We all know this cycle. Compose, write, revise, send, wait, fret, read, reread, repeat.

It is easier than ever now to spend hours poring over the online ephemera of a new crush or partner. Who has not attached operatic levels of hope and fear to the details of status updates and old photographs? *Look at that guitar he is holding! We knew he had a good job, but he must also be artistic. The picture with his niece proves how good he is with kids.* The problem of interpretation rarely occurs to us until later, when we realize that the guitar belonged to his ex-girlfriend and the child is his, from a previous relationship.

Love in this new medium trained people to let out sighs of ecstasy at every email. The age of *Online Seductions* left many computer users less in love with this or that particular partner than with the Internet itself.

In the 1990s, mainstream news sources told two kinds of sensational stories about online romance. One focused on improbable triumphs of cyberlove—or, as countless articles punned, "love at first byte." In April 1996, the "world's first digital wedding" took place when a thirty-four-year-old man named Bob Norris married twenty-seven-year-old Catherine Smylie in Times Square. The couple had met in a chat room the previous August. New York mayor Rudolph Giuliani officiated. Their vows were transmitted in real time on a message strip that the Joe Boxer company had added to its six-thousand-square-foot billboard for this occasion, and from there to the Internet.

Other tales of digital love were darker. There were accounts of online affairs splitting up previously happy marriages. Even more prominent were horror stories about online predators. In many ways fears that these inspired resembled the "white slave" panic that had struck around the dawn of dating, when many do-gooders warned young women that to accept a date was to put yourself in grave danger.

In the late 1990s, newspapers and magazines were filled with stories about online predators preying on white suburban children, in particular. Often, the heroes of these stories were online vigilantes who took it upon themselves to police chat rooms. In the early 2000s, the news show *Dateline NBC* created a whole reality series dedicated to this premise. Collaborating with a watchdog group called Perverted Justice, the staff of *To Catch a Predator* would impersonate underage people online. They approached users saying that they were thirteen or fourteen. After a few sessions of hot and heavy typing, the decoy kid would suggest meeting in real life. If the adult accepted, he would find himself confronted live on camera, and would be arrested by the police.

While a few cases of abduction and abuse surely did happen, they were hardly common. Early studies of chat rooms showed that some users misled the people they spoke to online, usually about their physical appearance or marital status. And of course cybersexters put on naughty personae like This Is A Naked Lady. But on average, people were in fact far *more* honest with strangers than they were in real life. It was this accelerated intimacy that was the problem. It was addictive.

Online dating addicts were often the butt of jokes, especially if they were still in high school. They made easy targets. But in retrospect, what was risible about cybersex was not that it was perverted. It was that it was so unproductive. It rarely created real-world couples; most participants never met IRL ("in real life"). And it squandered enormous amounts of potentially valuable attention.

The pioneers who commercialized the Internet rightly saw this wastefulness as an opportunity. When America Online and Prodigy introduced their services in the early 1990s, they offered a slew of "lifestyle" chat rooms aimed at singles, because they recognized that such conversations would be a huge draw. They quickly found ways to derive enormous profits from platforms where people could exchange erotic and romantic attention. Tech companies still do.

Let's be honest. It's not like we don't still spend hours using our computers and other devices to stalk our love interests. "He tweeted twice today and he still hasn't emailed me back," a friend seethed to me recently. She stopped and shook her head at her own absurdity. "I know that and I don't even follow him on Twitter!" It's not like it's any less pathetic to check the account of someone you've met once than it was to log on to a chat room hoping that the handle you cybersexted with last week might turn up. It's no less lonely. It's just less stigmatized, because now the economy runs on these kinds of feelings.

The same factors that let retailers like Amazon cater to the "long tail" economy enabled dating subcultures to thrive. In the 1950s, if you were one of the statistically small group of people who long for a partner to smear food on them during orgasm, you would likely have to forgo that fantasy. However, the Internet made it easy to find others who shared your fetish, or at least propose it to others at lower risk. The safe sex movement gave daters the vocabulary to examine and define their desires. The World Wide Web helped make these desires central to dating identity.

If people had long thought of dating as a form of shopping, during the 1990s they became more educated consumers. They were more likely to know what kind of sex they were in the market for and to believe that having their desires met was an important part of feeling fulfilled. Instead of just happening upon a sexual position in the throes of passion, lovers were more apt to sample from a series of predefined positions they had seen described or depicted. And they were likely to seek relationships with others who had similar interests. As a growing number of niche media channels, on cable television and online, displayed different lifestyles, a growing number of "sex educators" blurred the boundaries between advocacy and advertising.

Every dating lifestyle had its own expert. As early as 1987, the feminist Betty Dodson sang the praises of female masturbation in her book *Sex for One*. Like other feisty feminist "sex educators" of the era, Dodson traveled around the country teaching women to give themselves pleasure—and to demand the same from their partners. The long tail economy ensured that anyone interested could buy the tools that Dodson and others demonstrated. In 1993, the sex educators Claire Cavanah and Rachel Venning founded the sex toy boutique Toys in Babeland in Seattle. Their motivation was noble: There were few sex shops aimed at women, and the founders wanted to offer the curious information and encouragement. In 1995, Toys in Babeland started a mail-order business with a small print catalog; the website, www.babeland.com, followed soon after. The steady business it did generated the revenues that allowed them to open outposts in Los Angeles and New York.

The Internet made it possible to corner a national niche market, as long as you understood people's tastes specifically enough. Whatever your Thing might be, you no longer had to yearn for it alone. In 1991, a good friend of a gay video store clerk named Dan Savage told him that he was leaving Michigan, where they both lived, to move to Seattle and start a weekly newspaper. Savage jokingly pitched the friend an advice column and was invited to go with him. The column that he wrote for *The Stranger* was irreverent and hilarious. It got national syndication, and soon turned Savage into a celebrity. He went on to write books upon books of relationship advice, and, as of 2006, to host a podcast that still has thousands of followers.

Savage Love brings the specificity of the checklist to the advice column genre, promising to help readers navigate a seemingly infinite array of sexual preferences. When readers inquired after sex acts that did not have names yet, Savage invented them. He coined terms like "pegging" to fill in the gaps in an already-intricate taxonomy that readers wrote in about. (Pegging referred to female-on-male strap-on anal sex.) With new words at their disposal, Savage's readers could describe the acts they hoped for or hated in more and more detail.

Knowing and expressing one's sexual tastes, Savage told his audience, was a key part of dating. Better to confess a penchant for pegging to a new lover early on than risk suffering through decades of love unpegged. Better to know what kind of relationship a new crush is seeking before discovering a painful mismatch. If you wanted to be happy, you had to learn to understand your desires and express them clearly. If you did, you could renegotiate the terms of conventional romantic relationships.

Even marriage.

Savage has long recommended a model he calls "monogamish" to long-term couples, whether they are gay or straight. It means what it sounds like. The partners agree in advance that each is allowed to sleep with other people, occasionally, as long as they do not allow it to threaten the primary relationship. Savage insists that most long-term relationships are monogamish already; couples are simply unwilling to admit it. Other advice experts took things further. The 1990s saw a surge of interest in "polyamory"— maintaining multiple open and fluid relationships.

The Ethical Slut came out in 1997. It remains one of the most widely read how-to guides for "the lifestyle." The authors, Dossie Easton and Janet W. Hardy, argue that the world is suffused with enough sexual energy to satisfy everyone. "Many traditional attitudes about sexuality are based on the unspoken belief that there isn't enough of *something*," *The Ethical Slut* says. "We want everyone to get everything they want." The chapter "Varieties of Sluthood" insisted that the possible configurations are endless. But the different arrangements that the book describes do share certain basic traits. They are customized and flexible. "Relation-ship structures," the authors say, "should be designed to fit the people in them, rather than people chosen to fit some abstract ideal of the perfect relationship." Individuals freely link up to create new structures. "One woman of our acquaintance has a lifetime lifestyle of having two primary partners, one of each gender, with her other partners and her primaries' other partners forming a huge network."

"Relationships that add, and inevitably also subtract, mem-bers over time tend to form very complex structures with new configurations of family roles that they generally invent by trial and error." Rather than networks, Easton and Hardy say, they like to call these kinds of self-defining communities "constella-tions." But the utopia of linked communities based on abundant sexual energy, branching out unstoppably and constantly reor-ganizing themselves, sounds a lot like the Internet. The Web was not just a guide for the perplexed. It also was a model for dating in a global economy whose boundaries were growing increas-ingly fluid.

Needless to say, many Americans were horrified. Around the turn of the millennium, conservatives came back at the peggers and polyamorists with purity balls and chastity pledges. Conser-vative parents started hosting alternative proms on public school prom nights, which young women attended with their fathers; at these events, fathers publicly made vows that they would defend the virginity of their daughters. At colleges across the country, students in the True Love Waits movement began wearing "purity rings" that signaled their commitments to remaining chaste until marriage.

The media called these standoffs the "culture wars." But cul-ture wars was a misnomer. In the age of the network and the protocol, there was no single American culture left standing to defend. As panic about AIDS subsided from the mainstream, safe sex and the new culture of explicitness remained.

The frankness that AIDS activists had inspired, and the sense of infinite possibility that the Internet evoked, have continued to shape dating in the new millennium. You can make as many chastity pledges as you wish, and date only people who also have, but this will be just one consumer choice among many others. In the 1990s, the purist and the punk were just two kinks in the long tail of a market that was growing ever more segmented—and staying open 24/7.

CHAPTER 9. **PLANS**

Time is money. As schoolchildren, we learned that Benjamin Franklin said this. He did, in *Advice to a Young Tradesman, Written by an Old One*—a self-help manual that he published in 1748, to teach colonial Americans how they, too, could get rich. But the Founding Father was not the first to recognize that time was money. In fact, when the phrase made its debut in print, it was on the lips of a nameless housewife.

In 1739, a Pennsylvania periodical called *The Free-Thinker* recounted the sad story of "a notable Woman, who was thoroughly sensible of the intrinsick Value of Time. Her Husband was a Shoe-maker, and an excellent Crafts-man," the author recalled, "but never minded how the Minutes passed. In vain did his Wife inculcate to him, That *Time is Money*: He had too much Wit to apprehend her; and he cursed the Parish-Clock, every Night; which at last brought him to his Ruin."

This particular sensible wife may lie forgotten on the wayside of history. But we have all heard stories like hers. To this day, the male ne'er-do-well, who uses wit to avoid recognizing that it is high time he gets his life together, appears as the hero of count-less romantic comedies. A regular patron at the bars in many cities, he remains as lovable as he is indecisive. It is his female partner who will become the tragic victim, if she lets him get away with it. When it comes to romance, many of us still seem to believe that planning is a woman's work.

Love takes work, the therapists and self-help gurus tell us. It also takes time, and given that time is money, many daters seem understandably reluctant to gamble too much of it on any one romantic prospect.

Lovers today are less likely to be star-crossed than over-scheduled. How often have friends complained that they have "no time to date" or "to invest in a relationship"? How many have brushed one another off with the excuse that it was "not a good time" or they needed "time to think" or "to be alone for a while"?

Different people have proposed different ways of dealing with the problem of being too busy to find partners. Some have tried to turn the search into a game. In the late 1990s, an Orthodox rabbi named Yaacov Deyo became concerned that single mem-bers of his congregation in Los Angeles were struggling to meet other young Jewish professionals. In 1998, he invited a group of Hollywood friends to his house to brainstorm solutions. What they came up with, they called "speed dating."

A few weeks later, Deyo invited all the Jewish singles he could round up to come to a Peet's Coffee in Beverly Hills and brought a hand-cranked noisemaker—the *gragger* that Jews use during Purim celebrations. He paired the men and women off and in-structed them to chat for ten minutes each; after ten minutes he would whirl the gragger. These afternoon meet-ups at Peet's be-came so popular that Deyo began using an Excel spreadsheet to keep track of the feedback the daters provided about one another and their interactions. Within a year, copycat events were taking place all over the country. But some high-powered professionals say they do not have time for games. They do not have time even to manage their online dating accounts.

They can turn to Virtual Dating Assistants. The founder, Scott Valdez, started the company in 2012 after trying to hire an online dating assistant over Craigslist. In 2015, for $147 per date, or $1,200 per month, VDA consultants would help a client select prospects and plan the details of a date down to what outfit he should wear.

"Online dating's a part time job," a banner across their website trumpets. "Let our experts do it for you!"

The question remains: What's the dater who doesn't have hundreds or thousands of dollars to spare every month supposed to do?

Pragmatists preach that love is all timing. *You don't get married when you find the right one; you marry the one you find at the right time.* They say this as if it should be comforting to imagine that our hearts follow a secret schedule—that the right feelings will arrive at their appointed hour, to carry us away with whomever we happen to be standing next to on the platform. But what if the person we find ourselves dating at, say, twenty-eight, is not the "right" person? What if we fall in love long before the train is due to leave, or start looking only after it has departed? What if our lives are not on this track at all?

Romantics, on the other hand, insist that there is no use fretting about how or when we will find love. *It will happen when you least expect it!* It follows from this worldview that when you do find your special someone, you will "make time." A person in love will do anything and everything to be with his or her beloved. It is equally clarifying and distressing to believe the reverse: If your lover is not doing anything and everything to be with you, it must not be true love.

In 2004, Greg Behrendt, the author of the bestselling self-help book *He's Just Not That Into You*, called BS on men who professed to be too "busy" to be devoted boyfriends. "'Busy' is another word for 'asshole,'" he wrote. "'Asshole' is another word for the guy you're dating." In case the reader has missed the point, he later reiterates this cardinal "relationships rule" in all caps: "THE WORD 'BUSY' IS A LOAD OF CRAP AND IS MOST OFTEN USED BY ASSHOLES . . . Men are never too busy to get what they want."

Behrendt gained his expert credentials by serving as the sole straight male script consultant on *Sex and the City*. Given the fixation of that show on dating—and on female friendships that consist mostly of talking about dating—it makes sense that Behrendt assumes a straight woman can always find time to obsess about the men she is seeing. In the end, however, the romantics and the pragmatists are basically offering the same advice. The one tells you to bide your time until the lightning bolt strikes. The other suggests waiting until a moment that seems opportune. Either way, the point is, *Stop worrying.* Which is another way of saying: *Get back to work!*

As advice, it is not terrible, because the thing is, many daters are not just being "assholes." They really are busy. The ways that people spend their days and make their livings have always shaped how they experience time. In the decades since the era that the self-help experts have in mind when they refer to "traditional" dating, the rhythms of our lives have changed dramatically.

The custom of dating developed under a particular order. It came from an era when life was supposed to divide cleanly into work and leisure. Even the word "date" comes from the idea that there is a *point in time* when you will meet up with a love interest. So, too, does "going out" assume that there is a world of entertainment, separate from the world of home and work, for you to go out into.

Perhaps this is why today "dating" often sounds like a slightly sleazy euphemism. When a new boyfriend and I run into an ex of his, his vague use of the verb makes me feel hysterical.

"He said they dated for two weeks," I whine to a friend afterward. "And then he thought about it for a minute and was, like—actually, less! What does that even mean?"

"It means they had sex, like, three times," my friend shushes me. "Maybe four. Relax!"

A line like *I'll pick you up at six* bespoke a worldview. Dating was a departure from work. A kind of scheduled spontaneity, a date was recreation in its most literal sense: a kind of fun that was supposed to reproduce the workforce.

The patterns of "respectable" middle-class dating also implied a trajectory in time. As dating became the main form of courtship, daters implicitly promised each other that the time they spent together was an investment. It earned them closeness they could draw on in the future. A dater might date around awhile, but it was assumed that a couple would either grow more and more intimate, until its members were ready to get married and start a family, or they would break up and restart the process with someone else.

The advent of free love upset this time line. It allowed strangers to cut straight to sex and lovers to cohabit for years without getting married. The number of American couples "living in sin," without children, tripled between 1970 and 1979. At the same time, the corporations whose rhythms had dictated the pace of labor and leisure for decades were undergoing massive changes. In the Steady Era, large corporations had offered lifetime employment with good salaries and generous benefits. However, during the 1970s, this model gave way. As competitor manufacturing economies that had been destroyed during World War II recovered, stagflation mounted, and corporate profits crashed, more and more companies began to rely on temporary, contract, and freelance employees.

Older paths toward professional development dead-ended. And as employers began to contract more and more services out, *time itself changed*. All time might potentially be worth money, but none of it was sure to be. As more and more Americans went from being in-house employees with benefits, to being workers who moved from job to job, the future seemed newly precarious. Feeling precarious makes it difficult to fall in love.

Today, people do not just work differently from the way they did in the era of college dances or high school steadies. They also work a lot more. The 2014 nationwide Work and Education Survey conducted by Gallup found that 50 percent of Americans in full-time employment work more than forty hours per week. Twenty-one percent of the people surveyed reported working fifty to fifty-nine hours per week; 18 percent work sixty or more. And those are hours on the clock. These figures do not count time spent doing the things that many white-collar jobs require you to do without pay—tasks like commuting, checking and responding to voice messages and emails, or creating and maintaining a social media presence. Not to mention the housework that men earning a "family wage" once expected their stay-at-home wives to take care of.

When everyone has so little time to spare, dating starts to feel less like a pleasurable diversion and more like one more thing to fit in. It can feel risky—and strangely intimate—to spend time on someone new.

A columnist for *Elle* magazine recently confessed having spurned a date for no other reason than that the thought of spending an entire evening with a stranger made her nervous. "I recently declined a dinner invitation because I didn't think I knew the guy well enough to be alone with him for two hours." Her feelings are understandable. But they also seem to preclude ever going out with anyone you do not already know.

While part-time workers and freelancers have more flexibility, mostly they have it worse. Not only do they make less money and get few or no benefits. They are also under pressure to make themselves constantly available. A janitor can rarely afford to turn down an extra shift. A massage therapist who gets paid by the hour does well to keep her evenings free, in case a client suddenly throws his back out.

As the freelance worker hears the ticktock of every hour passing, so, too, do many daters fret about the opportunity costs of committing to any given partner. Young women, in particular, are warned to remain vigilant. We are constantly told that we are dating on a deadline. Let down your guard, and next thing you know you may have "wasted years."

I wasted years with [Name of Lover]. Has a straight man ever said this? Not that I know of, but when a woman does, after a breakup, everyone immediately understands what she means. Men and women alike are taught that female bodies are time bombs. Any time that a woman throws away on a relationship that does not pan out—which is to say, does not get her pregnant by a man who is committed to helping her raise their offspring— brings her closer to her expiration date. At the stroke of midnight, our eggs turn into dust.

———

The first warning came on March 16, 1978. "The Clock Is Ticking for the Career Woman," *The Washington Post* declared on the front page of its Metro section. The author, Richard Cohen, cannot have realized just how relentlessly this theme would come to dog daters. His article opened on a lunch date with a "Composite Woman" who is supposed to represent all women between the ages of twenty-seven and thirty-five.

"There she is, entering the restaurant," Cohen began. "She's the pretty one. Dark hair. Medium height. Nicely dressed. Now she is taking off her coat. Nice figure." Composite Woman has a good attitude, too. "The job is just wonderful. She is feeling just wonderful." But then her eyes fall.

"Is there something wrong?" he asks.

"I want to have a baby."

Cohen insisted that all the women he knew wanted to have babies, regardless of the kinds of romantic relationships they found themselves in.

"I've gone around, a busy bee of a reporter, from woman to woman," he attested. "Most of them said that they could hear the clock ticking. Some talked about it in a sort of theoretical sense, like the woman who said she wanted five children and didn't even have a boyfriend yet . . . Sometimes, the Composite Woman is married and sometimes she is not. Sometimes, horribly, there is no man in the horizon. What there is always, though, is a feeling that the clock is ticking . . . You hear it wherever you go."

Within months, the Clock was stalking Career Women everywhere.

A staff writer for *The Boston Globe*, Anne Kirchheimer, reported that "the beneficiaries of the women's movement, a first generation of liberated young ladies, this new breed of women who opted for careers, travel, independence rather than husband, home, and baby are older now and suddenly the ticking of the biological clock is getting louder and louder."

One woman Kirchheimer interviewed, a psychiatrist, jokingly diagnosed the affliction from which she and her other single friends were suffering as "withering womb syndrome."

Statistics did show that the birthrate had dropped precipitously over the previous two decades. In 1957, the average American woman had given birth to 3.5 children; by 1976, that number had fallen to 1.5. Even women who would eventually become mothers were waiting longer to do so. By 1977, 36 percent of women were giving birth to their first child at thirty or older. It was starting to look as if many might use birth control and abortion to put off motherhood indefinitely.

Would this be the way the world ended? *Not with a bomb but the pill?*

Stories about the biological clock said no.

In 1982, *Time* ran a cover story on "The New Baby Bloom" that reported that baby boomers were getting pregnant in droves and that anyone who aspired to motherhood had better get on it. "For many women, the biological clock of fertility is running near its end," the author, J. D. Reed, warned. "The ancient Pleistocene call of the moon, of salt in the blood, and genetic encoding buried deep in the chromosomes back there beneath the layers of culture—and counterculture—are making successful businesswomen, professionals and even the mothers of grown children stop and reconsider."

Time, *Time* said, stopped for no one. Women could dress up in pantsuits all we liked, but in the end, our bodies would call us out.

Even if women were now competing with men for high-paying jobs, and sleeping around outside of marriage, these stories said that free love and the feminist movement had not really changed the fundamentals of what women were. Women continued to be defined by motherhood; even the most successful Career Woman would eventually yearn for children.

This may have sounded like a description. It was an order.

Naturally, dating on the biological clock was stressful. The fact that women had this expiration date meant that they were not as free as men to enjoy a single life or to focus on their careers. Changing social mores and the pill might make it seem that way, but really they were just dating on borrowed time.

In August 1979, Anne Kirchheimer published another story on *The Boston Globe*'s front page: "Single Searching and Scared." The opening described a dire dating scene. A male and female friend decide to cohost a mixer for successful professionals. For twelve women, only two men show up, and one promptly gets stoned to take the pressure off.

Kirchheimer said that the odds were stacked against the "typical woman." "She's gotten those degrees, the high salary, and a sense of self-assuredness in the male-dominated working world and she's getting tired of dating around. She may want marriage and children and be hearing that biological clock ticking. She's ripe for what, in today's vernacular, is called 'a commitment.'" But, alas, "if a man isn't scared off or turned off by those standards then he probably has what it takes to play the field."

Commentators like Cohen and Kirchheimer warned female readers that they would feel pressure and panic if they put off getting pregnant too long. At the same time, they expressed a set of rather new ideas about masculinity. Namely, that men's bodies programmed them not to want relationships or offspring. Free of the time pressures that dictated the love lives of women, men naturally wanted no-strings sex. Never mind that as recently as the 1950s most American men had said that they considered marriage and family the cornerstones of personal happiness. Experts of the 1980s seemed to believe that men and women were destined by biology to approach dating with directly opposing goals. A man had forever to play. But if she hoped to catch a worthy partner, a Career Woman had to plan.

By the mid-1980s, baby boomer women had become an army of "clock-watchers." That was what the journalist Molly McKaughan called them. With the help of two psychology professors from Barnard, and editors at the glossy *Working Woman* magazine, McKaughan designed and distributed a survey that asked "How Do You Feel About Having a Child?" She received more than five thousand responses. She found that women's anxieties about finding partners to reproduce with determined how they were approaching their love lives, as well as their careers.

Her 1987 bestseller, *The Biological Clock*, reported that women who otherwise held widely diverging attitudes were all "consumed by the subject" of having children. A few expressed remorse for having waited too long to begin their hunt for a father. However, most women had recognized early that they had to date strategically.

A twenty-eight-year-old working in finance told McKaughan, "I have planned every day of my life since I entered college, knowing that I wanted to be extremely successful: first in my career, then in marriage, and finally, in my home life with children."

This Clock-Watcher accepted that to stand a chance of having the kind of life her male colleagues took for granted, she had to plan tirelessly.

"Time can literally pass a woman by," McKaughan reflected, "if she waits too long."

To this day, evidence of exactly how much female fertility declines with age remains hazy. As the psychologist Jean Twenge has pointed out, many frequently cited statistics concerning female fertility are misleading. In an article in *The Atlantic*, Twenge exposed the shaky bases of many facts handed down to women as gospel. After scouring medical research databases she discovered that, for instance, the oft quoted statistic that one in three women age thirty-five to thirty-nine will not be able to get pregnant after a year of trying came from a 2004 study that was itself based on French birth records kept from 1670 to 1830. The chance of remaining childless was also calculated from historical populations.

"In other words," Twenge wrote, "millions of women are being told when to get pregnant based on statistics from a time before electricity, antibiotics, or fertility treatment."

Another problematic element of data on fertility is that, in general, the information we have comes from patients who visit doctors because they are experiencing fertility problems. It is very difficult to assess what is going on with the population as a whole. How many couples are not conceiving because they do not want to? How many are practicing birth control? It is nearly impossible to know.

Strong scientific evidence has demonstrated that the quantity and quality of a woman's eggs do diminish over time. To this extent, the anxieties of the Clock-Watchers were well-founded, even if the exact time lines proposed to them could be dubious. But most of the vast body of writing about them fails to mention another, crucial fact: *Male fertility declines with age, too.*

A few famous men who fathered children when they were septuagenarians are often cited as proof that men have as long as they like to play the dating market. Early in the movie *When Harry Met Sally*, Sally confidently declares to two of her girlfriends that she is not worried about locking down a husband: "The clock doesn't *really* start ticking until you're thirty-six." However, when she learns that the longtime boyfriend who recently broke up with her plans to marry the next woman he takes up with, Sally becomes hysterical. She calls Harry and begs him to come over to her apartment to console her. He finds her pitching around her bed in a bathrobe.

"I'm gonna be forty!" she whimpers through her tears.

"When?" Harry asks.

"Someday."

He laughs kindly. "In eight years."

"But it's *there*," she insists. "It's just sitting there, like some big dead end. And it's not the same for men. Charlie Chaplin had kids when he was seventy-three."

Despite the famous exceptions, the widespread belief that male fertility is invulnerable to aging is simply false. Among couples seeking treatment for infertility, about 40 percent of cases are caused by the "male factor," 40 percent by the "female factor," and a final 20 percent cannot be explained. A large and growing body of research shows that sperm counts, and quality, also sharply diminish over the years. The children of older fathers have a much higher risk for autism and other conditions than those of younger ones do. And often "old sperm" simply flail around and perish around an egg they are trying to fertilize.

These facts have been reported occasionally—almost always as news of a "*male* biological clock." The need to include the adjective "male" hints at why this data has mostly gone ignored. *Our society speaks as if only women had bodies.* Our assumption seems to be that reproduction is a female responsibility first and foremost. Anything going wrong with it must be a woman's fault.

———

Female reproductive systems are not actually like clocks. Our bodies move roughly by the month, rather than precisely by the second hand. As anyone who has experienced PMS can attest, the way every four weeks pass does not feel uniform. Yet despite these inaccuracies, the metaphor of the biological clock captured something real and important that was happening in the American economy.

Two kinds of work time were clashing. The nine-to-five jobs that had been common for most of the twentieth century divided life into two kinds of time: on the clock and off the clock. In the 1950s and '60s, work done on the clock was thought of primarily as male. Women worked at home, providing care that followed different rhythms.

Anyone who has tried to work from home while tending to a child or an aging parent soon learns that you cannot schedule precisely when someone will need you. It is not easy to quantify exactly what you are doing while you wait for an infant to cry out so you can feed her, or to finish her food so that you can clean up. A time-use study would say that technically you are not performing child care during those moments. But neither are you free to turn to other tasks.

It is hard to focus on work you have brought home while waiting for an elderly person you love to need to be helped to the bathroom. Nor does the state of readiness in which a caretaker waits to perform such a task dissipate once she—it is usually she—has done so. The heart does not beat by the billable hour. *Is her bruise or cough or weight loss serious? Will he be all right?* Worries like these spill over, shadowing the parent long after she returns to her desk.

Many studies have shown that as middle-class women entered the workforce, they continued to do the vast majority of the housework that full-time wives and mothers once performed. Families that were able to afford help hired other women to as-

sist with housework and provide child care for them. These contractors were usually poorer immigrants and women of color,
who were expected to be grateful for the opportunity to leave
their own homes and children untended.

In an ideal world, having to pay strangers to do the things
that wives and mothers had done all along might have led society to recognize the value of that care and honor it accordingly.
Instead, it heightened the impression that care was drudgery and
did not deserve much compensation.

The rise of a select group of women in corporate workplaces
did not do much to change the belief that housework was women's
work. The hysteria over the biological clock helped make it seem
natural that every individual had to do her best to overcome the
liability of being female if she wanted to have a career. It made
the clash between the needs of human reproduction and corporate work seem like a personal problem—a pathology that struck
certain women ("withering womb syndrome"). In the process, it
distracted attention from the obvious truth that the real problem
was social.

In a country that mandates almost no parental leave and provides no support for child care, it is impossible for women who
elect to become mothers to participate equally in the economy.
The biological clock hysteria, with its image of a time bomb
lodged in every woman's ovaries, made each woman personally
responsible for dealing with that handicap. At the same time,
the emphasis that the media placed on motherhood told career
women that not having biological children was a devastating
failure. Many of them bought it. At least they did not opt out of
motherhood en masse or organize to demand better maternity
leave or state subsidized child care. Instead, they listened to
experts who told them what experts always tell women. *There is
something terribly wrong with you! But luckily, there is also something expensive you can buy to fix it.*

The assisted reproductive technology industry emerged in the 1970s. It started with sperm banks. During that decade, the development of liquid nitrogen had made it possible to transport and store human sperm for extended periods. Entrepreneurs saw the opportunity to accumulate and trade on human genetic material. Following the lead of farmers, who had been doing this with the semen of prize bulls for several decades already, the first banks called the product they sold "stock."

It did not take long for them to start opening near prestigious universities. Ads joked that they were offering undergrads the easiest gig in the world. "UC Men, get paid for something you are already doing! Call the Sperm Bank of California." In fact, a sperm donor could not just spend five minutes in a cubby with smutty magazines, take his money, and run. Most banks required the "contractors" they worked with to commit to donating regularly for at least twelve to eighteen months, provide a clean bill of health, and promise to abstain from alcohol, drugs, and sex for days or weeks before each donation. And of course they held the legal rights to keep a contractor's stock long after he finished coming in.

Originally marketed as a solution for couples who could not conceive, sperm banks soon began appealing to Career Women who could not find partners to reproduce with. Whether you were uninterested in men, or simply unlucky in dating, sperm banks sold you a chance to "do it on your own." Comedians joked that customers were likely to get screwed in the process. A *New Yorker* cartoon from the 1970s showed a glamorous woman in flapperish garb standing in front of an Artificial Insemination Clinic. She watches, aghast, as a diminutive bum slinks out cradling a small pouch marked "$."

In the 1993 romantic comedy *Made in America*, Whoopi

Goldberg plays a forward-thinking professor who used an anonymous sperm donation to conceive her daughter years ago. When the daughter, who is now a teenager, sets out to find her father, she is shocked to discover that even though her mother requested "black," she ended up with the sperm of a goonish car salesman played by Ted Danson.

"What do you mean he's white? Like, *white* white?" Whoopi demands, when the girl breaks the news.

"*White, white, white.*" She nods in tears.

In fact, sperm banks closely monitored their stock. They allowed their customers to shop for particular traits in a targeted fashion. Of course, you wanted to know the kinds of things you might learn by flirting with someone in a bar, like height, body type, and "dental regularity." Sperm banks kept computer databases that listed the physical and psychological qualities of each donor. But they also offered information that would be harder to pick up by simply going out on a date with someone, like his ethnic background and SAT scores. Banks kept baby pictures of donors on hand to show to prospective clients.

Long before people shopped online, these databases suggested a fantasy shopping spree on an Internet of Men. The Repository for Germinal Choice, better known as the "Genius Bank," opened in Escondido, California, in 1980, claiming to traffic only in the spunk of Nobel laureates; it stayed in business until 1997.

Today, a growing number of banks use 3-D facial recognition software to help customers find donors who resemble whomever they please. The aggregator DonorMatchMe lets users search dozens of databases of both sperm and egg banks in order to find the best one for them. ("The best bank to search," the website says, "is the one with the donor most like you.") The website of Fairfax Cryobank, one of the largest sperm banks in the industry, recently added lists of celebrity look-alikes next to their donors' (baby) profiles.

If it was true, as an article in *Newsweek* said, that women only date in order to answer "the ancient Pleistocene call of the moon" and "salt in the blood" summoning them to reproduce, Fairfax Cryobank would seem to have made dating obsolete. *Why slog through drinks with strangers when you could just upload a picture and get down with a Cary Grant or George Clooney clone?*

In fact, the industry quickly recognized that women who took longer to answer their "call" than the biological clock allowed them formed a growing potential market. Technologies for extracting eggs, or oocytes, and fertilizing them outside the human body soon followed.

Doctors performed the first successful in vitro fertilization (IVF) just months before reporters started clamoring about the biological clock. Richard Cohen's story on the clock ticking for Career Women ran in *The Washington Post* on March 16, 1978. On July 25, the world's first test-tube baby, Louise Brown, was born in Manchester, England. Baby Louise briefly became a global celebrity. But if a marketing team had been trying to come up with an advertising campaign to sell a broader population of women on IVF for the longer term, they could hardly have done better than the spate of stories that Cohen launched.

IVF had been designed to solve a specific medical problem. The mother of Louise Brown had been unable to conceive because of a blockage in her fallopian tubes; her doctors intercepted an egg released during her menstrual cycle, fertilized it, and reinserted it into her uterus. By 1981, however, researchers had figured out how to use hormones to stimulate the ovaries of any woman to release many eggs at once. Soon they were selling IVF to women who had no fallopian tube problems at all.

Different national and local laws govern how many embryos

a doctor is allowed to implant via IVF. To maximize the chances of a woman's carrying a baby to term, doctors usually want to use as many as possible and abort one or more of the fetuses if too many take hold. The chances that women who underwent the procedure might have to have abortions, and the fact that the procedure involved discarding fertilized embryos, led conservative political leaders to denounce it.

During the presidencies of Ronald Reagan and George H. W. Bush, Christians on whose votes the Republican Party depended pushed for the government to withdraw support for IVF research. They did not have to push hard. Government funding for the sciences was getting slashed across the board. The result was to create a massive market for assisted reproductive technologies that went almost entirely unregulated.

By the mid-1980s, clinics offering IVF treatments were opening across the country. While sperm banks encouraged women to contemplate having biological children without male partners, IVF let those who could afford it buy a little extra time to try to make their plans line up. But it was not a magic bullet for the problems that the biological clock posed. IVF is expensive; today, it can cost tens of thousands of dollars per cycle, and few health plans cover it. It is invasive. There have been few longitudinal studies of how the hormones IVF patients must take affect their bodies in the long term, and the most recent data suggests some cause for alarm. (In the fall of 2015, a team of British researchers who tracked over 250,000 IVF patients from 1991 to 2010 found that they were one-third more likely to develop ovarian cancer than women who had not.)

Finally, the risk is high that if you wait too long, IVF simply won't work. The most recent report by the American Society for Reproductive Medicine, published in 2012, shows that for women over forty, the success rates of IVF are dismal. For women over forty-two, the likelihood that a cycle will result in their carrying a baby to term is 3.9 percent. Go down to the forty-one- and forty-two-year-olds and the number is 11.8.

For a woman who has been counting on these procedures to start a family, discovering that she cannot do so can be devastating. Particularly after going to such lengths, many women who do not become biological mothers may suffer from crushing depression, self-accusation, and regret.

Studies show that since the turn of the millennium, women have been growing anxious about their fertility at younger and younger ages. In 2002, the CDC's National Survey of Family Growth reported that the number of women twenty-two to twenty-nine who had received fertility treatment had doubled over the previous seven years, to 23 percent. *Conceive*, a newly launched magazine aimed at women trying to get pregnant, found that 46 percent of readers were younger than thirty and 73 percent were younger than thirty-five. In 2006, *The Wall Street Journal* ran a story on women in their early twenties who were already seeking fertility treatments even if they had been off of hormonal birth control for only a few months.

Earlier generations of working women had accepted that both their careers and their love lives would require them to work on themselves. Advertisements and advice books taught them to see this as an exciting opportunity. It would be difficult to make IVF sound as fun as diet fads and makeup and fashions that the beauty manuals of the 1920s or the *Cosmo* articles of the 1960s touted. It is, rather, a fallback to which a woman can resort, if she has the means. Yet over the past decade, the ART industry has started marketing expensive interventions, to people who may not need them, as a luxury—or a chance to be proactive. *Have you frozen your eggs yet?*

In contrast to the language of "stocks" and "gifts" that we use to talk about sperm and egg donation, insurance is the metaphor that dominates discussions of egg freezing. Clinics that offer the treatment often use the language of high finance in their advertisements. They joke about "frozen assets" and speak earnestly about the wisdom of "hedging against" risk. Egg freezing is both a choice and an "option," in the specific sense that Wall Street traders use that term. When she freezes her eggs, a woman pays a certain amount of money—usually between $30,000 and $80,000, plus annual storage costs—in order to be able to get her eggs back for that price later.

Like IVF, egg freezing was developed for a specific purpose: Young female cancer patients who had to undergo chemotherapy or surgery sometimes elected to freeze eggs before doing so. But in recent years, clinics have started offering the experimental treatment as an option for healthy women, too. Indeed, they encourage women to freeze their eggs as early as possible. If you can afford it, why not buy yourself time?

The logic has convinced some of America's most successful corporations. In 2012, when Google, Facebook, and Citibank announced that they were considering covering up to $20,000 of the cost of egg freezing as a health benefit for female employees, many people touted this move as a miracle fix for the gender inequality that continues to plague corporate workplaces.

A *Time* magazine cover story on the subject declared that "Company-Paid Egg Freezing Will Be the Great Equalizer." The reporter quoted a source who worked in tech. "I have insurance policies in every other area of my life: my condo, my car, work insurance," she said. "This is my body, and arguably the most important thing that you could ever have in your life . . . Why wouldn't I at least protect that asset?"

Women who freeze their eggs report in overwhelming numbers that doing so has made them feel "empowered." Yet many of them seem to be motivated by romantic, rather than professional, ambitions. They say they are less worried about climbing the career ladder than about finding love.

In 2011, *Vogue* profiled "a willowy 35-year-old media company executive" who had just frozen her eggs. She stressed the benefits that doing so would bring her while dating. "Leah . . . knew she was coming dangerously close to the age when eligible men might search her eyes for desperation, that unseemly my-clock-is-ticking vibe. 'Freezing my eggs is my little secret,' she says. 'I want to feel there's a backup plan.'"

In 2013, the journalist Sarah Elizabeth Richards published *Motherhood, Rescheduled.* The book follows five women through the process. The author says that she herself is overjoyed at the pressure that having done so takes off. "Egg freezing . . . soothed my pangs of regret for frittering away my 20s with a man I didn't want to have children with, and for wasting more years in my 30s with a man who wasn't sure he even wanted children. It took away the punishing pressure to seek a new mate and helped me find love again at age 42." This makes egg freezing sound less like a tool for workplace equality than an expensive means to prolong the search for Prince Charming.

Evangelists for egg freezing suggest that the ultimate empowerment for women would be to work hard enough to be able to consume conspicuously and wait, dating forever. Can we really trust that good things come to those who plan?

In order to earn their happy ending, the women in these stories must be willing to go to any length to make things easy on the men they get involved with, just as they must in order to succeed professionally. The American workforce is now more than half female. Is egg freezing really the best fix that we can come up with for the problems that workplace conventions created for men cause for women? Is it not slightly incredible that between policy changes—say, health care and maternity leave policies like those in other developed countries—and an experimental "time-freezing" technology, American business leaders seem to think that *freezing time* is the more realistic fix?

In romance, the final step of planning is to make it seem spontaneous. Whatever she does, a woman on a date must not let her plan show. Richards, the evangelist of egg freezing, rhapsodizes about how the procedure made it possible for her to feel normal on dates. At least it let her feel normal enough to act normal on them. "It's a buzz kill on dates when you feel compelled to ask the guy sitting across from you, clutching his craft beer, 'So do you think you might want kids someday?'" she wrote.

The go-getting women who are cited as advertisements for egg freezing use the language of choice and self-empowerment—the same language that Helen Gurley Brown and Virginia Slims used in the 1960s. *You've come a long way*, indeed, when you can afford to spend tens of thousands of dollars in order to make your date more comfortable. But in practice, the only choice that egg freezing gives women seems to be the choice to buy into stereotypes that perpetuate gender inequality. Specifically, to be the one who does all the work of courtship and then hides the effort it costs her.

It is easy to understand why individual women might want to freeze their eggs. But freezing is never a solution to a problem. On the contrary, it is a way to prolong the existence of a problem. Any apparent problem that a society allows to go on and on must somehow be productive. The purpose of the biological clock has been to make it seem only natural—indeed, inevitable—that the burdens of reproducing the world fall almost entirely on women.

Another group of women, who were also receiving a lot of media attention during the heyday of the Clock-Watchers, prove it.

———

While 1980s Career Women fretted about fitting marriage and childbearing into their life plans, authorities constantly criticized other, younger women for failing to time pregnancy properly.

Enter the Teen Mom.

Around the same time that the story of the biological clock broke, policy makers and media outlets started reporting an "epidemic" of teen pregnancies. A press release from the President's Commission on Population Growth and the American Future announced that the rate of teen pregnancies *tripled* between 1971 and 1976. The number of teens who became pregnant every year hovered around one million for most of the 1980s, then spiked by about 20 percent around the turn of the decade.

In policy circles, and in the press, the panic escalated. Yet almost all the mainstream reports on these shocking statistics omitted one important detail. Teen birth*rates* were falling. While nearly 10 percent of girls who were teens in the 1950s had their first child before reaching twenty, in the 1980s, this figure was closer to 5 percent. It was actually the rate of teen *marriage* that was going down.

What was shocking was not that teens were having sex but that girlfriends were not staying with the boyfriends who fathered their children. In 1950, 13 percent of teen births were nonmarital. In 2000, 79 percent were. A culture of increasing sexual permissiveness may have played a role. But the economy surely did, too. In the 1970s, the shotgun wedding option that so many teens had been forced to take in the 1950s was no longer on the table. If a girl got pregnant in the Steady Era, the father could reasonably expect to find a job that could support her and their family. No longer. In a decade of double-digit inflation, stagnating wages, and unemployment, the solution to teen pregnancy was not marriage. Despite all evidence to the contrary, the conservatives who gained political power during the Reagan and Bush years insisted that it was also not comprehensive sex education or access to contraception and abortion. Republicans systematically blocked access to any of the means that have been shown to reduce teen pregnancy.

A consensus emerged that instead the best way to solve the crisis was to teach young women to manage their lives better. And so authorities started telling teen girls growing up in poor households that they had something in common with well-heeled Career Women. They, too, had to *plan*. Only, for the opposite outcome.

There is a long and troubling history of advocates of birth control appealing to eugenics. In the 1910s, Margaret Sanger, the founder of Planned Parenthood, tried to persuade authorities to legalize contraception by arguing that it would stop undesirable immigrants from reproducing. In the 1950s, the biologists who invented the oral contraceptive pill conducted dangerous clinical trials in Puerto Rico; they justified this choice by saying that the population needed to be reduced. In the 1970s, Latina activists claimed that 35 percent of that generation had been sterilized.

Campaigns against teen pregnancy may have been less overtly exploitative, but they had similar aims. While rich women were told that they would never be happy if they deprived themselves of the joys of motherhood, poor women were warned not to have children no matter what.

In 1980, the Girls Club of Santa Barbara decided that the mostly black and Latina teen girls they served were in dire need of instruction in "life planning." The board members decided that they had to "raise the level of their consciousness of today's world as it really is." In that world, these young women were extremely unlikely to marry men who would be able to support them. They would earn 59 cents to every dollar that their male peers earned, and if they headed their own households, they faced 70 percent odds of living in poverty. To make the most of their slim chance at a good life, they needed to develop a "flexible and aware mentality." To help them do so, the directors of the Girls Club developed a life-planning curriculum called Choices.

Choices: A Teen Woman's Journal for Self-Awareness and Personal Planning was published in July 1983. Festooned with pastel flowers, it was marketed as both a textbook and a trade book. When schools purchased *Choices*, they also received teacher-training materials. Because the creators wanted *Choices* to be used in public schools, they developed a companion program for boys, called *Challenges*. The pagination of the two volumes was coordinated. They used different gender pronouns and slightly different examples so that public schools could use them together to teach coed classes. By 1985, they had been adopted for life-planning programs in twenty-two states. They offered a picture of formal gender equality, separate but equal. *Challenges* for boys; *Choices* for girls.

Choices aimed to teach girls about all the career opportunities that were now open to women and get them into the right frame of mind to seize them. "One must remain flexible enough to change," the book admonished, "but once the basic decision-making skills are learned, the woman is empowered to make sound choices about anything."

Pages of worksheets allowed students to conduct "Attitude Inventories" on a wide variety of subjects. You were asked to tick off an option from "Strongly Agree" to "Strongly Disagree" in response to statements like "If a working couple buys a house, the husband should make the payments." "At work, women are entitled to use sick leave for maternity leave." "Men should not cry." You tried to answer questions like "How much does a dress cost?" to realize how much you would have to earn. The self-knowledge that you gained from the process was supposed to help you choose wisely in all aspects of life.

Chapter 7 was devoted to family planning. The teaching materials said that by the time the student reached this stage, "she has learned to create a decision-making model for when to have a baby; she has, through values clarification, thought about childcare options. Through an exercise in role-playing, the student learns how much commitment a family requires. *The young woman usually concludes that she is not ready emotionally or financially for the responsibility of a baby.*"

The authors added that by the time she completed the family-planning unit, the student "has learned to be assertive, a helpful skill in responses that prevent pregnancies." Being assertive enough to avoid being coerced into sex sounds like a good skill to learn. But you have to wonder what the corresponding page on *Challenges* said: *Try not to rape your girlfriend?*

The emphasis on planning and choice put the burden of policing romance on young women—precisely where it had been in the Steady Era. Only now, these women were also responsible for preparing themselves for careers.

Throughout the 1980s and '90s, life-planning techniques continued to be incorporated into the curricula in a wide range of public and private schools. These programs told young people to look at their romantic lives as part of a grand strategy. More important, they taught students to think that any deviation from that plan was a personal failing.

A future of debt and loneliness continues to be the main theme of outreach aimed at teen girls who might consider becoming mothers. An ad campaign that the New York City Human Resources Administration plastered on the subways in 2013 confronted them directly. *Got a good job?* one baby asks, bawling. *I cost thousands of dollars each year.* THINK BEING A TEEN

PARENT WON'T COST YOU? text slapped diagonally across the bottom reads. EXPECT TO SPEND MORE THAN $10,000 A YEAR TO RAISE A CHILD.

Another ad featured a tiny girl with an index finger pressed against her lips; she is looking off frame right, as if she is embarrassed for you. *Honestly Mom . . .* the thought bubble above her head says. *Chances are he* won't *stay with you. What happens to me?* The banner confirms: 90% OF TEEN PARENTS DON'T MARRY EACH OTHER.

Our culture sends very different messages to richer and poorer women about motherhood. Articles aimed at middle- and upper-middle-class women rhapsodize about the incomparable joy that having children will bring into their lives. Poor women, particularly women of color, are warned that having a baby will trap them in a lifetime of poverty. Both claims may be true. Motherhood may be a joyful experience if you can afford it. It may be ruinous if you cannot. But in both cases, the emphasis on planning serves to make the reproduction of the world look like a lifestyle choice—a purely private concern. The imperative to line up your life perfectly suggests that it is moral as well as practical to do so.

This fiction that it is female nature to take full responsibility for reproduction places a tremendous burden on women. And it strains many romantic relationships. The fiction that men and women who desire sexual and romantic relations are hardwired to want *opposing* things is not good for anyone. I bet you know at least one bachelor who has spent decades unable to commit to any relationship, despite professing that he yearns to do so; I know several. It turns out that even if cultural stereotypes say that a man can date around endlessly without lowering his stock, of course the experience will change him, just as it changes the partners whom stereotypes say he can dispose of at no cost to himself.

The success of the 2007 Judd Apatow comedy *Knocked Up* suggests how desperately men as well as women may want to get out of this impasse. In it, the young, hotshot career woman played by Katherine Heigl spends a wild night celebrating a recent promotion, falls into bed with the schlubby loser played by Seth Rogen, and several weeks later finds herself in the predicament that the title suggests. The first time I heard it summarized, I thought it was a horror movie. If we take the leap of faith that her character would not sprint to the nearest abortion clinic, we get to enjoy a fantasy in which two unappealing people can fumble their ways toward happiness without ever having to make any joint decisions whatsoever.

The unplanned pregnancy is not presented as a disaster. It is a godsend. Especially for Seth Rogen's character. Stereotypes say that the kind of man-child he epitomizes—unemployed, directionless—is terrified of the responsibilities of monogamy, marriage, and fatherhood. But it is clearly he, not Heigl, who is saved by their chance encounter. Knocking up a stranger rescues the man-child from himself.

The movie makes it clear that if, for whatever reason, the woman played by Katherine Heigl wanted to have a deadbeat's child at this juncture, she could have managed on her own. This is precisely what makes her a heroine. Indeed, if we thought that she was desperate to snag Seth Rogen, the movie would be unbearably depressing. It is her willingness to take on all the work of reproducing the world that is supposed to make her worthy of the happiness she stumbles into. She earns a man and a family by proving that she would have been willing to do everything herself.

Is it worth it? The greatest risk run by the Clock-Watcher who plans every day of her life, fearing that any misstep or wrong "choice" will derail her, is being disappointed.

How many Career Women have grown into exactly the women they planned, only to find that the future they thought they wanted was not what they expected? How could it not be disappointing after so much work? Like the housewife of Betty Friedan's *Feminine Mystique*, I imagine the Career Woman who returns to work two weeks after giving birth dismayed. The new Feminine Mystique has created a new problem with no name that feels disarmingly familiar. *Is this all? Is this what all of that was for?*

CHAPTER 10. HELP

There is a word for the route taken by the Clock-Watcher who decides that her time is up and bravely resolves to make the best life she can with whatever partner she has on hand. That word is *settling*.

The *Oxford English Dictionary* shows that "settle" has been used to mean "marry" since the 1600s. For centuries, settling did not necessarily sound like a bad thing. Indeed, many young men and women seemed to regard it as an opportunity. "The prudent gentlewoman . . . wishes to settle her daughter," the novelist Theodore Edward Hook observed in 1825. "I am come to years of discretion, and must think . . . of settling myself advantageously," a male character reflected in Thomas Love Peacock's satire *Crotchet Castle* six years later.

So why do we cringe at any hint that two people may be "settling for" each other today?

In recent years, the subject has seemed to come up more and more often. It started with an article by Lori Gottlieb that appeared in March 2008 in *The Atlantic.* "Marry Him!" the headline shrieked. "The Case for Settling for Mr. Good Enough."

Gottlieb declared that every woman she knew was preoccupied with the problem of finding a partner. "Every woman I know—no matter how successful and ambitious, how financially and emotionally secure—feels panic, occasionally coupled with desperation, if she hits 30 and finds herself unmarried," she claimed in the opening paragraphs. "If you say you're not worried, either you're in denial or you're lying."

To make matters worse, Gottlieb continued, her friends were approaching their husband hunts all wrong. She knew it, because she had, too. Gottlieb explained that she opted to have a child using an anonymous sperm donor in her late thirties so that she could hold out for a man she liked better than the men she had been dating. In retrospect, she says, she vastly overestimated the importance of sex and romance.

"Marriage isn't a passion-fest," she wrote. "It's more like a partnership formed to run a very small, mundane, and often boring nonprofit business." If they want to make it through this drudgery, she tells her readers that they should hurry up and lock a partner down.

Shared widely both by people who loved it and people who were enraged by it, "Marry Him!" spread rapidly around the Internet. It still inspires strong feelings. "Lori Gottlieb ruined my twenties!" a friend balks when I mention the article. She read it when she was twenty-five and falling out of love with the boyfriend she had been living with since college. Gottlieb persuaded her that she should slog through two more years. At that point, he confessed that he had been cheating and they both realized that there had been no point; they parted amicably.

In 2010, Gottlieb published a book of the same title. *Marry Him* invites us to accompany Gottlieb on her quest to find a man to settle for. The jacket copy describes it as a "wake-up call." But the book reads more like an odyssey of self-blame and regret. *Once upon a time I was a girl who had the whole world at her feet, but I was too picky and now look at me!* Along the way, Gottlieb makes occasional pit stops to criticize other high-achieving women.

Gottlieb uses two metaphors as touchstones for what these women do wrong when they date. The first is the "Husband Store." The second is the "Shopping List"—meaning the characteristics you want the husband you buy to possess. Citing a few statistics and anecdotes, she proposes that this kind of foolish choosiness may be why fewer and fewer American women are marrying. Gottlieb claims to have broken up with a man once for his taste in socks.

At some level, what Gottlieb is saying is unobjectionable. No, you should not go into dating thinking that you can find a partner premade to your highly detailed specifications. Yet *Marry Him* does not really offer an alternative to the logic that says dating is like shopping. It just tells readers to lower their expectations. Fast.

By the end, Lori Gottlieb seems ready to marry literally anyone. She says she would take a man who made bad jokes or had bad breath. But—spoiler alert—after 260 pages, she is still alone. She says that the moral is that she should have settled earlier. But to me, *Marry Him* reads more like an allegory of the limitations of the self-help genre. It tells its readers to mold themselves and their desires into very particular forms to try to attain a kind of happiness that is unimaginative at best.

Are straight women really still doomed to choose between a foolish, futile quest for Mr. Right and a mad dash after the equally elusive Mr. Anyone at All?

Some religions describe desire as a blessing. Others label it a curse. But none deny that all humans long for others with whom to share our lives. Almost all individuals seem to feel a deep need to live lives that include close and caring relationships. Given how vitally important this is, and how challenging it can be, it makes sense that they turn to experts. The intense, almost religious feelings that self-help gurus like Oprah Winfrey inspire in their fans reflect a real need that those fans experience to do something to address their frustrations.

America has a long tradition of bestsellers that offer readers guidance about how to cultivate their inner lives and achieve professional success. Over the twentieth century, a string of male self-help authors became household names. Napoleon Hill's *Think and Grow Rich* and Dale Carnegie's *How to Win Friends & Influence People* sold well even during the Great Depression. Norman Vincent Peale's *Power of Positive Thinking* became a bible to Company Men of the Steady Era. In 1989, Stephen Covey instructed readers in *The 7 Habits of Highly Effective People*; he promised that learning to attend to your inner voice can make you a better person and a better manager all at once.

Each of these books encourages readers to look inside themselves and trust their instincts. They advise you that you must have the strength to buck received wisdom and challenge authority— including the authorities in psychiatry or sociology who usually say that the folksy wisdom of these books is bogus. Romantic self-help, however, tends to offer the opposite advice.

Where business self-help says to trust your gut, romantic self-help warns you to question every instinct. Where the managers hear that they should listen to their coworkers, the daters hear that they should never trust a partner to mean what he says. If you hope to find love, you will have to learn to read between the lines and plot your actions accordingly. These books promise that they can help.

Courtship did not always seem this mysterious. Popular books of romantic advice are older than dating. During the Calling

Era, many publishers stayed in business by telling young people and their families how they should behave.

In *The Ladies' Home Journal*, an etiquette columnist who answered questions under the pen name the "Lady from Philadelphia" delivered firm instructions to female readers about how to manage their gentleman callers. The questions she answered showed that callers were just as capable of obsessing over the details of how to act as daters are today.

In July 1905, someone named Madge wrote asking how to react when a young man failed to show up after saying he would drop in. The Lady from Philadelphia advised her to "be charitable until you hear his explanation or apology," but "if no apology is ever made and he never comes you should treat him as the merest acquaintance, recognizing him when you pass, but without cordiality."

Sadie had the opposite problem. "What to do when a man persists in holding your hand in spite of all that you can say?" she pleaded.

The Lady from Philadelphia replied sternly that "no man, who is fit to be welcomed in your home, would refuse to release your hand if you asked him as if you meant it."

Single men, too, were eager for tips on how to conduct themselves. *Putnam's Handbook of Etiquette* (1913), a manual aimed at men, devoted a section to "The Question of the Hat, Gloves, and Stick."

"When a gentleman ventures a chance call upon women, and is asked by the servant to step into the drawing-room while she ascertains if the ladies are home, he retains his overcoat and gloves, and waits hat in hand," *Putnam's* instructed. "If the answer to his request is propitious, he then removes his top-coat and leaves it in the hall. With the coat, hat, stick, and gloves may also be left."

To the twenty-first-century reader, two things jump out

about Calling Era advice. The first is the tone of voice in which it is dispensed. This tone is confident. It suggests that there are clear protocols for how people pair up to reproduce society. To find a mate, all you have to do is follow them. In addition, the ritual of calling reflected and reinforced a set of strong beliefs about gender roles and relations. A long tradition argued that a man should always be running after the woman he desired—that he could not, by definition, want something that he had.

Barriers built into the ritual of calling ensured that during courtship, young men and women followed this script. The custom of calling rendered women passive and immobile. The setup required men to act in order to express interest. A woman did not have to pretend that she had somehow overlooked a text message in order to strike her crush as desirable. The mere fact that he was talking to her meant that he had already waited for her appointed day "at home," presented his calling card to her servant, and stood there fumbling with his hat, gloves, and stick.

The age of dating inherited its ideas about love and courtship from this earlier era. It held on to the idea that women were essentially passive and that men wanted to pursue them. But as women streamed into public workplaces and educational institutions, the real barriers that had made men into agents of desire and women into its objects were breaking down.

Men and women could now meet in many different settings; they might run into one another at work or on the street. A woman no longer had her family and her home to protect her against the embarrassing possibility of feeling attracted to a man who was not interested in her. Moreover, among the working-class pioneers of dating, men had the money that bought access to the spaces where courtship took place—bars or restaurants or dance halls. This meant that in order to have any fun, women had to chase men.

"The lure of the stage, of the movie, of the shop, and of the office make of it the definite El Dorado of the woman," the sociologist Frances Donovan wrote in 1919. "Owing to present day conditions of city life, the man is the one pursued, the woman the pursuer."

As more middle-class women with disposable income began dating, the idea that men paid remained the norm. This made men the hosts of courtship. In order to be wooed, women had to woo men—without ever giving away that they were doing it.

To many observers, this reversal of traditional gender roles seemed to pose a threat to romance. Therefore, early books of dating advice urged women that in order to make themselves desirable, they would have to create the illusion that they were still feminine. That meant, still as passive as they had been when they were homebound.

To save courtship, women had to cover up the fact that changes in the economy were changing gender roles and relations. To the extent that their work and their new mobility did empower them, they had to hide it. Otherwise they risked a fate that women had long been taught to fear: growing old without finding a husband.

Elinor Glyn, the writer who coined the term "It Girl," published a popular manual of romantic advice in 1923. *The Philosophy of Love* included chapters aimed at both men and women. Glyn warned female readers that with the men they truly desired, they should make every effort not to show it. While the Lady from Philadelphia had told readers of *Ladies' Home Journal* how they should behave with men, Glyn emphasized all the things that a woman must *not* do.

"She cannot be altogether irresponsibly natural."

She must not be "affected at all."

"She must never show her eagerness."

"She must never try to keep him one instant when he suggests leaving."

"She must never show that she desires to hold him in any way."

"She must not be vague."

She "must not become peevish and complaining, selfish and demagnetised, and indifferent to her appearance . . ."

She must not be "wearing 'any old thing'" when he comes over.

Glyn said that the point of all these prohibitions was to sustain the fiction that men were in control of courtship. "She must always make him feel that *he* must make the advance, and that she is something to be schemed for," she concluded.

Doris Langley Moore agreed. The British socialite and fashion icon won the admiration of her friends by managing to keep men falling all over her, even after World War I wiped out a generation of eligible bachelors. In 1928, Moore anonymously published a dating advice manual that divulged the secrets of her romantic success, *The Technique of the Love Affair*. "A woman has not made a conquest until she finds herself pursued," Moore advised.

When Dorothy Parker reviewed the book for *The New Yorker*, she expressed dismay at her own ignorance about the laws of dating. "From this book I have learned that not once have I been right," she wrote. "Not one little time."

The short stories that Parker was publishing around 1930 suggested otherwise. Again and again, Parker chronicled how hard ordinary women tried to win love from men by keeping them in pursuit.

"A Telephone Call" consists of a two-thousand-word prayer.

A Shopgirl begs God for strength as she waits to hear from a man she has been seeing.

"Dear God, let him call me now," the narrator begins. "I won't ask anything else of You, truly I won't."

So she claims. But she soon switches to pleading for help controlling herself.

"Please, God, keep me from telephoning him."

In a rush of short, staccato sentences, Parker captures all the urges and orders fighting with one another in this young woman's head. "I'll think about something else. I'll just sit quietly. If I could sit still. If I could sit still. Maybe I could read. Oh, all the books are about people who love each other."

This woman knows that restraining herself is crucially important. Expressing her desire would be more than a turnoff. It would inspire hatred.

"I know you shouldn't keep telephoning them," she says. "I know they don't like that. When you do that, they know you are thinking about them and wanting them, and that makes them hate you."

She keeps repeating that men *hate* female feelings.

"They hate sad people."

"They don't like you to tell them they've made you cry."

"They hate you whenever you say anything you really think."

Another story that Parker published in the same collection hints at why that might be. In "Advice to the Little Peyton Girl," a Shopgirl named Sylvie despairs when her boyfriend, Bunny Barclay, grows distant.

"You showed him how much you cared for him, Sylvie," her older and wiser friend explains. "[You] showed him he was all-important to you. Men do not like that."

Sylvie learns the hard way that Bunny took her love for him as a kind of demand—a threat to his autonomy.

"You must be light and you must be easy," her friend continues, as Sylvie's heart breaks. "Ease is the desire of all men."

Parker saw that making things easy for men could be hard work. Moreover, a woman's desire to "seem easy" with a love interest could produce the opposite effect. It could make her completely neurotic. By the end of "A Telephone Call," the narrator has shut her clock in the bathroom and is trying to distract herself by counting to five hundred by fives.

Nonetheless, virtually all of the most popular romantic self-help books aimed at women today still offer some version of the same advice that Glyn and Moore gave, and Parker parodied, in the 1920s. They address their readers in a scolding tone. If you browse bestselling career advice in a bookstore or on Amazon, you will find titles that burst with affirmation. *Brag!* their titles cheer. *Ask for It! Lean In!* By contrast, the books about dating seem calculated to discourage any acts of self-expression. *He's Just Not That Into You*, they say.

It's Not Him, It's You begins berating its reader before she has even made it past the table of contents. Each chapter is named for one of the "fundamental mistakes" that the book says women make.

"Your Attitude Sucks," one chapter declares.

"You Think Men Have a Clue."

In this context, a book like *Ignore the Guy, Get the Guy* starts to sound optimistic.

The Rules, which came out in 1995, probably remains the best-known dating advice franchise in America. The authors, Ellen Fein and Sherrie Schneider, elevated the kinds of prohibitions that Elinor Glyn and Dorothy Langley Moore offered into a philosophy of life.

The Rules instructs you in how to become a "Rules Girl"—

the type of woman who effortlessly attracts and keeps men—by elaborating all the things you must not do: "Don't talk to a man first." "Don't ask him to dance." "Don't stare at men or talk too much." "Don't call him, and rarely return his calls." "Don't accept a Saturday night date after Wednesday." "Don't see him more than once or twice a week." "Don't rush into sex." "Don't open up too fast." "Don't tell him what to do."

The farther you continue down this list, the more the book starts to sound like the founding scripture of a cult of self-hatred. "Don't talk to your therapist about *The Rules*," the authors warn more than once. And for anyone who feels herself wavering, there is Rule #32: "Don't break *The Rules*."

Restraining and repressing every instinct you have is hard work, and the Rules Girls are the first to admit it. "We know we're asking you to go against your feelings here," Fein and Schneider concede in their introduction. "But you want to get married, don't you?" The supermodel Kate Moss famously quipped that *nothing tastes as good as skinny feels. The Rules* offers a kind of emotional equivalent for Single Girls. *Nothing could feel worse than being alone.*

In this genre of advice, love serves as a kind of disciplinary instrument. The prospect of a long-term partnership is dangled in front of women as the prize of a lifetime of self-denial. Should a single woman think of straying, the authors remind her of the possibility of future loneliness to put her back on track. The possibility that any woman might be interested in anything other than getting married to a man never comes up.

Meanwhile, however, another danger goes entirely unmentioned. This is that a Rules Girl becomes so expert at ignoring her feelings that she forgets what she wanted from dating in the first place. The surest way to make it seem like you do not care is to actually not care. The surest way to cover up that you are feeling the first stirrings of love is to try to actually not feel them. Ironically, dating advice sometimes seems to be training its reader how to steel herself against the very emotions that she says she hopes to experience.

When the sociologist Arlie Hochschild wrote her pioneering study of service workers in the 1980s, she observed that the kind of "emotional labor" that their jobs required could be exploited, just as physical labor can be exploited. More than a century earlier, Karl Marx had described in detail how workers who perform repetitive, exhausting tasks for too little money gradually develop sensations of being estranged from their own bodies. For Marx, the essence of what makes us human lies in our labor—in the ways that we purposefully shape the world around us. So when a worker finds himself compelled to perform too much work for too little, the process not only exhausts him but in fact dehumanizes him. It deforms his spirit. The parts of his body with which he works become like tools, mere instruments, and it is his employers who profit from them, rather than himself.

Hochschild studied a group of female flight attendants who worked for Delta Airlines throughout the late 1970s and early '80s. The most strenuous exertions that their jobs required were not physical. They were emotional. Flight attendants had to maintain an attractive appearance and adhere to strict codes regarding body shape and dress. But most important, they had to express warmth toward passengers, calming them when they were disruptive or comforting them if they were scared. Delta training materials instructed attendants to treat their smiles as their "greatest assets."

The women, Hochschild reported, could become deranged with grinning. Some found that after returning home from a transatlantic flight, they were literally incapable of laughing with their children. This is the extreme to which the kinds of emotional labor that are meant to seem natural and effortless can lead. Take it too far and you have too much taken from you. You realize that your emotions themselves are no longer your own.

Meanwhile, the most cunning men have gotten wise to the ruses of the Rules Girl. They see that beneath her cool exterior, she is highly vulnerable. If you have been conditioned to believe that your life derives value only from male attention and affection, you will presumably go to great lengths to get it. If you are used to thinking that the only way you can pursue your desires is by making yourself into an object of desire for someone else, being ignored can quickly make you feel desperate.

The Pickup Artist (PUA) tries to manipulate women by stealing a page from the *Rules* playbook. In the early 2000s, the *New York Times* reporter Neil Strauss spent two years immersed in a PUA subculture centered around Los Angeles. The guru who initiated him was a Toronto native who went by the name of Mystery. For the purposes of his PUA education, Strauss also gets a nickname: "Style." Recounting his story, Style offers a secondhand seduction guide for men who are as lonely and desperate as he once was. The PUAs call them AFCs—"average frustrated chumps."

The central principle of PUA "game theory" boils down to this: In order to attract attractive women, men must first destroy their self-esteem by feigning indifference to them. To sleep with an HB (a hot babe, anywhere from a 7 to a 10, on their scale), a PUA simply follows a sequence that Mystery calls FMAC: find, meet, attract, close.

PUAs like acronyms. They like jargon in general. A lot of the fun of reading Strauss's *The Game* lies in mastering its vocabulary.

For instance, a night out chasing HBs is called "sarging." One of the best "approaches" is the "neg."

"Neither compliment nor insult, the neg is something in between—an accidental insult or backhanded compliment. The purpose of a neg is to lower a woman's self esteem while actively displaying a lack of interest in her—by telling her that she has lipstick on her teeth, for example, or offering her a piece of gum after she speaks."

I love a woman who can eat.

Aren't you cold in that?

You get the idea.

On the surface, *The Game* seems like the antithesis of *The Rules*. *The Rules* are prissy and self-consciously retro; they appeal to old-fashioned ideas of chivalry and chaperonage. *The Game* is frankly ruthless in its pursuit of no-commitment sex. Yet these books share a worldview. The system of beliefs regarding hetero-sexual relationships that they espouse are almost identical.

Both *The Rules* and *The Game* present the battle of the sexes as a kind of market competition, where women barter sex for love and men do the opposite. In this exchange, not only is dating work for women and recreation for men. Desire is a liability. If a seller knows you want to buy, he knows he can get more.

Strauss presents the game as a way to fulfill a male fantasy of having an easy time getting women into bed. In the opening chapter, he describes how pitiful and helpless he was before his PUA education. He stresses that he is physically unattractive.

"My nose is too large for my face . . . to say that my hair is thinning would be an understatement . . . my eyes are small and beady . . . I am shorter than I'd like to be and so skinny that I look malnourished to most people." He spills all this in the first few paragraphs.

"So for me, meeting girls takes work."

In addition to advertising the effectiveness of his methods, even for the balding and beady-eyed, Straus is apologizing in advance, using self-deprecation to encourage readers to feel sorry enough for pre-PUA Neil to go easy on him for all the bad behavior that follows. He explains that because his appearance did not inspire lust, he often felt overwhelmed by his own emotions and sense of neediness.

"I can't seem to evolve to the next state of being because I spend far too much time thinking about women," Style laments. "I'd turn a one-night stand into a two-year stand because I didn't know when it was going to happen again."

It was dealing with emotions like uncertainty that he found unmanning. In order to help an AFC get out of his state of vulnerability and desperation, the PUAs recommend that he pretend that his feelings are *unreal*.

"Think of tonight as a video game," Mystery admonishes his protégés. It works.

"The bars and clubs became . . . just different levels on a video game I had to get through," Style recalls later.

"All your emotions are there to try to fuck you up," Mystery eggs him on. "Know that they cannot be trusted at all."

This kind of *Revenge of the Nerds* story has been around for a long time. Such stories often revolve around how men feel about how women make them feel. More specifically, they offer male readers a fantasy of being able to refuse to feel anything—and, thus, become invulnerable to the anxiety that can paralyze an average frustrated chump during an "approach."

Already in 1933, Nathanael West had connected the dots between the male rage he felt seething all around him in New York City and what political economists now call the "feminization of labor." During the Great Depression, the entrance of women into formerly male workplaces put new pressure and competition on their colleagues. In addition, the nasty hero of *Miss Lonelyhearts* is asked to perform a female kind of work—attending to the feelings, and assuaging the anxieties, of others.

Miss Lonelyhearts is a nameless writer who once had literary aspirations. Instead, in the midst of the Depression, he finds himself eking out a living by ghostwriting a romantic advice column in the voice of a middle-aged matron. The resentment that Miss Lonelyhearts expresses toward real women cannot be separated from his sense of being emasculated by his job.

When one day, early on, Miss Lonelyhearts heads to a speakeasy to meet his friends after work, he finds his colleagues complaining about female competitors like Dorothy Parker.

"Someone started a train of stories by suggesting that what they all needed was a good rape."

He tells about a girl who was "regular" until she "went literary." "The guys on the block got sore and took her into the lots one night. About eight of them. They ganged her proper . . ."

Someone else talks about an ambitious female novelist who tried to go undercover to do research in a speakeasy. "They got her into the back room to teach her a new word and put the boots to her. They didn't let her out for three days. On the last day they sold tickets to niggers."

Miss Lonelyhearts is so accustomed to these conversations that he hardly notices. In case we doubt that this is a numbing strategy these sad men use to protect themselves against their sense of impotence, Nathanael West tells us: "They would go on telling these stories until they were too drunk to talk."

The practice of holding up this kind of hateful language as proof of immunity to feeling has not gone away. Every decade may get the *American Psycho* that no decade deserves. Since the beginning of the Great Recession, the bestselling author, public speaker, and professional misogynist Tucker Max has earned millions of readers by dishing out stories of his frat-boyish sexual escapades. Every day his website offers tweetable swipes that he has taken at women he has slept with. When I visit his website, this is the most recent:

"I know this really sexy move you can do with your mouth. It's called 'shutting the fuck up.'"

The rudeness of these men is part of the revenge fantasy that they offer. It plays a key role in their refusal to perform the emotional labor that the women in their lives expect.

Men more polite than Miss Lonelyhearts and Tucker Max also reject women who do not manage to "seem easy." How many times have you heard a man explain why he left a woman by saying that, in some way, she demanded too much emotional labor of him? How many female exes became unbearable because they were "too much work," "not worth the effort," "difficult," "oversensitive," "intense," or "tiresome"? Still more criticisms imply that women fail to manage their own emotions properly; they are "hysterical," "illogical," "shrill," "unreasonable," "overwhelmed," "all over the place," "confused." At some point every woman seems to become "crazy."

Ease may still be the desire of every man.

For almost a century, dating self-help books have warned women that they must repress their emotions in order to avoid making their partners think that they expect something. This clearly places a burden on women who want to be involved with men. It is not good for men either. For one thing, it frankly infantilizes them.

In 1928, Doris Langley Moore wrote that a man could not be trusted to control his impulses or anticipate his own feelings. "Men, like children, soon tire of what is soon obtained."

The Rules give the same warning. "He might think he wants to see you every night," the authors say. "He doesn't." The Rules Girl must not only sustain her man's desire by making herself scarce. She also must understand it better than he does himself.

This philosophy of love assumes that men are as emotionally helpless as boys are practically helpless. As a child needs his mother to cook and clean and care for him, so, too, does an adult man need a woman to manage his feelings. Otherwise, like the bachelor who lives in filth and lets laundry pile up and orders Chinese takeout every night, he will be a complete mess.

This gendered division of labor makes women emotionally overworked and makes men emotionally incompetent. At the same time, it burdens men with the sole responsibility for making decisions about their sexual and romantic liaisons. As the kind of woman Parker captured in "A Telephone Call" frets in maddened silence, we can easily imagine a man growing overwhelmed with the pressure of the decision that has been left up to him. More often than not, the men in these stories start strong, waver, and then fade out.

This kind of mutual mystification is not good for men or for women. What it is good for, however, is a multibillion-dollar self-help industry that profits off of their loneliness and uncertainty.

Self-help books have an obvious incentive to mystify men to women, and vice versa. Elinor Glyn's *Philosophy of Love* was aimed at a general audience. But the bestselling advice franchises of recent decades all insist that men and women have radically different approaches to romance—and therefore require specific advice on how to approach one another.

Men Are from Mars, Women Are from Venus, one of the bestselling advice books of all time declared.

"Men and women differ in all areas of their lives," the author

John Gray explains in his introduction. "They almost seem to be from different planets." The book even includes a "Venusian/ Martian Phrase Dictionary."

Many dating experts since have followed this lead, presenting gender difference as the most helpful rubric for understanding relationships. (The bestselling books rarely acknowledge that anyone might be interested in anything other than heterosexual monogamy headed toward marriage.) There are obvious reasons why this formula helps sell books. It suggests that there is some secret to dating. And it turns the author into an authority, simply on the basis of being a man or woman.

In *Act Like a Lady, Think Like a Man*, Steve Harvey promises to tell readers *What Men Really Think About Love, Relationships, Intimacy, and Commitment*. Like John Gray, Harvey says that all dating difficulties boil down to gender difference. But compared with Gray, who strives to sound neutral and empathetic, Harvey seems inclined to side with Team Boys over Team Girls.

"Women are complicated creatures," Harvey writes. "Now men, by contrast, are very simple creatures. It really doesn't take much to make us happy."

For the view from neuroscience, you can read *The Male Brain* and *The Female Brain*. Even *Sex Tips for Straight Women from a Gay Man* sticks to the idea that desire works straightforwardly along gender lines. Cowritten by two friends who match the description in the title, and illustrated with cheeky line drawings, it suggests that male pleasure is a secret a gay man could simply let a woman in on.

"Think of this book as your personal trainer, at a fraction of the cost," the introduction tells the reader.

The training that most self-help books offer is how to make yourself malleable. Self-help tells you to bow to the world as it is. The approach that says that the sources of all your frustrations are in you is supposed to feel empowering. It tells readers that they can do something. Yet when addressing problems that are clearly social in origin, what it trains you best in is self-blame. It scolds you, while it offers you a hand.

The reason that the advice in books like *Philosophy of Love* or *The Rules* or *Act Like a Lady* is so repetitive is not simply that their authors are dull. The reason that the genre seems incapable of imagining any kind of desire that falls outside a very narrow spectrum—looking for sex or looking for marriage—is not simply that the authors are prejudiced. Rather, this form of self-help precludes the possibility that a connection between two or more people might be capable of changing the conditions in which they live. The genre exists to help perpetuate those conditions. As a result, the love that self-help books hold out as the prize for following all their rules rarely sounds worth it when you get there. It seems average to the point of emptiness.

AFTERWORD: **LOVE**

The premise of the romantic self-help industry is that the problems we encounter in dating are individual. The history of dating reveals that the opposite is true. We inherit the roles we play in the theater of dating from those who came before us and take stage directions from those who live around us. Every person may experience intimate feelings intimately. But this does not mean that those feelings are merely individual. Our intimate feelings reflect the power of forces that shape every other aspect of our lives. The possibilities of how we feel arise from those we feel among.

Self-help literature usually ignores the fact that the frustrations that cause people to seek self-help are often not just their problems. They are social in origin. They do not lie somewhere deep within us but reflect the many relationships that constitute our world. Some authors acknowledge that sources of the dissatisfaction their readers experience lie outside their control. Yet once they have, they almost immediately push this fact aside. They say, *Okay, but let's focus on what you can do.* Then they proceed to tell you how to adapt to get by as best you can with things the way they are.

This approach seems self-defeating when you consider that the goal is love—opening and merging your one life with the lives of others. Love requires openness. The point is to be changed by, and to witness change in, one another. Slowly, this back-and-forth transforms the shared reality we call the world. Love is less noun than verb: not a thing to get, but a process to set in motion. Yet many of the experts who take for granted that love is the highest goal of every life—the happy ending that will make all efforts worth it—seem to doubt the possibility of changing anything. Ironically, they place little faith in love itself.

I began to feel a need to write this book when I sensed that I was trying to make a life according to rules I did not understand and that the process had blinded me to my desires. Following my desires was supposed to be the point. Yet I had never reflected long enough to discover whether the feelings that I believed should be there actually were. I had no idea who I was. And as long as I kept impersonating all the women I thought I should be, I could not receive love, much less give it. I had no self to choose to give it from.

I did not know then what book I was writing. That became clear only as I read and talked with friends and strangers and began to notice that they, too, felt anxious and confounded by the roles that dating pushed them into. They were especially exasperated by how often these roles seemed to follow strictly gendered scripts that pitted them against their partners.

Through these conversations, I came to see that American culture sends deeply mixed messages about our courtship system. A huge number of products are devoted to depicting, discussing, and facilitating dating. An archaeologist unearthing our artifacts eons hence would have to conclude that it was a crucially important part of life in our civilization, if only from the number of dating apps on our disintegrating smartphones. Yet as a subject of inquiry, dating usually remains confined to venues marked as frivolous, like women's magazines or romantic comedies. In practice, we treat it as recreation—an individual pursuit rather than a collective concern. The result has been to put an enormous amount of pressure on people to date, while providing little support for them.

As I neared the end of my research, where the history of dating caught up with the present, I began to notice that our culture has a similarly split attitude toward love. On the one hand, we fixate on it. Americans gorge on romance novels, sentimental movies, and bride-themed reality shows; couples take on debt to stage industrial-size weddings, then slog through years of costly therapy trying to keep the promises they made at them. On the other hand, we accept social arrangements that leave many people little time to devote to personal relationships. Images and narratives about love that we consume constantly reinforce the message that only certain kinds of love can count.

Self-help books, movies, and pop songs alike tend to focus on love that is romantic, monogamous, usually heterosexual, and ideally headed toward marriage and reproduction. The writer and activist Laurie Penny has dubbed this "Love™." I think of it as *Love: The End*, the final frame that supersedes all the awkward or heartbreaking scenes that came before and blots them gently away. "Nobody remembers anything about dating, once they're out" a married friend laughs. "It's like we all have posttraumatic shock." Many single people speak of love as if it were an escape route or a prize they hope to get for making it through dating's trials.

Some feminists claim that love is bad for us. In her book *Against Love*, the Northwestern University professor Laura Kipnis argues that the ideal of a lifelong romantic relationship dupes its adherents into living lives in which they feel unfree and

264 LABOR OF LOVE

unfulfilled. "When did the rhetoric of the factory become the language of love?" Kipnis asks. "When it comes to love, trying is always trying too hard: work doesn't work." Kipnis celebrates the spontaneity of flirting and erotic play as a source of joy and growth. She sees compulsory monogamy as a tool of social control that renders Americans desexed and docile.

Women in particular are often exhorted to work at Love™ in ways that feel coercive. Both material realities and sexist socialization tell women that living without it will be worse for them than it would be for a man. Single women earn less money than their male counterparts; if they have children, they usually bear most of the responsibility and expense of raising them. While our culture may be becoming more comfortable with the idea that women might opt out of long-term coupledom, the figure of a spinster continues to elicit pity. By contrast, the image of the lifelong bachelor still exudes dusty glamour.

The problem that Kipnis highlights is not with love per se. The problem is with a world where Love™ is the only love going, and where structural inequalities compel the individuals who buy into it to put in different amounts of work. We may need more words for all the forms love can take.

The Ancient Greeks had three: *eros*, *philos*, and *agape*. These meant desire, friendship, and the love of God for the world he created. The Romans translated *agape* as *caritas*, "charity." Love can be given without expectation of return. We might start by being kinder and more generous toward ourselves. Women in particular must unlearn the ways that we are taught to devalue our own wishes and well-being—to see ourselves as too fat, too loud, too ambitious, too needy, and so on.

This book has shown how many of the things that trouble daters about their personal lives are more than personal. To improve them we would need to make the kinds of political changes that can be achieved only by banding together and organizing. Rather than directing the critical energies that we apply to self-help inward, if we directed them outward, we might come up with concrete fixes that could make dating—and much besides dating—better. If there were better health care, child care, and maternity leave policies, for instance, would dating on the biological clock be nearly as nerve-racking as it is now? If the demands of school and work were not so grueling, would young people feel so much pressure not to "waste time" on relationships? Perhaps—or perhaps not. They would almost certainly feel freer to explore.

Our challenge is to find ways to honor love properly without falling back into outdated patterns. We might think of this as a third sexual revolution. We should certainly not corral sex back into marriage. Though I have criticized the "dating market," I am not saying that everyone should get out of it by "settling down." Rather, we must find ways to celebrate the myriad kinds of love that sex and romance lead to. We must be mindful, kind, and appreciative toward our partners. One of the things we ought to appreciate about them is the work they do in appreciating us.

The logic of transactions deep in the structure of dating encourages us to see love as something we compete against others to get. The illusion that we can only win love and never will it leaves many people feeling paralyzed. The way that our culture has divided labor and desire, assigning one to history and the other to biology, renders us helpless: It tells us that love is a mere feeling, fleeting and uncontrollable. If you see love as the most important event of your life and believe that you cannot influence it, of course any difficulties you encounter in a relationship will seem terrifying. Any problem you and your partner encounter means your feelings have already ebbed. But this way of seeing love and emotion as absolutely separate from labor is mistaken.

Love consists of acts of care you can extend to whomever you choose, for however long your relationship lasts. Over the past century, dating has changed, changing how people imagine they must be in order to be loved. As it has, love has not stood still. Love changes in time, too.

The point of recognizing the labor of love is not to reject it but to reclaim it, to insist that it be distributed equally and directed toward the ends that we in fact desire. In dating or a relationship, seeing the labor of love for what it is allows you to conduct a simple test: Is what you are doing worth it? How much do you want, and how much is too much to give? There is a difference between putting off something that is bothering you until a time when you are confident you and your partner can discuss it productively and burying it because you fear that admitting anger will make you undesirable. There is a difference between making constant demands on a partner and admitting when you feel vulnerable. The difference is exploitation. Love demands that we recognize and refrain from it.

When we have the freedom to direct the ways we perform it, labor is not a liability. It is a source of strength. Once we have clarity, we benefit from acknowledging the ways in which love itself is work. It is a productive force. In order to harness it, we must be vulnerable. To feel incomplete, and thus to yearn for others, always means being able to be hurt. It is through the fearful process of recognizing our needs and showing them to others that we grow.

I fell in two kinds of love while writing this book. The first was with a friend. We had crossed paths a few times before we *met* met—before something she said or I said over the kind of lunch date half-strangers politely schedule sparked and gave us a glimpse of our potential. In movies and on television, women often seem to treat their friendships as fallbacks, like focus groups they use to work through romantic problems and dissolve once they find a partner. But a passionate friendship can be just as powerful as a romantic passion. You turn the lens on your life just a bit and a whole new plane leaps into focus. Tilt the page and you see shapes you did not know were there. It was that friendship that inspired and sustained me as I wrote this book.

The second was with the person I have since married. To have come to know him and to know myself through him has been the greatest joy of my life yet. I had always feared that love would require ceding more of myself than I wanted, or would require losing my identity. It turned out that the opposite was true. It was through this relationship that I first came to see who I was and what happiness meant.

Both experiences took me by surprise. It was not only that they happened, as they say, when I least expected it. Love itself was not what I expected. It was not the end of a search but the beginning. In love, I began to feel desire as a movement in me that reached outward, yearning to act upon the world.

If we can be brave enough to honor love, we might begin to change all the things that people hate about dating. By treating the work of reproduction with the seriousness that it deserves, we might begin to see how productive—and truly *creative*—it can become. One thing is clear: Whatever we can do cannot be done alone.

SELECTED BIBLIOGRAPHY

There are so many books that helped me write this book. In the following pages, I would like to give a brief account of works that have broadly shaped my thinking on feminism, gender, sexuality, and work (in other words, everything). Then I will offer a list of references for books that directly guided my research.

When I first started to articulate the idea for *Labor of Love*, a wise person told me to read Beth L. Bailey's *From Front Porch to Back Seat*. That book, and her *Sex in the Heartland*, provided an invaluable introduction to the field. So, too, did John D'Emilio and Estelle B. Freedman's *Intimate Matters*. Stephanie Coontz's books *Marriage, a History* and *The Way We Never Were* helped me begin to think about how emotions that we often presume to be unchanging and eternal, like love between romantic partners or family members, in fact change dramatically over time. Alice Kessler-Harris's classic *Out to Work* and Ruth Schwartz Cowan's *More Work for Mother* provided helpful overviews of the history of labor performed by American women in the paid workforce and outside it.

Kathy Peiss's *Cheap Amusements* gave me a vivid view into the lives of working-class women in New York City in the early twentieth century, introducing me to the phenomenon of "Charity Girls" who were "treated" to dates. Ruth Rosen's pioneering study on prostitution, *The Lost Sisterhood*, and *The Maimie Papers*, a collection of letters that the ex-prostitute Maimie Pinzer wrote in the 1910s and 1920s, which Rosen edited with Sue Davidson, provided a window into the lives of women doing sex work during that period. The more recent work of Elizabeth Bernstein (*Temporarily Yours*) and Melissa Gira Grant (*Playing the Whore*) updated my understanding of "sex work as work," the evolution of which often anticipates broader trends in the American economy.

It would be difficult to account for all the works of Marxist and feminist theory that have influenced my thinking about gendered forms of labor. But I want to acknowledge the ones that have been most important to me.

Arlie Hochschild first defined and described the phenomenon of "emotional labor" in *The Managed Heart*, a sociological account of the work performed by flight attendants and debt collectors. That study and her more recent book *The Outsourced Self* have deeply shaped my perspective on these matters. So, too, has the work of the feminist activist Silvia Federici. Her essay collection *Revolution at Point Zero* provides an overview of her thinking on how capitalism exploits women. Her fascinating history *Caliban and the Witch* offers a longer view on how modern economies have subjugated female and nonwhite bodies, making their work seem like part of their nature in order to justify expropriating its fruits from them.

Shulamith Firestone's *The Dialectic of Sex* stunned me with the scope of its ambition. Its argument for understanding women as an underclass that must "seize the means of reproduction" gave me new perspectives on fertility and ways of child rearing, as well as on the history of feminism more broadly. The writings of Angela Davis on sexism and racism in the United States provided me with an invaluable framework for understanding certain limitations of the liberal feminist movements whose history I was taught in school. Her classic volume of essays *Women, Race, & Class* crystallized many things for me about how these categories intersect. So did the essays of bell hooks, particularly those collected in *Feminist Theory* and *Ain't I a Woman*. The friend who first recommended hooks's beautiful book *All About Love* to me described it as "a field guide to still being able to experience love under capitalist patriarchy." Its prose is more graceful and moving than that makes it sound. I strongly recommend it to everyone. Approaching the subject from a different direction, Laura Kipnis's *Against Love* gave me rich food for thought.

Below is a list of bibliographic information for the books I have mentioned, as well as other scholarly works that I drew on during my research.

Almeling, Rene. *Sex Cells: The Medical Market for Eggs and Sperm*. Berkeley: University of California Press, 2011.

Aschoff, Nicole. *The New Prophets of Capital*. New York: Jacobin/Verso, 2015.

Bailey, Beth L. *Sex in the Heartland*. Cambridge, MA: Harvard University Press, 2002.

———. *From Front Porch to Back Seat: Courtship in Twentieth-Century America*. Baltimore: Johns Hopkins University Press, 1988.

Bartell, Gilbert D. *Group Sex: A Scientist's Eyewitness Report on the American Way of Swinging*. New York: P. H. Wyden, 1971.

Bernstein, Elizabeth. *Temporarily Yours: Intimacy, Authenticity, and the Commerce of Sex*. Chicago: University of Chicago Press, 2007.

Bogle, Kathleen A. *Hooking Up: Sex, Dating, and Relationships on Campus*. New York: New York University Press, 2008.

Boyd, Nan Alamilla. *Wide Open Town: A History of Queer San Francisco to 1965*. Berkeley: University of California Press, 2005.

Chauncey, George. *Gay New York: Gender, Urban Culture, and the Making of the Gay Male World, 1890–1940*. New York: Basic Books, 1994.

Cherlin, Andrew J. *Labor's Love Lost: The Rise and Fall of the Working-Class Family in America*. New York: Russell Sage Foundation, 2014.

———. *The Marriage Go-Round: The State of Marriage and the Family in America Today*. New York: Alfred A. Knopf, 2009.

Cohen, Lizabeth. *A Consumers' Republic: The Politics of Mass Consumption in Postwar America*. New York: Vintage Books, 2003.

Coontz, Stephanie. *Marriage, a History: How Love Conquered Marriage*. New York: Penguin, 2006.

———. *The Way We Never Were: American Families and the Nostalgia Trap*. New York: Basic Books, 1992.

Cooper, Melinda, and Catherine Waldby. *Clinical Labor: Tissue Donors and Research Subjects in the Global Bioeconomy*. Durham, NC: Duke University Press, 2014.

Cowan, Ruth Schwartz. *More Work for Mother: The Ironies of Household Technology from the Open Hearth to the Microwave*. New York: Basic Books, 1983.

Davis, Angela Y. *Women, Race, & Class*. New York: Random House, 1981.

———. *Angela Davis: An Autobiography*. New York: Random House, 1974.

D'Emilio, John, and Estelle B. Freedman. *Intimate Matters: A History of Sexuality in America*. New York: Harper and Row, 1988.

Faderman, Lillian, and Stuart Timmons. *Gay L.A.: A History of Sexual Outlaws, Power Politics, and Lipstick Lesbians*. Berkeley: University of California Press, 2009.

Fass, Paula S. *The Damned and the Beautiful: American Youth in the 1920's*. New York: Oxford University Press, 1977.

Federici, Silvia. *Revolution at Point Zero: Housework, Reproduction, and Feminist Struggle.* Oakland, CA: PM Press, 2012.

———. *Caliban and the Witch: Women, the Body and Primitive Accumulation.* Brooklyn: Autonomedia, 2004.

Freitas, Donna. *The End of Sex: How Hookup Culture Is Leaving a Generation Unhappy, Sexually Unfulfilled, and Confused About Intimacy.* New York: Basic Books, 2013.

Fronc, Jennifer. *New York Undercover: Private Surveillance in the Progressive Era.* Chicago: University of Chicago Press, 2009.

Gould, Deborah B. *Moving Politics: Emotion and ACT UP's Fight Against AIDS.* Chicago: University of Chicago Press, 2009.

Grant, Melissa Gira. *Playing the Whore: The Work of Sex Work.* New York: Jacobin/Verso, 2014.

Halberstam, David. *The Fifties.* New York: Ballantine Books, 1994.

Haraway, Donna J. *Simians, Cyborgs, and Women: The Reinvention of Nature.* New York: Routledge, 1991.

Hochschild, Arlie Russell. *The Outsourced Self: What Happens When We Pay Others to Live Our Lives for Us.* New York: Picador, 2013.

———. *The Managed Heart: The Commercialization of Human Feeling.* Berkeley: University of California Press, 2012.

hooks, bell (Gloria Watkins). *Feminist Theory: From Margin to Center.* New York: Routledge, 2015.

———. *Ain't I a Woman: Black Women and Feminism.* New York: Routledge, 2014.

———. *All About Love: New Visions.* New York: William Morrow, 2000.

Johnson, David K. *The Lavender Scare: The Cold War Persecution of Gays and Lesbians in the Federal Government.* Chicago: University of Chicago Press, 2004.

Kessler-Harris, Alice. *Out to Work: A History of Wage-Earning Women in the United States.* New York: Oxford University Press, 1982.

Kipnis, Laura. *Against Love: A Polemic.* New York: Pantheon, 2003.

Lawrence, Tim. *Love Saves the Day: A History of American Dance Music Culture, 1970–1979.* Durham, NC: Duke University Press, 2003.

May, Elaine Tyler. *Homeward Bound: American Families in the Cold War,* rev. ed. New York: Basic Books, 2008.

Meyerowitz, Joanne J. *Women Adrift: Independent Wage Earners in Chicago, 1880–1930.* Chicago: University of Chicago Press, 1988.

Peiss, Kathy. *Hope in a Jar: The Making of America's Beauty Culture.* Philadelphia: University of Pennsylvania Press, 2011.

——. *Zoot Suit: The Enigmatic Career of an Extreme Style*. Philadelphia: University of Pennsylvania Press, 2011.

——. *Cheap Amusements: Working Women and Leisure in Turn-of-the-Century New York*. Philadelphia: Temple University Press, 1986.

Penny, Laurie. *Unspeakable Things: Sex, Lies and Revolution*. New York: Bloomsbury, 2014.

——. *Meat Market: Female Flesh Under Capitalism*. Alresford, U.K.: Zero Books, 2011.

Power, Nina. *One-Dimensional Woman*. Ropley, U.K.: Zero Books, 2009.

Ramirez-Valles, Jesus. *Compañeros: Latino Activists in the Face of AIDS*. Champaign: University of Illinois Press, 2011.

Rosen, Ruth. *The Lost Sisterhood: Prostitution in America, 1900–1918*. Baltimore: Johns Hopkins University Press, 1982.

Sears, Clare. *Arresting Dress: Cross-Dressing, Law, and Fascination in Nineteenth-Century San Francisco*. Durham, NC: Duke University Press, 2014.

Serano, Julia. *Whipping Girl: A Transsexual Woman on Sexism and the Scapegoating of Femininity*. Emeryville, CA: Seal Press, 2007.

Shilts, Randy. *And the Band Played On: Politics, People, and the AIDS Epidemic*. New York: St. Martin's Press, 1987.

Talbot, David. *Season of the Witch: Enchantment, Terror, and Deliverance in the City of Love*. New York: Free Press, 2012.

Thurber, James, and E. B. White. *Is Sex Necessary? Or, Why You Feel the Way You Do*. Garden City, NY: Blue Ribbon Books, 1929.

Turner, Fred. *From Counterculture to Cyberculture: Stewart Brand, the Whole Earth Network, and the Rise of Digital Utopianism*. Chicago: University of Chicago Press, 2006.

Wallace, Michele. *Black Macho and the Myth of the Superwoman*, rev. ed. New York: Verso, 1990.

Weekley, Ayana K. *Now That's a Good Girl: Discourses of African American Women, HIV/AIDS, and Respectability*. PhD diss., University of Minnesota, 2010.

ACKNOWLEDGMENTS

I should probably thank everyone I have dated or who spilled the secrets of their own dating lives to me. But they know who they are.

The real inspiration for this book was my friendship with Mal Ahern. It grew out of a period of intense collaboration that we spent reading, writing, thinking, talking, and often staying together. Mal contributed key ideas, salient facts, astute edits, and spot-on jokes; from the beginning, *Labor of Love* was her labor, too. I cannot imagine what my life would be like if I had not met Mal. Thank you.

I also want to thank *The New Inquiry*, which published the essays that grew into this book, and everyone associated with it. I feel very fortunate to have encountered people with their ambition, generosity, and intelligence. I am especially grateful to Atossa Araxia Abrahamian for being a top-notch editor, interlocutor, and running partner, and to Sarah Leonard and Rachel Rosenfelt for their friendship and support.

Thank you to my agent, Chris Parris-Lamb, who understood at once what I wanted to do with this project, helped me see it more clearly, and shepherded it along. I am so glad that Emily Bell, my brave and brilliant editor, took it on. She steered me deftly through the tricky process of revising and refining heaps of research, and her vision for the book gave me confidence. I feel lucky to have had her by my side.

I wrote this book in the New York Public Library's Frederick Lewis Allen Memorial Room. Thanks to Jay Barksdale and Melanie Locay for making my time there possible. Thank you also to my advisers at Yale University, who put up with my working on this alongside my PhD, and particularly to Dudley Andrew, Harold Bloom, and Katie Trumpener, who stunned me by reading a monster first draft within days and offering detailed, helpful feedback.

My mother-in-law, Mathea Falco, was an unfailingly enthusiastic and insightful first reader; her encouragement kept me going. When my delightful father-in-law, Peter Tarnoff, laughed at something, I knew I had to keep it in.

My dear friend Hesper Desloovere endured my talking about historical dating endlessly, generously read and commented on chapters, and provided invaluable moral support. Rebecca O'Brien and Lauren Schuker Blum did the same. Mike Thompson was just the cheerleader I needed when I needed reassurance.

Thank you to Marco Roth for having always encouraged my writing and, though he probably does not remember it, telling me long ago that I should try my hand at love and polemics. To Shirin Ali for keeping me sane. To Ava Kofman for reading and helping me get my facts straight. To Joanna Radin and Kate Redburn for offering expert insights and advice. Jenna Healey generously offered guidance on researching the history of the idea of the biological clock. Other women contributed their intelligence and experience in many ways: Ana Cecilia Alvarez, Kate Siegel, Tess Takahashi, and Tess Wood.

I owe my parents, Bill and Kathy Weigel, big-time for falling in love, bringing me into being, and then reading more books to me than any human should have to read to another one. I am deeply grateful, as I am sure they were, to Eileen Folan for teaching me to read myself. Ever since I declared my intention to become a writer of historical fiction at age six or seven, these people have supported and believed in me even though I didn't. My younger (and cooler) sister, Julia Weigel, has been my steadfast partner in crime and beloved consultant on psychology, biology, and Kids These Days.

Only Ben Tarnoff can know how much I owe him. For gamely discussing the ins and outs of my most arcane finds and cockamamie theories. For being my go-to American historian and policy expert, not to mention in-house editor. Smarter, kinder, and funnier than I imagined a person could be before I knew him, Ben makes every day of work into a joy.

INDEX